Brand Management
in Canadian Law

John S. McKeown, B. Comm., LL.B.
of the Ontario Bar

THOMSON
™
CARSWELL

Library and Archives Canada Cataloguing in Publication

McKeown, John S., 1948-
   Brand management in Canadian law / John McKeown.

Includes index.

ISBN 0-459-24156-7

1. Brand name products—Canada.   2. Trademarks—Canada.
I. Title.

KE2779.M35 2004   346.7104'88   C2004-904778-7
KF2979.M35 2004

Composition: Computer Composition of Canada Inc.

THOMSON

CARSWELL

One Corporate Plaza
2075 Kennedy Road
Toronto, Ontario
M1T 3V4

Customer Relations:
Toronto 416-609-3800
Elsewhere in Canada/U.S. 1-800-387-5164
Fax 1-416-298-5094
World Wide Web: http://www.carswell.com
E-mail: carswell.orders@thomson.com

PREFACE

Many textbooks deal with trade mark law and other legal doctrines that apply to a brand and the components which make it up. However, this material does not typically provide any assistance concerning how the legal doctrines relate to the underlying concepts relating to brand management. This book is an attempt to bring these competing concepts together so that practitioners will have a clearer understanding of the big picture.

The idea for the book arose as a result of a number of seminars which I presented to clients in conjunction with other non-legal professionals involved in the branding process. The components that make up a brand, a consumer's perception of a brand, brand equity, brand leverage and integration are discussed initially. Additional chapters deal with legal considerations relating to choice of a brand name, branding on the internet, protecting the components of a brand and developing effective brand management policies.

As a practicing lawyer and advocate, my approach to writing is always to present the law in a clear and understandable fashion. This approach has been applied in the preparation of this text.

Unless constrained by a statutory reference, I have used the dictionary word "trade mark" rather than the statutory "trade-mark".

The law is stated as of December 2003.

I must thank my wife and our sons for their patience during the time I worked on this text.

DEDICATION

To My Wife and Sons

TABLE OF CONTENTS

CHAPTER 3: Branding on the Internet

CHAPTER 4: Protecting Brand Names — Registration

CHAPTER 5: Protecting Brand Names — Enforcement

CHAPTER 6: Protecting Product Shape and Appearance

CHAPTER 7: Protecting Product Packaging

CHAPTER 8: Protecting Brand Advertising

CHAPTER 9: Developing Effective Brand Management Policies

TABLE OF CASES

Chapter 1: The Brand

1. INTRODUCTION

This book considers brand management from a legal perspective. The components which make up a brand, the consumer perception of the brand, brand equity, how a brand can be leveraged and its integration into a system of brands are initially discussed. The chapters which follow discuss the legal considerations relating to choosing a brand name, branding on the internet, protecting the components of a brand and developing effective brand management policies.

In Canada there is no single legislative framework dealing with brands but there are a number of specific acts and common law doctrines which apply to the components which make up the brand. These laws and how they apply in a brand context are considered.

The discussion is intended to be sufficiently comprehensive to allow a thorough understanding of the applicable concepts and to be available in one convenient place. Each chapter concludes with a summary and check list intended to assist in implementing the suggestions contained in the chapter.

2. BRAND COMPONENTS

While there may be no universally accepted definition of a "brand", the term is traditionally associated with a distinguishing name or symbol intended to identify the wares or services of the seller from those of its competitors. It signals to the customer the source of the product and protects both the customer and the seller from competitors who may attempt to sell products that appear to be identical.[1]

---

[1] David Aaker, *Managing Brand Equity*, (New York: The Free Press, 1991) at 7.

A "brand" is made up of the brand name, the product and its shape, the packaging, and the image and positive associations associated with these elements. Each of these components contributes to making a brand distinctive. However, the product or service must be the primary brand communication. To be effective, the offering must provide competitive functional performance. A brand is not static and must be innovative to remain competitive.

The brand is also an aggregation of both tangible and intangible values which exist in the minds of consumers. The brand name should symbolize to consumers the image and values associated with the brand. When properly managed, the brand influences consumer decisions and generates value for consumers and the brand owner.

The tangible attributes of a brand are frequently referred to as brand expression. Brand expression is typically the visual identity of the brand which includes:

(a)   the brand name;
(b)   the design presentation of the brand name and associated symbols;
(c)   product shape and appearance;
(d)   product packaging; and
(e)   product advertising.

Brands vary in strength. Traditionally, extensive sales of the product and significant advertising are considered as a measure of the distinctiveness of the brand and its strength. However, the object, from a business perspective, is to develop a brand which is so valued by consumers that they will not willingly accept substitutes even when they are cheaper in price. Such famous and trusted brands as LEVI'S, BAYER, KODAK, and CAMPBELL'S transmit price, quality and other information directly to consumers.

Modern marketing has focused upon creating differentiated brands. Market research has been used to help identify and develop the components which lead to brand differentiation. Unique brand associations have been established using product attributes, names, packaging, distribution strategies and advertising.

It has been suggested that one of the goals of branding is to make a brand unique on dimensions that are both relevant and welcomed by consumers. Success in an overcrowded market will depend on effective brand differentiation based on the identification, internalization and communication of unique brand values that are relevant and desired by consumers.[2]

---

[2] L. de Chernatony and M. McDonald, *Creating Powerful Brands in Consumer, Service and Industrial Markets,* (Oxford: Butterworth-Heinemann, 1999).

Brand values should be periodically reviewed and adjusted to ensure that they remain relevant and contemporary.

A brand has to be linked with a business strategy. The brand strategy must support the business strategy. As observed by Kotler, marketing thinking should not begin with a product or a product class but with a need.[3] The management of the components which make up the brand is vital in a competitive economy.

3. BRAND IMAGE

Brand image is the consumer perception of brand attributes and associations from which consumers derive symbolic value.[4] Once established, the brand image defines the meaning consumers associate with the brand or what the brand stands for. Brand image is like an individual's reputation. It is subjective in nature and changes over time.

From the consumer's point of view the brand must deliver the image and the values it symbolizes. The brand is the brand owner's promise to consistently deliver the components which make it up. The promise operates at different levels which vary from product to product. For items which are commodities, tangible attributes and price may be more important but for products driven by image the emphasis is on the intangible.

The term "brand execution" is used to refer to the communication of brand image to customers. The term "brand position" or "brand positioning" is used to mean the message that a brand owner wishes to imprint in the minds of customers about its brand. Frequently, this is accomplished through advertising consisting of a motivating, persuasively communicated message that provides targeted prospects with a reason why they should consider and remember the advertised product as being able to deliver the brand owner's promise.

4. BRAND EQUITY

There is no universal definition of "brand equity". However, there is a commonality in the definitions which have been put forward by writers in the field. David Aaker, an authority on branding, has described brand equity as "a set of brand assets and liabilities linked to a brand, its name and symbol, that add to or subtract from the value provided by a product or

---

[3] P. Kotler, *Marketing Management Analysis, Planning, Implementation, and Control*, (Prentice Hall, 1988).

[4] M. Patterson, "Re-appraising the Concept of Brand Image" (1999) Volume 6, No. 6 *The Journal of Brand Management*, at 409–26.

service to a firm and/or to that firm's customers".[5] Kevin L. Keller has defined customer-based brand equity as the differential effect of brand knowledge on consumer response to the marketing of the brand. Customer-based brand equity involves consumers' reaction to an element of the marketing mix for the brand in comparison with the reactions to the same marketing mix elements attributed to a fictitiously named or unnamed version of the product or service. Positive brand equity occurs when the consumer is familiar with a brand and holds some favorable, strong or unique brand associations in memory.[6] The Marketing Science Institute has described brand equity as being a "set of associations and behaviors on the part of a brand's consumers, channel members and parent corporation that permits the brand to earn greater volume or greater margins than it could without the brand name and that gives a strong, sustainable, and differentiated competitive advantage".[7]

Keller suggests that brand equity may be built in three ways: through selection of the brand elements; the mix employed in the brand marketing program; and secondary associations. [8]

Brand knowledge is linked to brand equity. For Keller, brand knowledge is made up of two components, brand awareness and brand image. Brand awareness relates to the likelihood that a brand will come to mind and the ease with which it does so. Brand awareness consists of brand recognition and brand recall performance. Brand recognition relates to the consumer's ability to confirm prior exposure to the brand when given the brand as a cue. Brand recall relates to the consumer's ability to retrieve the brand when given the product category or some other type of probe as a cue.[9] Brand image, which has been previously discussed, consists of the perceptions about a brand shared by consumers.

Brand equity is important for a number of reasons. First, brand equity serves as an estimate of the value of a brand. A brand may become more valuable than the physical assets which make up a business. There have been many corporate acquisitions where the amount paid for the subject

---

[5] David Aaker, *Managing Brand Equity*, (New York: The Free Press, 1991), at 15.

[6] Kevin L. Keller, "Conceptualizing, Measuring and Managing Customer Based Brand Equity" (1993) 57 *Journal of Marketing*, January at 1.

[7] Rajendra Srivastava, Allan Shocker, "Brand equity: a perspective on its meaning and measurement", Cambridge Massachusetts: Marketing Science Institute Working Paper, 91-124.; Leslie de Chernatony & Fiona Harris, *Measuring the consumer-based equity of financial services brands* (2001).

[8] Kevin L. Keller, *Strategic Brand Management*, (Upper Saddle River, New Jersey: Prentice Hall 1998) at 68.

[9] Kevin L. Keller, "Conceptualizing, Measuring and Managing Customer Based Brand Equity" (1993) 57 *Journal of Marketing*, January.

companies was significantly greater than the balance sheet values of the concrete assets owned by the companies. The difference represented the value of the brand portfolios owned by the target companies.

Second, considering brand equity can assist in the management of the components which make up the brand and allow those engaged in marketing decisions to make more efficient use of corporate resources. Brand owners are expected to create brand equity and to justify investments in marketing strategies by reference to increased brand equity.

Finally, the concept of brand equity can be important in the context of enforcing rights. In the case of *IMAX Corp. v. Showmax, Inc.*,[10] the plaintiff brought an action for trade mark infringement relating to trade marks it owned consisting of the word IMAX used in association with a variety of motion picture related wares and services, including motion picture theatre services. The defendant announced its intention to operate large-format theatres in Toronto and Vancouver in association with the trade mark SHOWMAX. The plaintiff sought an interlocutory injunction to restrain the defendant from using the SHOWMAX as the name of the large-format motion picture theatre it proposed to open in Montreal.

As part of its evidence supporting the motion for an injunction, the plaintiff relied on survey evidence to support its contention that use of the term SHOWMAX as the name of a giant movie screen theatre in Montreal would be likely to cause visitors and potential visitors to such a theatre to believe that the theatre was owned or operated by or had some business association with the plaintiff. Survey data showed that about half the people surveyed held this belief. The plaintiff also filed expert evidence to show irreparable harm. In this regard, its experts stated that the use of the trade mark SHOWMAX by the defendant would damage the brand meaning or equity of the IMAX mark, that is, the ability of the IMAX mark to act as a distinctive unique signifier of the plaintiff's movie theatres. The IMAX mark would no longer identify and distinguish theatres controlled by IMAX as strongly and clearly as it did before use began of the confusing SHOW-MAX mark. This damage to goodwill and the value of the mark was categorized as impossible to calculate in monetary terms or to remedy by restorative measures. The Court accepted that this evidence was sufficient

---

[10] (2000), 5 C.P.R. (4th) 81 (Fed. T.D.); and see *Midas Equipment Ltd. v. Zellers Inc.* (1991), 35 C.P.R. (3d) 543 (Alta. Q.B.); *Canadian Jersey Cattle Club v. George Weston Ltd.* (1991), 38 C.P.R. (3d) 113 (T.M. Opp.Bd.); *Petals, Inc. v. Winners Apparel Ltd.* (1999), 2 C.P.R. (4th) 92 (Ont. S.C.J.); *Warner-Lambert Co. v. Concord Confections Inc.* (2001), 11 C.P.R. (4th) 516 (Fed. T.D.); *Sydneywide Distributors Pty Ltd v Red Bull Australia Pty Ltd*, [2002] FCAFC 157 (F.C.A.).

to show irreparable harm and granted an interlocutory injunction pending trial.

5. BRAND EXTENSIONS

Brand extensions are closely related to brand equity. The equity of the brand is leveraged by extending the brand to additional wares and services or expansion into new geographical markets.[11]

Brand extensions capitalize on the brand image of the core product or service to efficiently inform consumers and retailers about a new product or service. Brand extensions can facilitate acceptance of the new product or service by providing two benefits. First, awareness for the extension may be higher because of previously established brand awareness. Second, consumers may form expectations for the extension on the basis of what they already know about the core brand.[12]

The decision to extend the brand can be a difficult one. It is suggested that once multiple products or services are associated with a brand, the congruence among the associations becomes an important determinant of the consistency and cohesiveness of the brand image. It is argued that an appropriate extension can help the core brand image by improving the nature of the associations and clarifying the business definition and core benefits for the brand. For example, brand extensions helped to fortify the brand image of the WEIGHT WATCHERS and SUNKIST brands. On the other hand, extensions may harm the core image if the brand becomes associated with a large number of unconnected products or services.

Aaker has suggested that when a product is tied closely to a product class, its potential for extension is limited, but that if the brand relies heavily on intangible associations or an idea such as a mark like HEALTHY CHOICE or HEALTHY EATING, it may be a better candidate for extensions to new categories because the intangible image or idea applies in a wide variety of contexts.[13]

There may be other adverse implications associated with an extension. For example, it is suggested that the successful introduction of MILLER

---

[11] For a case where the plaintiff attempted to argue that its trade mark should be given a wider ambit of protection on the basis of brand extension theory, see *Veuve Clicquot Ponsardin c. Boutiques Cliquot Ltée* (2000), (sub nom. *Veuve Clicquot Ponsardin Maison Fondée en 1772 v. Boutiques Cliquot Ltée*) 7 C.P.R. (4th) 189 (Fed. T.D.).

[12] Kevin L. Keller, "Conceptualizing, Measuring and Managing Customer Based Brand Equity" (1993) 57 *Journal of Marketing*, January.

[13] David Aaker, *Brand Leadership*.

LITE beer may have had a negative impact on MILLER HIGH LIFE beer as "less hearty".[14]

6. BRAND SYSTEMS

A company may have a system or hierarchy of brands which are used concurrently. For example, General Motors has a number of branded divisions which include CADILLAC and CHEVROLET, among others. Within each division there are separate brands for different models of vehicles such as SEVILLE or LUMINA. Finally, in some cases specific features or components are branded such as MAGNETIC RIDE CONTROL suspension or a NORTHSTAR engine. This type of approach is not specific to the automotive industry and is frequently adopted by larger brand owners. Such an approach provides the advantages of simplicity and relatively low costs. However, it may be inappropriate if it prevents the growth of differentiated brands within the system.

The top brand in such a hierarchy is frequently referred to as a "corporate brand" and the other brands as subsidiary or secondary brands. The number of subsidiary brands can vary from large families of brands, such as all CHEVROLET branded vehicles, to specific sub-brands which are only used on one type of product. Where there is a distinct set of customers who are provided with a distinct product, often through distinct channels, a sub-brand may be the most effective choice.

Another strategy is to develop and manage a system of strong autonomous brands relating to specific products. Such an approach is more flexible and allows specific brands to develop. These brands may be directed at specific segments of the relevant market.

Private label brands, which are also referred to as distributor's brands, were initially developed in the grocery and retail drug industries, but more recently have expanded to mass merchandisers and specialty stores among others. Private label brands are associated with a retailer and the branding of the retail outlet including the products sold there. Loblaws' PRESIDENT'S CHOICE brand is an example of a successful private label. The expansion of warehouse retailers, price clubs and "category killers" has added to the number of private label offerings.

National brands, which are also referred to as manufacturer's brands, have been predicated on developing brand equity associated with the perceived manufacturer of the products in issue. COCA-COLA and BUDWEISER are examples of well known national brands.

---

[14] Kevin L. Keller, "Conceptualizing, Measuring and Managing Customer Based Brand Equity" (1993) 57 *Journal of Marketing*, January.

Aaker has suggested that the corporate brands frequently play an endorsement role.[15] For example, General Mills is an endorser for CHEERIOS brand breakfast cereal. In this context, the primary role of the General Mills brand is to reassure the customer that the product will deliver the promised functional benefits because General Mills, the company behind the brand, is a substantial, successful organization. Another example is the use by Dow Corning of a bisected branding approach involving the use of a separate brand to sell mature products perceived to be commodities via the internet. Dow Corning's endorsement of the new brand provides credibility but is distanced from Dow Corning's existing market approach.[16]

It can be difficult to determine the best mix of brands within a portfolio. Some companies use their corporate brand to the exclusion of sub-brands. When the brand owner acquires a new business, it is immediately brought within the existing corporate brand umbrella. This may stunt the growth of highly differentiated brands within a portfolio. It can also put more pressure on the corporate brand to be relevant when it is extended to the new wares or services. On the other hand, some brand managers attempt to increase incremental market share by launching new brands and targeting new customers. This may create overlap with other brands in the portfolio to the detriment of both brands. It is difficult to find the right balance between products, sub-brands and the corporate brand.

In addition to this balance, there are economic considerations. Brands are an economic asset whose function is to create value for shareholders. Each specific brand should be managed to maximize the discounted value of its future cash flows and decisions should be based on key economic measures, including market share, price premiums, scale economies and other financial variables as well as brand equity.[17] More assets should be made available to the successful power brands. Secondary brands which do not perform should be sold or eliminated or their wares or services transferred to another brand in a neighboring category.

7. CO-BRANDING

Co-branding occurs when two brand names are used together at the same time. In the most extreme form of co-branding, two brands are presented together to create synergies and increase consumer demand. In cer-

[15] David Aaker, *Building Strong Brands*, (The Free Press, 1996) at 245.

[16] Randal Rozin & Liz Magnusson , "Practice Paper Processes and Methodologies for Creating a Global Business-to-Business Brand" (February 2003), Volume 10, No. 3 *Brand Management* at 185-207, Henry Stewart Publications.

[17] Peter Doyle, "Shareholder-Value-Based Brand Strategies" (September 2001), Volume 9, No. 1 *Brand Management* at 20-30, Henry Stewart Publications.

tain franchised businesses, co-branding has become popular and consumers are familiar with the concept of ordering their favorite franchised brand of hamburgers, submarine sandwiches, ice cream or frozen yogurt at the same location where they purchase gasoline for their automobiles. MasterCard International Inc. has also used co-branding as a means to segment the credit card market. The GM card, which allows the user rebates on General Motors' vehicles, is an example of this approach.

Co-branding allows the participants to leverage their respective brands. Each of the participants in the co-branding scheme relies on the other's image, products, services or location to increase their own market penetration and share. Each of the brands can potentially gain access to new markets. However, there are concerns that co-branding may result in mixed consumer perceptions leading to possible confusion and diminution of the value of the participating brands. In addition, if one of the participants is viewed negatively by the public such negative publicity may be attributed to the other participant.

It is important to keep in mind that it may be difficult to unwind the co-branding arrangement in the event that the participant's businesses change and the co-branding arrangement is no longer advantageous. There may be significant costs associated with educating consumers when the co-branding arrangement is discontinued.

A less extreme form of co-branding occurs when a branded ingredient is referred to in the presentation of another brand.[18] Two common examples of this type of approach involve the NUTRASWEET and INTEL INSIDE brands. Both of these brand names are widely used in their respective fields to indicate the presence of branded components. A related concept is branding product features, components or service programs. In this type of situation the brand owner attempts to distinguish its product from that of others by virtue of these features. For example, General Motors uses its MR. GOOD WRENCH service program in this fashion.

There have been relatively few cases which have considered situations involving co-branding. In the United States, there is some authority for the proposition that a product may be associated with multiple marks owned by different firms. A common example is a familiar manufacturer's mark and a merchant's mark appearing at the same time on a product, with one mark identifying the manufacturer and the other mark identifying the retail merchant. The use of multiple marks is appropriate so long as the separate identifying function of each mark is made apparent to consumers.[19]

---

[18] See *Service Intelpro v. Procter & Gamble* (1992), 47 C.P.R. (3d) 118 (T.M. Bd.).

[19] J. Thomas McCarthy, *Trademarks and Unfair Competition*, 2nd ed. (Rochester, N.Y.: Lawyers Cooperative, 1984) at 181.

The leading case is *Yardman, Inc. v. Getz Exterminators Inc.*,[20] where a lawnmower was manufactured by Yardman, Inc. and sold exclusively by Sears Roebucks & Co. The YARD-MAN trade mark and the Sears trade mark CRAFTSMAN were used on the mowers and their packaging. However, each machine bore a nameplate indicating that Yardman Inc. was the source of the mowers. This was accomplished by using the legend "Product of Yard-Man, Inc. . . . for Sears, Roebuck & Co.".

There have been very few reported cases in Canada dealing with the issues associated with co-branding. Relying on the United States jurisprudence and principles established under the Canadian *Trade-marks Act,* it appears that co-branding should not be objectionable by itself as long as the following steps are taken:

(a)   Each participant should be licensed to use the trade-marks which are used in the co-branding. The licensing arrangements must satisfy the requirements of the *Trade-marks Act* dealing with control and quality of the goods or services; and

(b)   The trade marks must be used in such a fashion as to maintain the distinctiveness of each mark. For example, if a manufacturer's and distributor's marks are used the manufacturer's mark must be identified with the manufacturer and the distributor's mark must be identified with the distributor. An appropriate trade mark legend similar to that used in the *Yardman* case should be developed and used. The message to the public is vital.[21]

8. SUMMARY AND CHECKLIST

The following matters should be considered in order to understand brand management.

1.   A "brand" is made up of the brand name, the product and its shape, the packaging, and the image and positive associations associated with these elements. A brand is also an aggregation of both tangible and intangible values which exist in the minds of consumers.

2.   A brand can be managed to influence consumer decisions and generate value for consumers and the brand owner.

---

[20]   157 U.S.P.Q. 100 (TTAB 1968)

[21]   See article by John R. Morrissey, "Double Trade Marking" (1982), Volume 15 No. 8 Series P.T.I.C. Bull. 957.

3. The management of the components which make up the brand is vital in a competitive market place.

4. There are a number of legal considerations relevant to managing a brand. In Canada there is no single legislative framework dealing with brands but there are a number of specific acts and common law doctrines which apply to the components which make up the brand.

5. The brand must deliver the image consumers associate with it and the values it symbolizes.

6. Brand equity serves as an estimate of the value of a brand. Brand owners must create brand equity and justify investments relating to marketing strategies by reference to increased brand equity.

7. The equity of the brand may be leveraged by extending the brand to additional wares and services or expanding it into new geographical markets.

8. Brand equity must be protected from the activities of competitors.

9. If there is a portfolio of brands, an appropriate balance must be maintained between each of the brands. Each brand should be managed to maximize the discounted value of its future cash flows.

10. Co-branding allows the participants to leverage their respective brands but there are concerns that co-branding may result in mixed consumer perceptions, leading to possible confusion and diminution of the value of the participating brands. If co-branding is carried out, specific steps must be followed to maintain the distinctiveness of each brand name.

Chapter 2: Selecting A Brand Name

1. INTRODUCTION

Consumers are faced with a multitude of product choices. Typically they seek to reduce the complexity of their buying decisions by focusing on key pieces of information. In order to influence the decision making process, a brand name should symbolize the image and values desired to be associated with the brand. The brand name chosen should reinforce the brand's desired positioning by associating it with attributes which will influence consumer buying behavior. The brand name should also assure the customer that the goods or services associated with it will be of the quality or value the customer has come to expect.

A brand name must distinguish the brand owner's goods or services from those of its competitors. In this sense the brand name should be unique so that it is clear to consumers that all goods bearing the brand name or services provided in association with it come from or are sponsored by the brand owner. This will not occur if the brand name selected is confusingly similar with a brand name already in use by another.

A brand name may also be presented in connection with a design component or logo. The design may become a symbol which represents the brand. Many people remember and respond to symbols more consistently than to words. The arch-shaped design used by McDonald's Corporation is a good example of the effectiveness of a symbol as part of a brand.

2. CHOOSING A BRAND NAME

New product ideas or concepts must be identified and evaluated in the context of industry dynamics and the competitive environment. Once it is decided that the concept is viable, an assessment can be made of what is expected of the new brand. Typically this will be expressed in terms of anticipated sales but other basic considerations must be addressed. For example, will the brand be a manufacturer's brand or a distributor's brand, a specialty brand or a low price brand? The assessment should be made in conjunction with market research directed to external market forces such as the state of competition, the nature of the product and substitutes for it and current economic conditions.

The geographical markets in issue will be particularly important. In a global market there are a multitude of linguistic and cultural issues to be considered. The pronounceability and the meaning of the brand name in each relevant language must be considered.

Matters specific to the brand owner need to be considered such as the extent of corporate assets and the nature of its business and its current brands. The end result should be a written business plan specifying anticipated sales, distribution channels and customer demographics which will set out the criteria that the brand must satisfy.

Once a plan is in place potential brand names need to be generated. Sources of such names include employee suggestions, group discussions and studies, and input from advertising agencies or other specialists. Proposed names can be ranked in terms of anticipated effectiveness against the plan.

a) Desirable Brand Name Characteristics

Ideally, a proposed name should have the following characteristics:

(a) *Brevity*. A brand name should be simple and easy to understand. Long brand names, at least the ones that survive, tend to be simplified by consumers, for example COCA COLA becomes COKE.

(b) *Easily remembered*. Consumers have limited time and energy to devote to brand names. They are faced with a multitude of product choices. It is advantageous to choose a brand which is memorable and distinctive.

(c) *Easily readable and pronounceable*. As more markets are considered and additional linguistic and cultural issues arise the more difficult it will be to achieve this characteristic. Care must be taken to avoid unintended connotations. For example, PUFFS brand tissues may be acceptable in North America, but PUFF in German is a colloquial term for whorehouse and in England it sounds similar to "poof", a derogatory term for a homosexual.

(d) *Be meaningful*. A name should communicate positive product attributes and avoid unpleasant connotations. Brands names such as LEAN CUISINE or DIE HARD are good examples.

(e) *Allow for some flexibility.* If possible, a brand name should allow for adaptation to changing market needs. For example, Anderson Consulting changed its name to ACCENTURE to communicate the emphasis it placed on the future and BOSTON CHICKEN changed its name to BOSTON MARKET to reflect a shift to family meals. These changes allowed for more flexibility of the brand. LASTMINUTE.COM for travel services may be too limiting.

(f) *Be suggestive of the product class.* It may advantageous to choose a brand name which suggests the attributes of the class of product in issue. Frequently, this type of brand name is easy to recall, for example, TICKETRON for use in association with vending tickets for sports and entertainment events. However, if such a mark is descriptive it may be difficult to protect. In addition, it may be difficult to expand such a mark into other product categories.

(g) *Work with a symbol or slogan.* It is advantageous if a brand name works well with a symbol or slogan. For example, the trade mark APPLE has been widely used in association with computers and computer software together with a stylized representation of an apple.

(h) *The proposed name must be legally available in the countries in which it is proposed to be used.* Consideration must also be given to the availability of domain names which include the brand name or a substantial part of it. In addition, the mark should be legally strong. For example, marks that are descriptive or common to the trade, even if protectable, will only be entitled to limited protection.

(i) *The proposed name should also be protectable under the* Trademarks Act *or registrable as described in part 9 of this chapter.*

b) Cautions

A brand owner should be cautious in choosing a coined word as a brand name. If a brand name is chosen which consists of a coined or invented word with no inherent meaning, such as EXXON, considerable financial resources and time may be required before the name becomes known. Similar considerations apply to initials. However, coined words may be the only viable choice to avoid linguistic and cultural problems faced by international brands.

A brand name which is descriptive of the product, the brand owner or the geographic locality from which the product originates may not be a good choice. A brand name which suggests but does not describe characteristics or properties of the product may be more acceptable. An example is the trade mark TALON for zippers. A suggestive name may be potentially more appealing to the customer and more easily remembered.

A brand name should not have any undesirable associations. The potential response by all segments of the market for the product should be considered. If some portion of the market will react negatively to the brand name, it should not be chosen.

There are advantages to be gained by tying the brand name to the brand owner's name. If goodwill has been built up over the years, new brand extensions can gain acceptance by being linked with this historical goodwill. Consumers will feel more confident in purchasing wares or services which are associated with a well established firm. For example, H.J. Heinz Company has consistently used the HEINZ component of its name as part of the brand name for a multitude of products. However, care must be taken to ensure that such a brand name is used as a trade mark and is not simply a trade name. The use of a business name may not support a trade mark registration unless the trade name is given special typographical treatment or prominence.[22]

This strategy is not adopted by all brand owners. For example, Procter & Gamble has always used individual brand names in association with product formulations and positionings which appeal to different segments of different markets. Further, if the individual brand approach is adopted and the new brand is unsuccessful, goodwill associated with the firm as a whole will be damaged less than if the brand had been directly tied to the corporate name.

3. BRAND EXTENSIONS

There are significant risks and costs associated with launching a new product or service. Many new products fail. One method of reducing the risk is to extend an existing brand to a new category of products or a service.[23] When this is done the core brand is extended to the new product. A consumer seeing the core brand will attribute its qualities to the new product.

---

[22] *Road Runner Trailer Manufacturing Ltd. v. Road Runner Trailer Co.* (1984), 1 C.P.R. (3d) 443 (Fed. T.D.).

[23] See the discussion of Brand Equity and Brand Extensions, **parts 4 and 5 of Chapter 1**.

The promotion of the new product will benefit all of the products in the product line. For example, the VIRGIN and NIKE brands have been extended across a diverse group of products and services. Such extensions may be carried out directly or by licensing a third party to manufacture and sell the new products under a licence from the brand owner.

Developing a brand name which is derived from an existing brand name to create a family of brands with a common denominator is conceptually similar to a brand extension. An example is KODAK and KODACHROME. Care must be taken to ensure the variant is legally protected to avoid any negative impact on the distinctiveness of the lead brand name.

Unfortunately, there are potential costs associated with leveraging a brand in this fashion. First, if one of the products loses credibility, all of the products and services associated with the brand may be affected. Second, the core brand may be become diluted. For example, it has been suggested that the HEWLETT-PACKARD brand for use in association with high-end scientific instruments has been diluted by the use of the brand in association with value priced printers.

4. NAME CHANGES

The considerations relating to a change of the brand name are very similar to those associated with choosing a new brand name. In many instances, because of changes in the way a company does business, mergers and acquisitions or because of negative associations with an existing brand name, it may become necessary to change that name.

Unlike evaluating a new idea or concept, in this context long term business objectives will be more important. The market opportunities for differentiation and strategic naming objectives must be used to evaluate proposed brand names.

A well planned and well executed communications campaign will be required in order to implement the change. The campaign must extend to communicating the strategic vision behind the new name to employees and other internal audiences who will have to live with the new brand name. Internal communications must be effectively used to generate excitement about the new name as well as generating acceptance and sustaining commitment.

The brand owner must also consider the potential market responses which may result when a brand name is discontinued. A U.S. case illustrates some of the relevant considerations.[24] In this case the plaintiff used the trade

---

[24] *Cumulus Media, Inc. v. Clear Channel Communications, Inc.*, 304 F.3d 1167 (United States Court of Appeals for the Eleventh Circuit, 2002).

mark BREEZE to identify its radio broadcasts, but changed its on-air name from the BREEZE to STAR 98 and announced the change through on-air advertisements. Other aspects of the plaintiff's programming such as call-in shows and the like remained unchanged. In addition, the BREEZE mark continued to appear on some of the plaintiff's materials including the sign at its headquarters, business cards and promotional materials.

Shortly after the change the defendant, which also operated a radio station, changed its on-air name from the MIX to the BREEZE and adopted a design trade mark very similar to the plaintiff's design presentation of its mark. When the plaintiff learned of the defendant's activities, it immediately instituted proceedings and sought an interlocutory injunction. In response to the motion for an injunction, the defendant argued that the plaintiff had abandoned the BREEZE mark. The motion judge disagreed and granted an injunction and the defendant appealed.

On appeal, the Court observed that an infringer must prove two separate elements in order to succeed with a defence based on abandonment: that the plaintiff had ceased using the mark in dispute and that it had done so with an intent not to resume its use.[25] On the facts before it, the Court was not prepared to interfere with the judge's grant of an interlocutory injunction.

While the plaintiff was successful, it remains to be seen whether it succeeded as a result of a conscious plan or because it had not completed all aspects of its changeover in a timely fashion. A conscious plan to maintain use of the brand name to a degree sufficient to support the registration would be preferable.[26]

5. INTERNATIONAL CONSIDERATIONS

a) Brand Names

Although much has been said concerning global brands, the fact remains there are relatively few of them. It has been observed that despite the alleged homogenization of the world market, less than 4% of the numerous brands marketed by six of the world's most powerful consumer goods companies, Procter & Gamble, Nestle, Kraft, Colgate and Quaker could be classified as global brands.[27]

---

[25] The law is similar in Canada see **Chapter 4, part 9(d)(iv)**.

[26] Mere token use is not sufficient see **Chapter 4, part 8(c)**.

[27] J. Lannon, "Three Cultures International Marketing" (1998) Volume 5, No. 5 *The Journal of Brand Management* at 346 –357.

Any time a brand name will be used in more than one country consideration must be given to cultural and linguistic issues.[28] Similar considerations apply to the design presentation of the brand name. A presentation may appeal to one culture but not necessarily appeal in others.

Consideration must also be given to the legal issues relating to intellectual property and trade marks in particular. Trade marks are territorial and limited to the country in which they are used unless a specific treaty or international convention is in place which provides for protection in other countries. As a result, the availability of the mark for use and registration must be assessed in each country in which it is proposed to use the brand name.

b) Brand Image

Brand image is determined by consumer experience with the brand, including exposure to advertising and promotion, packaging and the situations in which the brand is used. Consumers in different cultures may associate fundamental attributes to a brand in different ways according to situational factors. Also, brand knowledge gained from marketing activities can differ substantially from one culture to another and culturally specific mental associations may be linked to this knowledge.[29]

It has been suggested that while global brands may be driven by similarities among countries, local fine tuning needs to be done to accommodate national differences.[30] For example, recent advertisements for VOLVO automobiles emphasize safety in some markets and excitement elsewhere. Competitive intensity may also influence brand perception since the greater the extent of local competition, the greater the risk that consumers may fail to differentiate between various brands.

---

[28] The linguistic issues are frequently assessed by carrying out native speaker checks, but this is only part of the analysis.

[29] R. Bennett, "Market Closeness, Commitment and the International Customization of Brand Image: The case of Western Brands and the Czech Republic" Volume 8, No. 1 *Brand Management* at 56.

[30] R. Bennett, "Market Closeness, Commitment and the International Customization of Brand Image: The case of Western Brands and the Czech Republic" Volume 8, No. 1 *Brand Management* at 56.

6. TRADE MARK PROTECTION IN CANADA

A brand owner should understand how the trade mark system works when selecting a brand name since the decisions made will affect the rights potentially available in the future.

In Canada, the *Trade-marks Act*[31] applies to a brand name and is of fundamental importance. Obtaining a trade mark registration facilitates the protection of the brand name. There are also common law rights associated with a brand name which may be asserted independently.

The *Trade-marks Act* provides for a public registry system which is national in scope, showing proscribed information for each registered trade mark. The Act facilitates the protection of trade marks by granting exclusive rights to owners and providing for public notice of the rights.

This registration system co-exists with common law trade mark rights. Common law rights are acquired through actual use of the common law mark in association with wares or services. As a common law trade mark becomes known and goodwill is associated with it, the owner of the mark will be able to assert claims against others who use confusing trade marks in the specific region or area that the common law trade mark owner has built up goodwill. Common law trade mark rights may be helpful on a case-by-case basis or may be impediments to overcome in other cases.

7. BASIC CONCEPTS

a) The Trade Mark

The Act contains a restrictive definition of this term. It provides that a trade mark means: (a) a mark that is used by a person for the purposes of distinguishing or so as to distinguish wares or services manufactured, sold, leased, hired or performed by him from those manufactured, sold, leased, hired or performed by others; (b) a certification mark; (c) a distinguishing guise; or (d) a proposed trade mark.

The definition is of fundamental importance in determining what can be registered and protected as a trade mark. The ordinary grammatical meaning of the word "mark" suggests that what is being referred to is a symbol. The definition is not in conflict with the concepts associated with branding but focuses on the differences between brand names. A certification mark, a distinguishing guise and a proposed trade mark are included in the statutory definition even though they have different attributes.

---

[31] R.S.C. 1985, c. T-13, as amended.

The definition also incorporates the concept of "use" which is defined by the Act.[32] The words "for the purposes of distinguishing or so as to distinguish" incorporate the definition of "distinctive" and all that the concept of distinctiveness means in trade mark law.[33]

Manufacturers' marks are expressly referred to but distributors' marks are also included. A trade mark may become known to consumers by virtue of the involvement of the distributor when the manufacturer is not known. A typical example of a distributor's mark is the private label offerings sold to consumers by numerous retailers.

There is nothing in the Act which prevents a slogan or a tagline from being used as a trade mark. Whether the use of a slogan in a particular case is in fact trade mark "use" depends on whether the use is trade mark "use" as defined by subsection 4(1) of the Act and whether the slogan is a "trade-mark" as defined in section 2 of the Act.[34]

The Act contains a parallel definition of a "proposed trade-mark".[35] Under the Act it is possible for a person who has not yet begun to use a trade mark to file an application based on an intention to use it in Canada. There are a number of advantages to filing an application prior to actually using the trade mark.[36] A proposed trade mark owner may only obtain rights, apart from a right to claim priority, by actually using the trade mark, which is a condition precedent to obtaining a registration.[37]

b) Distinctiveness and Secondary Meaning

The Act provides that "distinctive" in relation to a trade mark, means a trade mark that actually distinguishes the wares or services in association with which it is used by its owner from the wares or services of others or is adapted so to distinguish them.[38] The definition recognizes that a trade mark may acquire distinctiveness, which is also referred to as secondary meaning. The definition also recognizes that the concept applies to a trade mark, which is adapted to distinguish wares or services, because the trade mark is

---

[32] Section 4 of the *Trade-marks Act* and see **part 3 of Chapter 4.**

[33] See **part 7(b) of this chapter.**

[34] *General Mills Canada Ltd. v. Procter & Gamble Inc.* (1985), 6 C.P.R. (3d) 551 (T.M. Opp. Bd.); *Hudson's Bay Co. v. Sears Canada Inc.* (2002), 26 C.P.R. (4th) 457 (T.M. Opp. Bd.).

[35] Section 2 of the *Trade-marks Act.*

[36] See **Chapter 4.**

[37] Subsection 40(2) of the *Trade-marks Act.*

[38] Section 2 of the *Trade-marks Act.*

inherently distinctive.[39] The term "inherent distinctiveness" is not defined in the Act, but is frequently referred to in cases considering the provisions of the Act.

The essence of a protectable trade mark is its distinctiveness.[40] In order to be protected, a trade mark must be distinctive within the meaning of the definition set out above. When an application for a trade mark is submitted, the Registrar of Trade-marks may not directly refuse it on the basis of lack of distinctiveness but an application may be opposed on the grounds that the applied-for mark is not distinctive.[41] In addition, a registration may subsequently be found to be invalid if the trade mark is not distinctive at the time the proceedings bringing the validity of the registration into question are commenced.[42]

In applying the definition, the critical factor is the message actually given to the public:[43] the name which appears on the address line on product packaging will be important.[44]

The courts have stated that three conditions must be met to show distinctiveness:

(a)   that a mark and a product are associated;

---

[39] *AstraZeneca AB v. Novopharm Ltd.* (2003), 24 C.P.R. (4th) 326 (Fed. C.A.), leave to appeal refused (2003), 2003 CarswellNat 3110 (S.C.C.); *Novopharm Ltd. v. AstraZeneca AB* (2003), 28 C.P.R. (4th) 129 (F.C.); *Boston Pizza International Inc. v. Boston Chicken Inc.* (2003), 24 C.P.R. (4th) 150 (Fed. C.A.). To be distinctive, a trade mark must be either inherently distinctive or used in Canada so as to have acquired distinctiveness.

[40] *Steinberg Inc. v. J.L. Duval Ltée.* (1992), 44 C.P.R. (3d) 417 (Fed. T.D.).

[41] Subsection 37(1) and subsection 38(2)(d) of the *Trade-marks Act.* See *Smith, Kline & French Canada Ltd., Re,* [1987] 2 F.C. 633 (Fed. T.D.); *Novopharm Ltd. v. Astra AB* (2000), 6 C.P.R. (4th) 16 (Fed. T.D.), affirmed (2001), 15 C.P.R. (4th) 327 (Fed. C.A.), leave to appeal refused 2002 CarswellNat 1251 (S.C.C.); *Apotex Inc. v. Monsanto Canada* (2002), 6 C.P.R. (4th) 26 (Fed. T.D.); *Novopharm Ltd. v. Bayer Inc.* (2000), 9 C.P.R. (4th) 304 (Fed. C.A.).

[42] Subsection 18(1) of the *Trade-marks Act.*

[43] *Royal Doulton Tableware Ltd. v. Cassidy's Ltd.–Cassidy's Ltée.* (1984), 1 C.P.R. (3d) 214 (Fed. T.D.); *Heavy Duty Cycles Ltd. v. Harley Davidson Inc.* (1997), 72 C.P.R. (3d) 527 (Fed. T.D.); *Consorzio del Prosciutto di Parma v. Maple Leaf Meats Inc.* (2001), 11 C.P.R (4th) 48 (Fed. T.D.), affirmed (2002), 18 C.P.R. (4th) 414 (Fed. C.A.).

[44] *Moore Dry Kiln Co. v. United States Natural Resources Inc.* (1976), 30 C.P.R. (2d) 40 (Fed. C.A.); *White Consolidated Industries Inc. v. Beam of Canada Inc.* (1991), 39 C.P.R. (3d) 94 (Fed. T.D.).

(b)   that the "owner" uses this association between the mark and its product and is manufacturing[45] and selling the product; and

(c)   the association enables the owner of the mark to distinguish its product from that of others.[46]

The distinctiveness of a trade mark may change over time. An initially non-distinctive mark may acquire distinctiveness and a registration may be obtained. A mark is not registrable if it is primarily merely the name or the surname of an individual who is living or has died within the preceding thirty years, or is either clearly descriptive or deceptively misdescriptive in the English or French language of the character or quality of the wares or services in association with which it is used or of the conditions of or the persons employed in their production or their place of origin.[47] However, a trade mark which is not registrable because it falls into one of these categories may be registrable if it has been used in Canada by the applicant or its predecessor in title so as to have become distinctive at the date of filing of an application for registration.[48]

In addition, a mark which is distinctive or which has acquired distinctiveness, may lose its distinctiveness. Such a loss may occur because of misuse or mismanagement by the trade mark owner. Communicating an inappropriate message to the public may result in a loss of distinctiveness.[49]

The concept of inherent distinctiveness is not expressly mentioned in the provisions of the Act dealing with registrability. However, in the context of determining whether two trade marks are confusing, the Court or the Registrar must consider, among other things, the inherent distinctiveness of the trade marks in issue and the extent to which they have become known. An inherently distinctive mark will only refer the consumer to the wares or services in issue. Typically, such a mark will be a unique coined word. A mark with less inherent distinctiveness will refer the consumer to other sources.

---

[45]   Distributing would also be sufficient.

[46]   *Philip Morris Inc. v. Imperial Tobacco Ltd.* (1985), 7 C.P.R. (3d) 254 (Fed. T.D.), affirmed (1987), 17 C.P.R. (3d) 289 (Fed. C.A.), leave to appeal refused (1988), (sub nom. *Philip Morris Inc. v. Imperial Tobacco Ltd. (No. 1)*) 19 C.P.R. (3d) vi (note), (sub nom. *Morris (Philip) Inc. v. Imperial Tobacco Ltd.*) 87 N.R. 398 (note) (S.C.C.); *AstraZeneca AB v. Novopharm Ltd.* (2003), 24 C.P.R. (4th) 326 (Fed. C.A.), leave to appeal refused (2003), 26 C.P.R. (4th) vi (S.C.C.); *Novopharm Ltd. v. AstraZeneca AB* (2003), 28 C.P.R. (4th) 129 (F.C.).

[47]   Subsection 12(1)(a) and (b) of the *Trade-marks Act.*

[48]   Subsection 12(2) of the *Trade-marks Act;* also see **part 9(d) of this chapter**.

[49]   For example, see *Heintzman v. 751056 Ontario Ltd.* (1990), 34 C.P.R. (3d) 1 (Fed. T.D.).

A foreign trade mark owner may file an application for a trade mark and obtain a registration in Canada based on a trade mark which has been duly registered in the applicant's country of origin, if among other things, the mark applied for is not without distinctive character, having regard to all of the circumstances including the length of time during which it has been used in any country.[50] The courts have found that the onus of proving that a trade mark is not without distinctive character is a heavy one to discharge.[51] In order to satisfy the onus, at least some evidence that the mark has become known so as to distinguish the applicant's wares is required.[52]

c) Certification Mark

A certification mark is a specialized type of trade mark used to distinguish wares or services which comply with a defined standard, in contrast to a trade mark which is used to distinguish wares or services of the owner from wares or services of others.[53] Use of the certification mark is intended to assist in selling the wares or services sold or performed in association with it by taking advantage of the reputation acquired by the certification mark.[54] A well-known example is the GOOD HOUSEKEEPING SEAL OF APPROVAL.

The Act provides that the term certification mark means a mark that is used for the purpose of distinguishing or so as to distinguish wares or services that are of a defined standard with respect to

---

[50] Subsection 14(1)(b) of the *Trade-marks Act*.

[51] *Union Carbide Corp. v. W.R. Grace & Co.* (1987), 14 C.P.R. (3d) 337 (Fed. C.A.); *Molson Breweries, a Partnership v. John Labatt Ltd.* (2000), 5 C.P.R. (4th) 180 (Fed. C.A.), leave to appeal refused (2000), 7 C.P.R. (4th) vi (S.C.C.). The standard of proof remains on the balance of probabilities and reference to a heavy burden appears to refer to the exceptional aspect of subsection 12(2).

[52] *Canadian Counsel of Professional Engineers v. Lubrication Engineers, Inc.* (1992), 41 C.P.R. (3d) 243 (Fed. C.A.). Distinctiveness can only be acquired through use in Canada; see *Boston Pizza International Inc. v. Boston Chicken Inc.* (2003), 24 C.P.R. (4th) 150 (Fed. C.A.).

[53] *Life Underwriters Assn. of Canada/Assoc. des assureurs-vie du Canada v. Provincial Assn. of Quebec Life Underwriters/Assoc. Provinciale des assureurs-vie du Québec* (1988), (sub nom. *Life Underwriters Assn. of Canada v. Provincial Assn. of Quebec Life Underwriters*) [1989] 1 F.C. 570 (Fed. T.D.), reversed (1990), (sub nom. *Life Underwriters Assn. of Canada v. Provincial Assn. of Quebec Life Underwriters*) 33 C.P.R. (3d) 293 (Fed. C.A.), reversed (1992), (sub nom. *Life Underwriters Assn. of Canada v. Provincial Assn. of Quebec Life Underwriters*) 40 C.P.R. (3d) 449 (S.C.C.).

[54] *Wool Bureau of Canada Ltd. v. Queenswear (Canada) Ltd.* (1980), 47 C.P.R. (2d) 11 (Fed. T.D.).

(a)   the character or quality of the wares or services;

(b)   the working conditions under which the wares have been pro-
       duced or the services performed;

(c)   the class of persons by whom the wares have been produced or
       the services performed; or

(d)   the area within which the wares have been produced or the ser-
       vices performed.

The certification mark must distinguish the wares or services it is used
with from wares or services that are not of the defined standard.[55]

A certification mark may be adopted and registered only by a person
who is not engaged in the manufacture, sale, leasing or hiring of wares or
performance of services such as those in association with which the certification mark is used.[56] The owner cannot use the certification mark in the
sense contemplated by the Act.[57] The owner of the certification mark may
license others to use the mark in association with wares or services that
meet the defined standard. Such licensed use is deemed to be use by the
owner.[58]

The owner of a registered certification mark may prevent its use by
unlicensed persons or by licensed persons who use the mark in association
with wares or services in respect to which the mark is registered but to
which their licence does not extend.[59]

A geographical certification mark descriptive of the place of origin of
wares or services may be registered by an administrative authority or commercial association for a country, state, province or municipality including
or forming part of the area indicated by the mark; however, the owner of
such a mark must permit the use of the mark in association with any wares
or services produced or performed in the area of which the mark is descriptive.[60]

---

[55] Section 2 of the *Trade-marks Act.*

[56] Subsection 23(1) of the *Trade-marks Act.*

[57] *Wool Bureau of Canada Ltd. v. Queenswear (Can.) Ltd.* (1980), 47 C.P.R. (2d)
       11 (Fed. T.D.); *Mister Transmission (International) Ltd. v. Registrar of Trade
       Marks* (1978), 42 C.P.R. (2d) 123 (Fed. T.D.).

[58] Subsection 23(2) of the *Trade-marks Act.*

[59] Subsection 23(3) of the *Trade-marks Act.*

[60] Section 25 of the *Trade-marks Act.*

d) Prohibited Marks

The adoption and use, as well as the registration of certain types of marks, is prohibited by the Act.[61] Subsection 9(1) of the Act provides that no person shall adopt in connection with a business, as a trade mark or otherwise, any mark consisting of, or so nearly resembling as to be likely to be mistaken for, a variety of regal, governmental or public words, crests, symbols, marks or other devices.[62]

---

[61] Sections 9, 10, 10.1, 11, 11.1, 11.14, 11.15 and subsection 12(1)(e) of the *Trademarks Act*.

[62] The list includes

a) the Royal Arms, Crest or Standard;

b) the arms or crest of any member of the Royal Family;

c) the standard, arms or crest of His Excellency the Governor General;

d) any word or symbol likely to lead to the belief that the wares or services in association with which it is used have received, or are produced, sold or performed under, royal, vice-regal or governmental patronage, approval or authority;

e) the arms, crest or flag adopted and used at any time by Canada or by any province or municipal corporation in Canada in respect of which the Registrar has, at the request of the Government of Canada or of the province or municipal corporation concerned, given public notice of its adoption and use;

f) the emblem of the Red Cross as used by the Medical Service of armed forces and by the Canadian Red Cross Society, or the expression "Red Cross" or "Geneva Cross";

g) the emblem of the Red Crescent on a white ground adopted for the same purpose as specified in paragraph (f) by a number of Moslem countries;

h) the equivalent sign of the Red Lion and Sun used by Iran for the same purpose as specified in paragraph (f);

h.1) the international distinctive sign of civil defence (equilateral blue triangle on an orange ground);

i) any territorial or civic flag or any national, territorial or civic arms, crest or emblem, of a country of the Union if the flag, arms, crest or emblem is on a list communicated under article 6ter of the Convention of the Union of Paris or pursuant to the obligations under the Agreement on Trade-related Aspects of Intellectual Property Rights set out in Annex 1C to the WTO Agreement stemming from that article, and the Registrar gives public notice of the communication;

i.1) any official sign or hallmark indicating control or warranty adopted by a country of the Union, if the sign or hallmark is on a list communicated under article 6ter of the Convention or pursuant to the obligations under the Agreement on Trade-related Aspects of Intellectual Property Rights set out in Annex 1C to the World Trade Organization Agreement stemming from that article, and the

The Registrar of Trade-marks must, at the request of the relevant interested party, give public notice of the adoption and use of the following devices in order for subsection 9(1) to apply to them;

(a)   the arms, crest or flag adopted and used at any time by Canada or by any province or municipal corporation in Canada;[63]

Registrar gives public notice of the communication;

i.2) any national flag of a country of the Union;

i.3) any armorial bearing, flag or other emblem, or any abbreviation of the name, of an international intergovernmental organization, if the armorial bearing, flag, emblem or abbreviation is on a list communicated under article 6ter of the Convention or pursuant to the obligations under the Agreement on Trade-related Aspects of Intellectual Property Rights set out in Annex 1C to the World Trade Organization Agreement stemming from that article, and the Registrar gives public notice of the communication;

j) any scandalous, obscene or immoral word or device;

k) any matter that may falsely suggest a connection with any living individual;

l) the portrait or signature of any individual who is living or has died within the preceding thirty years;

m) the words "United Nations" or the official seal or emblem of the United Nations;

n) any badge, crest, emblem or mark
    (i) adopted or used by any of Her Majesty's Forces as defined in the *National Defence Act*,
    (ii) of any university, or
    (iii) adopted and used by any public authority, in Canada as an official mark for wares or services,in respect of which the Registrar has, at the request of Her Majesty or of the university or public authority, as the case may be, given public notice of its adoption and use;

n.1) any armorial bearings granted, recorded or approved for use by a recipient pursuant to the prerogative powers of Her Majesty as exercised by the Governor General in respect of the granting of armorial bearings, if the Registrar has, at the request of the Governor General, given public notice of the grant, recording or approval;

q) the name "Royal Canadian Mounted Police" or "R.C.M.P." or any other combination of letters relating to the Royal Canadian Mounted Police, or any pictorial representation of a uniformed member thereof.For these provisions "country of the Union" means
    (a) any country that is a member of the Union for the Protection of Industrial Property constituted under the Convention of the Union of Paris made on March 20, 1883 and any amendments and revisions thereof made before or after July 1, 1954 to which Canada is party; or
    (b) a Member of the World Trade Organization established by Article I of the World Trade Organization Agreement.

[63] Subsection 9(1)(e) of the *Trade-marks Act*.

(b)   any badge, crest, emblem or mark
    (i)   adopted or used by any of Her Majesty's Forces as defined in the *National Defence Act*,
    (ii)   of any university, or
    (iii)   adopted and used by any public authority, in Canada as an official mark for wares or services;[64]
(c)   any armorial bearings granted, recorded or approved for use by a recipient pursuant to the prerogative powers of Her Majesty as exercised by the Governor General in respect of the granting of armorial bearings.[65]

These devices may be adopted, used or registered as a trade mark in connection with a business, with the consent of Her Majesty or the entity intended to be protected by the Act.

Section 10 provides that where a mark has by ordinary and *bona fide* commercial usage become recognized in Canada as designating the kind, quality, quantity, destination, value, place of origin or date of production of any wares or services, no person shall adopt it as a trade mark in association with such wares or services or others of the same general class or use it in a way likely to mislead. In addition, no one may adopt or so use any mark so nearly resembling that mark as to be likely to be mistaken for it.

Section 10 is designed to prohibit the adoption of such marks as the hallmark for silver and such other well-known marks indicative of quality or origin. Such a mark or a mark which resembles it should be open for use by any party and is not available for adoption as a trade mark by any one person. Under this provision, registration of the trade mark HABANOS in association with cigars was prohibited since the words habana and habanas are commonly used in Canada to denote cigars made in Cuba.[66]

The mark as a whole must be considered and a compound mark which includes a prohibited mark as a component combined with a disclaimer of it may be acceptable.[67] The party claiming the applicability of the section must support its claim with appropriate evidence.[68]

Section 10.1 of the Act prohibits the use of a denomination registered under the *Plant Breeders' Rights Act* to designate a plant variety. No person

---

[64]   Subsection 9(1)(n) of the *Trade-marks Act*.
[65]   Subsection 9(1)(n.1) of the *Trade-marks Act*.
[66]   *Benson & Hedges (Canada) Ltd. v. Empresa Cubana Del Tabacco* (1975), 23 C.P.R. (2d) 274 (T.M. Opp. Bd.).
[67]   *Jordan & Ste-Michelle Cellars Ltd./Caves Jordan & Ste-Michelle Ltée v. Andres Wines Ltd* (1985), 6 C.I.P.R. 49 (Fed. T.D.).
[68]   *Canteen of Canada Ltd. v. Montreal Mobile Canteen Wholesale Supplies Ltd.* (1978), 46 C.P.R. (2d) 128 (T.M. Opp. Bd.).

may adopt such a denomination as a trade mark in association with the plant variety or another plant variety of the same species or use it in a way likely to mislead. In addition, no one may adopt or use any mark so nearly resembling that denomination as to be likely to be mistaken for it.

Sections 11.11 to 11.20 describe procedures for obtaining protected geographical indications for wines and spirits. No person shall adopt or use in connection with a business, as a trade mark or otherwise, a protected geographical indication identifying a wine or a spirit in respect to a wine or a spirit not originating in the territory indicated by the protected geographical indication or a translation in any language of the geographical indication in respect to that wine or spirit.[69] The Act also contains a proscribed procedure for obtaining protection after notice to the public, a number of exceptions and transitional provisions.

e) Official Marks

This term is used to describe marks adopted and used by a public authority, in Canada as an official mark for wares or services.[70] A request for an official mark may only be filed by a public authority. There are a large number of these marks and their existence can cause problems for businesses seeking new marks.[71] They can also cause problems for applications for a trade mark or registrations filed or obtained prior to the filing of the official mark since the publication of the official mark may preclude expansion and, in the case of a pending application, registration but not use of the mark.

In considering what is required to be shown to be a "public authority", the courts have found that there must be a significant degree of public control and the entity must not exist for private profit.[72] In order to satisfy this test there must be power which enables the government, directly or indirectly through its nominees, to exercise a degree of ongoing influence in the body's governance and decision-making similar to that often found in legislation dealing with statutory bodies that regulate the practice of a profession in which only those whom they license may engage, such as

---

[69] Sections 11.14 and 11.15 of the *Trade-marks Act*.

[70] Subsection 9(1)(n) of the *Trade-marks Act*.

[71] See *Explosion of Section 9(1) Notices* by R. Brant Latham, (1985), 2 C.I.P.R. 74; *Official Marks Are There Any Limits to this Branding Power?*, Colin P. McDonald (2003), 17 I.P.J. 83.

[72] *Canadian Olympic Assn. v. (Canada) Register of Trade Marks* (1982), 67 C.P.R. (2d) 59 (Fed. C.A.).

architecture and law. The fact that a body is created by statute subject to legislative amendment from time to time is not sufficient.[73]

When an application under subsection 9(1) of the Act is submitted, the Register of Trade-marks must be satisfied that the applicant is a public authority and must give public notice of the adoption and use of the mark by the public authority.[74] Such applications are not subject to limitations relating to registrability and, for example, an official mark may be clearly descriptive. In addition, official marks are not subject to opposition proceedings.[75]

The procedure to be followed to challenge the decision of the Registrar to publish an official mark was previously uncertain, but the Federal Court of Appeal has stated that it is subject to judicial review.[76] However, the time for action is limited since the application must be made within thirty days of the communication of the decision or such further time as a judge of the Federal Court may allow.

There are few, if any, limitations on what constitutes an official mark, but it must be derived from a proper office or officer or authority. It is not necessary that the mark have the connotation of officiality.[77] An official mark must have been adopted and used in Canada in association with wares or services before a request for publication is made.[78]

Subparagraph 9(1)(n)(iii) of the Act forbids the adoption of a trade mark so nearly resembling as to be likely to be mistaken for a mark adopted by a public authority in respect of which the Register has given public

---

[73] *Assn. of Architects (Ontario) v. Assn. of Architectural Technologists (Ontario)* (2002), 19 C.P.R. (4th) 417, 9 C.P.R. (4th) 496 (Fed. T.D.), leave to appeal refused (2003), 2003 CarswellOnt 1061 (S.C.C.); also see Trademark Office practice notice dated October 2, 2002.

[74] *Stadium Corp. of Ontario v. Wagon-Wheel Concessions Ltd.*, [1989] 3 F.C. 132 (Fed. T.D.).

[75] *Insurance Corp. of British Columbia v. Canada (Registrar of Trade Marks)* (1979), 44 C.P.R. (2d) 1 (Fed. T.D.).

[76] *Assn. of Architects (Ontario) v. Assn. of Architectural Technologists (Ontario)* (2002), 19 C.P.R. (4th) 417 (Fed. C.A.), reversing (2001), 9 C.P.R. (4th) 496 (Fed. T.D.), leave to appeal refused (2003), 2003 CarswellOnt 1061 (S.C.C.); *Canadian Jewish Congress v. Chosen People Ministries Inc.* (2002), 19 C.P.R. (4th) 186 (Fed. T.D.), affirmed 2003 CarswellNat 1881 (Fed. C.A.).

[77] *Insurance Corp. of British Columbia v. Canada (Registrar of Trade Marks)* (1979), 44 C.P.R. (2d) 1 (Fed. T.D.).

[78] *Pisticelli v. Ontario (Liquor Control Board)* (2001), 14 C.P.R. (4th) 181 (Fed. T.D.); *FileNET Corp. v. Canada (Registrar of Trade-marks)* (2001), 13 C.P.R. (4th) 385 (Fed. T.D.), affirmed (2002), 22 C.P.R. (4th) 328 (Fed. C.A.); and subsection 9(1)(n) of the *Trade-marks Act*.

notice. It does not operate retroactively to prohibit the adoption of a mark.[79] As a result, there is nothing to prevent the continued use of a trade mark adopted or registered before the publication of a similar official mark. However, the existence of such an official mark will preclude the expansion of an existing registration to additional wares or services[80] or any pending application which was not registered at the time of the publication of the official mark even if previously adopted, used and applied for.[81]

The test of resemblance under section 9 "consisting of, or so nearly resembling as to be likely to be mistaken for" is different from the test for registered trade marks set out in section 6 of the Act and the absence of similarity of services or wares between the parties is irrelevant.[82] The Court will consider whether a person, on first impression having only an imperfect recollection of the official mark, would likely be confused by the impugned mark.[83]

8. AVAILABILITY SEARCHES

Once a potential brand name is selected, searches should be conducted to determine whether or not it is available for use and whether it can be registered under the Act.[84] It is extremely important to conduct these searches at as early a stage as possible and certainly prior to any use of the brand name. Searches should also be carried out if a brand is being extended to additional wares or services not included in the initial registration.

Reference must be made to existing registrations and pending applications in the countries where it is contemplated the mark will be used. Consideration must also be given to elements or components which make

---

[79] *Canadian Olympic Assn. v. Allied Corp,* (1990), 28 C.P.R. (3d) 161 (Fed. C.A.); *Royal Roads University v. R.* (2003), 27 C.P.R. (4th) 240 (F.C.). Section 11 of the *Trade-marks Act* precludes the use of a trade mark adopted contrary to section 9, but it does not operate retroactively. Subsection 12(1)(e) of the *Trade-marks Act* precludes registration, but speaks in the present tense and does not apply in the same fashion as subsection 9(1)(n) and section 11 of the *Trade-marks Act.*

[80] *Canadian Olympic Assn. v. Konica Canada Inc.* (1991), 39 C.P.R. (3d) 400 (Fed. C.A.), leave to appeal refused (1992), 41 C.P.R. (3d) v (S.C.C.); *Royal Roads University v. R.* (2003), 27 C.P.R. (4th) 240 (F.C).

[81] *Canadian Olympic Assn. v. Allied Corp.* (1990), 28 C.P.R. (3d) 161 (Fed. C.A.).

[82] *Canadian Olympic Assn. v. Allied Corp.* (1990), 28 C.P.R. (3d) 161 (Fed. C.A.).

[83] *Big Sisters Assn. of Ontario v. Big Brothers of Canada* (1997), 75 C.P.R. (3rd) 177 (Fed. T.D.), affirmed (1999), 86 C.P.R. (3d) 504 (Fed. C.A.); *Techniquip Ltd. v. Canadian Olympic Assn.* (1999), 3 C.P.R. (4th) 298 (Fed. C.A.).

[84] Searches can be conducted online at *http://strategis.ic.gc.ca/cipo/trademarks/search/tmsearch.do.*

up the mark as well as any phonetic equivalents. If a French or foreign language equivalent of the mark is likely to be used, a separate search for these forms of the mark will be required.

The following information will be required in order to carry out a search:

(a) the proposed brand name and any French or foreign language equivalents and any proposed design presentations;

(b) a description of the wares or services with which the brand name is proposed to be used. For searching purposes in Canada, general categories will be sufficient and are preferable to an overly specific list which may be changed;

(c) a list of countries in which the mark is likely to be used and when such use will occur; and

(d) any information which may be available concerning the use of similar marks by competitors.

It is also useful to search legal databases, directed to intellectual property matters, to ascertain whether the mark or marks similar to it have been the subject matter of previous litigation.

If the words making up the brand name are unusual, reference should be made to standard dictionaries so that the brand owner has a clear idea of the meaning of the mark being sought. Dictionary definitions can also help in making the assessment of whether the mark is clearly descriptive of the wares and services or whether it is merely suggestive.[85] In addition, as previously discussed, if the mark will be used in other countries an assessment must be made of the meaning which will be attributed to the mark in those countries.[86]

Frequently, preliminary screening searches can be conducted on an online basis to ascertain whether there are any obvious impediments. The trade mark offices of numerous countries make available to the public their database of marks for searching purposes.[87] Commercial service providers also provide access to such information.

If the screening search does not disclose any conflicts which cannot be overcome, a complete trade mark search can be carried out. Such a search will include a more complete review of existing trade mark registrations and their possible impact.

In addition, searches may be carried out directed to the common law rights of individuals or businesses who have used similar marks or business

---

[85] See **Chapter 4, part 9(c)**.

[86] See **Chapter 2, part 5**.

[87] See the WIPO Ecommerce trade mark database Portal at *http://ecommerce.wipo.int/databases/trademark/output.html* for a representative listing.

names but have not obtained trade mark registrations. Online searches may be done of corporate and business names (NUANS searches), telephone directories, the internet, domain names and trade directories. This type of search is frequently referred to as a common law search. Common law searches can also be conducted using the services of a search firm but availability will vary by country.

All searches are subject to limitations relating to the timeliness of the searched data and its accuracy. For example, there will be delays in the noting of filed applications in the records available to be searched. Such searches cannot cover the possibility that a foreign applicant may file an application in Canada within six months of its filing date of the application in their own country and claim the benefit of this date in Canada in accordance with the Act.[88] Unless a decision to file a trade mark application is made immediately, the search should be updated to check for new applications.

In addition, the interpretation of the data requires that assessments must be made on the basis of relatively limited information. For example, in most cases there will be little or no evidence as to how the trade marks disclosed in the search are actually used. In some cases, additional specific investigations may be appropriate.

Once these searches have been carried out, an opinion should be obtained from counsel qualified in providing opinions concerning the potential availability and registrability of the proposed mark. If multiple countries are involved, separate opinions should be obtained from counsel in each country. Since the process of obtaining a registration can frequently take a substantial period of time, in the vast majority of cases, a decision to move forward must be made on the basis of such opinions.

If potential impediments to obtaining a registration are disclosed, and if it is warranted, an assessment can be made concerning whether the impediments can be removed. If the impeding mark has been registered under section 9, a consent may be obtained from Her Majesty or the entity protected by the section. If a registered trade mark is not in use, consideration can be given to initiating proceedings under section 45 of the *Trade-marks Act* for its expungement.[89] If the proposed trade mark is important, it may be possible to obtain assignments of the rights associated with the registered trade marks which are impediments. In addition, particularly for common law rights, investigations can be carried out to ascertain the extent to which the brand name in issue has been used in association with specific wares or services. It is possible to purchase the rights associated with a common law

---

[88] See **Chapter 2, part 2(d)**.
[89] See **Chapter 4, part 8(a).**

mark but this can be more cumbersome than obtaining an assignment of a registered mark particularly if the mark is used as a trade name.[90]

The failure to adequately search can result in considerable trouble and expense. If money is invested to launch a brand in the market place without knowing whether the brand name is available for use and registration, that investment will be at risk. Further, if the brand name infringes another party's right, the threat of litigation and exposure to claims will exist. Stopping a campaign to launch a brand can be both expensive and embarrassing.

9. REGISTRABILITY

a) The Concept

The right to registration is not inherent in a trade mark, but depends upon compliance with the terms of the Act. Subsection 12(1) sets out characteristics which may preclude obtaining a registration. A brand owner must be aware of these restrictions. More specifically, subject to section 13 which deals with distinguishing guises, a trade mark is not registrable if it is:

(a)   a word that is primarily merely the name or the surname of an individual who is living or has died within the preceding thirty years;

(b)   whether depicted, written or sounded, either clearly descriptive or deceptively misdescriptive in the English or French language of the character or quality of the wares or services in association with which it is used or proposed to be used or of the conditions of or the persons employed in their production or of their place of origin;

(c)   the name in any language of any of the wares or services in connection with which it is used or proposed to be used;

(d)   confusing with a registered trade mark;

(e)   a mark of which the adoption is prohibited by section 9 or 10, which deal with prohibited marks;

(f)   a denomination under the *Plant Breeders' Rights Act*[91] the adoption of which is prohibited by section 10.1;

(g)   in whole or in part a protected geographical indication, where the trade mark is to be registered in association with a wine not

---

[90] See **Chapter 4, part 7(a)**.
[91] S.C. 1990, c. 20.

originating in a territory indicated by the geographical indication; or

(h) in whole or in part a protected geographical indication, where the trade mark is to be registered in association with a spirit not originating in a territory indicated by the geographical indication.

b) Primarily Merely a Name or a Surname

A trade mark is registrable if it is not a word that is primarily merely the name or the surname of an individual who is living or has died within the preceding thirty years.[92] The question to be answered is whether the primary or principal meaning of the word is merely a surname. If the answer to the question is yes, then the trade mark is not registrable.[93] In answering this question, the Registrar or the Court, as the case may be, must take the perspective of a person in Canada of ordinary intelligence and education and determine whether they would likely respond to the word by thinking of it as being the surname of one or more individuals.[94]

In order to establish that a trade mark is primarily merely the name or surname of an individual who is living, there must be evidence that an individual bearing that name is living or is recently dead.[95] It is immaterial whether the name is rare or in common use, as long as it is a name and nothing else.[96]

Even if a trade mark is primarily merely the name or surname of an individual who is living or has died within the preceding thirty years, it is still possible to register the trade mark upon proof of a secondary meaning.[97]

The subsection does not prevent the registration of foreign words[98] or the names of historical characters who have died prior to the preceding thirty

---

[92] Subsection 12(1)(a).

[93] *Canada (Registrar of Trade Marks) v. Coles Book Stores Ltd.* (1972), [1974] S.C.R. 438 (S.C.C.).

[94] *Standard Oil Co. v. Canada (Registrar of Trade Marks)* (1968), 55 C.P.R. 49 (Can. Ex. Ct.).

[95] *Gerhard Horn Investments Ltd. v. Canada (Registrar of Trade Marks)*, [1983] 2 F.C. 878 (Fed. T.D.).

[96] *Forge Moderne Inc. v. Canada (Registrar of Trade Marks)* (1967), 51 C.P.R. 193 (Can. Ex. Ct.).

[97] Subsection 12(2) and see *Labatt Brewing Co. v. Molson Canada* (2003), 24 C.P.R. (4th) 496 (Fed. T.D.).

[98] *Galanos v. Canada (Registrar of Trade Marks)* (1982), 69 C.P.R. (2d) 144 (Fed. T.D.).

year period[99] or a Christian name alone.[100] The name of a fictitious person is not precluded from registration unless the fictitious name coincides with the name of a living person or a person who bore such name and has been dead for less than thirty years.[101] If the mark is both a surname and a dictionary word, each of which are of substantial significance, it is not "primarily merely" a surname.[102]

Section 9(1) prohibits the adoption of a trade mark consisting of, or so nearly resembling as to be likely to be mistaken for, the portrait or signature of any individual who is living or has died within the preceding thirty years.[103] This prohibition may be overcome by obtaining the consent of the individual involved[104] but a signature is *prima facie* unregistrable by virtue of subsection 12(1)(a).[105]

c) Descriptive or Deceptively Misdescriptive Trade Marks

i) General Principles

A trade mark is not registrable if it is, whether depicted, written or sounded, either clearly descriptive or deceptively misdescriptive in the English or French languages of the character or quality of the wares or services in association with which it is used, or proposed to be used or of the conditions of or the persons employed in their production or of their place of origin.[106] The purpose of the section as it applies to descriptive marks is to prevent traders from monopolizing descriptive words and precluding competitors from using such words which are part of the common

---

[99] *Gerhard Horn Investments Ltd. v. Canada (Registrar of Trade Marks)*, [1983] 2 F.C. 878 (Fed. T.D.).

[100] *Leo Chevalier International Ltd. v. St. Lawrence Textiles Ltd.* (1984), 79 C.P.R. (2d) 270 (Fed. T.D.), affirmed (1987), 14 C.P.R. (3d) 448 (Fed. C.A.).

[101] *Gerhard Horn Investments Ltd. v. Canada (Registrar of Trade Marks)*, [1983] 2 F.C. 878 (Fed. T.D.).

[102] *Elder's Beverages (1975) Ltd. v. Canada (Registrar of Trade Marks)* (1979), 44 C.P.R. (2d) 59 (Fed. T.D.); *Molson Cos. v. John Labatt Ltd.* (1981), 58 C.P.R. (2d) 157 (Fed. T.D.); *Miller Brewing Co. v. T.G. Bright & Co.* (1983), 78 C.P.R. (2d) 55 (T.M. Opp. Bd.); *Cooper v. Mark's Work Warehouse Ltd.* (1985), 5 C.I.P.R. 194 (T.M. Opp. Bd.).

[103] Subsection 9(1)(l) and subsection 12(1)(e).

[104] Subsection 9(2).

[105] *Murjani International Ltd. v. Universal Impex Co.* (1985), 5 C.P.R. (3d) 115 (T.M. Opp. Bd.).

[106] Subsection 12(1)(b); *S.C. Johnson & Son Ltd. v. Marketing International Ltd.* (1979), [1980] 1 S.C.R. 99 (S.C.C.); *101482 Canada Inc. v. Canada (Registrar of Trade Marks)*, [1985] 2 F.C. 501 (Fed. T.D.).

language.[107] The restriction relating to deceptively misdescriptive marks appears to be designed to protect potential purchasers of the wares or services.

A trade mark that is not registrable by reason of this provision is registrable if it has been so used in Canada by the applicant or a predecessor in title as to have become distinctive at the date of filing of an application for its registration.[108]

In order to determine whether a trade mark is either clearly descriptive or deceptively misdescriptive, one must consider the first impression of such a trade mark upon the ordinary user or dealer in such wares or services.[109] It is not appropriate to carefully or critically analyze the trade mark.[110] The common meaning of words in their ordinary and popular sense must be ascertained, which may not be their etymological meaning.[111]

The word "clearly" in the Act is not synonymous with "accurately" but means "easy to understand, self-evident or plain".[112] Registration will be refused only if the trade mark is clearly descriptive or deceptively misdescriptive.[113]

The word "character" as used in the subsection means a feature, trait or characteristic of the product.[114] The trade mark should not be considered by itself, but rather in relation to the wares or services in association with which

---

[107] *Clarkson Gordon v. Canada (Registrar of Trade Marks)* (1985), 5 C.I.P.R. 167 (Fed. T.D.); *Fibergrid Inc. v. Precisioneering Ltd.* (1991), 35 C.P.R. (3d) 221 (Fed. T.D.).

[108] Subsection 12(2).

[109] *Staffordshire Potteries Ltd. v. Canada (Registrar of Trade Marks)* (1976), 26 C.P.R. (2d) 134 (Fed. T.D.); *Thomson Research Associates Ltd. v. Canada (Registrar of Trade Marks)* (1982), 67 C.P.R. (2d) 205 (Fed. T.D.), affirmed (1983), 71 C.P.R. (2d) 288n (Fed. C.A.).

[110] *John Labatt Ltd. v. Carling Breweries Ltd.* (1974), 18 C.P.R. (2d) 15 (Fed. T.D.); *Oshawa Group Ltd. v. Canada (Registrar of Trade Marks)* (1980), 46 C.P.R. (2d) 145 (Fed. T.D.); but see *Drawing the Line in the Wake of the OFF Decision (S.C. Johnson & Son, Ltd. v. Marketing International Ltd. - Supreme Court of Canada)* by Gerald O.S. Oyen, 65 C.P.R. (2d) 193 (1982).

[111] *John Labatt Ltd. v. Carling Breweries Ltd.* (1974), 18 C.P.R. (2d) 15 (Fed. T.D.).

[112] *Drackett Co. v. American Home Products Corp.*, [1968] 2 Ex. C.R. 89, 55 C.P.R. 29 (Can. Ex. Ct.).

[113] *Thomas J. Lipton Ltd. v. Salada Foods Ltd. (No. 3)* (1979), [1980] 1 F.C. 740, 45 C.P.R. (2d) 157 (Fed. T.D.).

[114] *Drackett Co. v. American Home Products Corp.*, [1968] 2 Ex. C.R. 89, 55 C.P.R. 29 (Can. Ex. Ct.); *Jordan & Ste. Michelle Cellars Ltd. v. T.G. Bright & Co.* (1984), 81 C.P.R. (2d) 103 (Fed. C.A.).

it is used or intended to be used.[115] A mark which describes a condition or manner in which the wares are used by consumers may not be clearly descriptive of the character or quality of the wares.[116]

To be deceptively misdescriptive, a trade mark must initially be found to be descriptive and then be found to mislead the public as to the character or quality of the wares.[117] The test applied is whether the general public in Canada would be misled concerning the product with which the trade mark is associated.[118] For example, the trade mark SHAMMI applied for use in association with a transparent polyethylene glove, which did not contain any chamois or shammy, was deceptively misdescriptive.[119]

Laudatory words such as superior, super, supreme etc. may be clearly descriptive or deceptively misdescriptive and not registrable;[120] however, the fact that a trade mark has a laudatory connotation does not necessarily mean that registration is precluded. The mark must be considered in its entirety as a matter of immediate impression in the context of the wares or services referred to in the application in order to determine whether the mark, either clearly describes or deceptively misdescribes, the character or quality of the applicant's wares or services.[121]

The question of whether a trade mark is clearly descriptive in the English or French languages must be determined in the context of English or French usage on an international basis, and not simply English or French

---

[115] *Thomas J. Lipton Ltd. v. Salada Foods Ltd. (No.* 3) (1979), [1980] 1 F.C. 740, 45 C.P.R. (2d) 157 (Fed. T.D.).

[116] *Provenzano v. Canada (Registrar of Trade Marks)* (1978), 40 C.P.R. (2d) 288 (Fed. C.A.).

[117] *Oshawa Group Ltd. v. Canada (Registrar of Trade Marks)* (1980), 46 C.P.R. (2d) 145 (Fed. T.D.); *Canada (Deputy Attorney General) v. Biggs Laboratories (Canada) Ltd.* (1964), 42 C.P.R. 129 (Can. Ex. Ct.).

[118] *Atlantic Promotions Inc. v. Canada (Registrar of Trade Marks)* (1984), 2 C.P.R. (3d) 183 (Fed. T.D.).

[119] *Canada (Deputy Attorney General) v. Biggs Laboratories (Canada) Ltd.* (1964), 42 C.P.R. 129 (Can. Ex. Ct.).

[120] *Canada (Registrar of Trade Marks) v. G.A. Hardie & Co.,* [1949] S.C.R. 483 (S.C.C.); *Mitel Corporation v. Canada (Registrar of Trade Marks)* (1984), 79 C.P.R. (2d) 202 (Fed. T.D.); *Café Suprême F. & P. Ltée. c. Canada (Sous-procureur general)* (1984), 3 C.I.P.R. 201 (Fed. T.D.), affirmed (1985), 4 C.I.F.R. xlii (Fed. C.A.).

[121] *Nabisco Brands Ltée. — Nabisco Brands Ltée. v. Perfection Foods Ltd.* (1986), 12 C.P.R. (3d) 456 (Fed. T.D.), affirming (1985), 7 C.P.R. (3d) 468 (T.M. Opp. Bd.); *Canadian Tire Ltée v. Uni-Select Inc.* (1998), 85 C.P.R. (3d) 120 (T.M. Opp. Bd.); *Canadian Bankers' Assn. v. Richmond Savings Credit Union* (2000), 8 C.P.R. (4th) 267 (T.M. Opp. Bd.).

meanings current in Canada.[122] A descriptive connotation in a foreign language should not preclude registrability unless the mark would be understood in Canada as being descriptive.[123]

While the principles applicable to determine whether a trade mark is either clearly descriptive or deceptively misdescriptive are relatively clear, their application may not be. In addition, there are many reported cases in this area which can be difficult to reconcile.

ii) Suggestive Words

A suggestive connotation does not necessarily make a trade mark "clearly" descriptive.[124] A mark which contains a covert and skillful allusion to the character or quality of the wares may be permissible.[125] However, a trade mark that refers to the character or quality of wares or services in an elliptical way may be held to be clearly descriptive.[126]

iii) Coined or Invented Words

If a word is new to the English or French languages, it may not be clearly descriptive. However, the word must not be a dictionary word and be without a clearly discernible meaning.[127]

---

[122] *Home Juice Co. v. Orange Maison Ltée.*, [1970] S.C.R. 942 (S.C.C.).

[123] *Gula v. B. Manischewitz Co.*, [1946] Ex. C.R. 570 (Can. Ex. Ct.), affirmed (1947), 8 C.P.R. 103 (S.C.C.); *B. Manischewitz Co. v. Hartstone* (1952), [1953] Ex. C.R. 1 (Can. Ex. Ct.); *Jordan & Ste-Michelle Cellars Ltd. v. Gillespies & Co.* (1985), 6 C.P.R. (3d) 377 (Fed. T.D.).

[124] *Canada (Deputy Attorney General) v. Jantzen of Canada Ltd.* (1964), [1965] 1 Ex. C.R. 227 (Can. Ex. Ct.); *Great Lakes Hotels Ltd. v. Noshery Ltd.* (1968), [1968] 2 Ex. C.R. 622 (Can. Ex. Ct.); *Thomas J. Lipton Ltd. v. Salada Foods Ltd. (No. 3)* (1979), [1980] 1 F.C. 740, 45 C.P.R. (2d) 157 (Fed. T.D.); *Jordan & Ste-Michelle Cellars Ltd. v. T.G. Bright & Co.* (1984), 2 C.I.P.R. 45 (Fed. C.A.).

[125] *Eastman Photographic Materials Co. v. Comptroller-General of Patents, Designs & Trade Marks,* [1898] A.C. 571 (U.K. H.L.); *GWG Ltd. v. Canada (Registrar of Trade Marks)* (1981), 55 C.P.R. (2d) 1 (Fed. T.D.); *Thomson Research Associates Ltd. v. Canada (Registrar of Trade Marks)* (1982), 67 C.P.R. (2d) 205 (Fed. T.D.), affirmed (1983), 71 C.P.R. (2d) 287 (Fed. C.A.).

[126] *S.C. Johnson & Son Ltd. v. Marketing International Ltd.* (1979), [1980] 1 S.C.R. 99 (S.C.C.).

[127] *Eastman Photographic Materials Co. v. Comptroller-General of Patents, Designs & Trade Marks,* [1898] A.C. 571 (U.K. H.L.); *Pizza Pizza Ltd v. Canada (Registrar of Trade Marks)* (1982), 67 C.P.R. (2d) 202 (Fed. T.D.); *Clarkson*

The mere joining together of two descriptive words to form a single word[128] or the adding of a short, meaningless syllable or other trifling addition[129] will not be sufficient to avoid the prohibition. Similarly, misspelling or changes in the orthography of clearly descriptive words will not be sufficient to make them registrable trade marks.[130] In each case the first impression created by the trade mark, whether depicted, written or sounded, must be taken into consideration. A mark may be registrable as a whole although it includes a word which is clearly descriptive which is disclaimed.[131]

iv) Geographical Words

A trade mark which is clearly descriptive or deceptively misdescriptive of the place of origin of the wares or services it is sought to be registered in association with is not registrable.[132] The fact that words indicate origin does not necessarily preclude registration.[133] The purpose of the prohibition is to prevent one person from acquiring a monopoly with respect to a trade mark that is generally recognized as a locality connected with the wares or services in issue.

v) Conditions of or the Persons Employed in Production of Wares

A trade mark which is clearly descriptive or deceptively misdescriptive of the conditions of production or of the persons employed in the production

---

Gordon v. Canada (Registrar of Trade Marks) (1985), 5 C.P.R. (3d) 252 (Fed. T.D.).

[128] Unless the new word creates an impression separate and distinct from its components; see *General Motors Corp. v. Bellow*, [1948] Ex. C.R. 187 (Can. Ex. Ct.), affirmed [1949] S.C.R. 678 (S.C.C.); *Oshawa Group Ltd. v. Canada (Registrar of Trade Marks)* (1980), 46 C.P.R. (2d) 145 (Fed. T.D.).

[129] *Thomson Research Associates Ltd. v. Canada (Registrar of Trade Marks)* (1982), 67 C.P.R. (2d) 205 (Fed. T.D.), affirmed (1983), 71 C.P.R. (2d) 288n (Fed. C.A.).

[130] *Thorold Concrete Products v. Canada (Registrar of Trade Marks)* (1961), 37 C.P.R. 166 (Can. Ex. Ct.).

[131] *Lake Ontario Cement Ltd. v. Canada (Registrar of Trade Marks)* (1976), 31 C.P.R. (2d) 103 (Fed. T.D.); *GWG Ltd. v. Canada (Registrar of Trade Marks)* (1981), 55 C.P.R. (2d) 1 (Fed. T.D.).

[132] *Dower Brothers Ltd. v. Canada (Registrar of Trade Marks)*, [1940] Ex. C.R. 73 (Can. Ex. Ct.); *Atlantic Promotions Inc. v. Canada (Registrar of Trade Marks)* (1984), 2 C.P.R. (3d) 183 (Fed. T.D.).

[133] *Great Lake Hotels Ltd. v. Noshery Ltd.* (1968), 56 C.P.R. 165 (Can. Ex. Ct.).

of the wares or in the provision of the services, is not registrable. For example, the trade mark KILNCRAFT was not registrable in association with tableware. [134]

vi) *Disclaimer*

The Registrar of Trade-marks may require an applicant for registration of a trade mark to disclaim the right to the exclusive use of a portion of the trade mark which is not independently registrable. Such a disclaimer does not prejudice or affect the applicant's rights in the disclaimed matter.[135] The remaining portion of the mark must contain distinctive matter.[136]

A disclaimer of part of a trade mark may be used to overcome an objection based on descriptiveness or the use of a name or surname. However, a disclaimer may not be used in relation to a deceptively misdescriptive trade mark so as to make the trade mark as a whole registrable when the unregistrable matter is the dominant feature of the trade mark.[137]

d) Acquired Distinctiveness — Secondary Meaning

Trade marks that are not registrable because they are personal names or surnames or clearly descriptive or misdescriptive of the character or quality of wares or services or the conditions of or the persons employed in their production or of their place of origin may become registrable. If a mark within these categories has been used in Canada by the applicant or its predecessor in title such that it has become distinctive at the date of filing an application for its registration, it may be registered.[138] The issue is whether the mark has acquired distinctiveness through use so that it has "become" distinctive at the date of filing of an application,[139] not whether the mark is inherently distinctive or adapted so to distinguish[140] wares or services. Acquired distinctiveness through use is also referred to as secondary meaning.

---

[134] *Staffordshire Potteries Ltd. v. Canada (Registrar of Trade Marks)* (1976), 26 C.P.R. (2d) 134 (Fed. T.D.); *Canadian Council of Professional Engineers v. Lubrication Engineers Inc.* (1992), (sub nom. *Lubrication Engineers Inc. v. Canadian Council of Professional Engineers*), 41 C.P.R. (3d) 243 (Fed. C.A.).

[135] Section 35.

[136] *Molson Cos. v. John Labatt Ltd.* (1981), 58 C.P.R. (2d) 157 (Fed. T.D.).

[137] *Lake Ontario Cement Ltd. v. Canada (Registrar of Trade Marks)* (1976), 31 C.P.R. (2d) 103 (Fed. T.D.).

[138] Subsection 12(2).

[139] Subsection 12(2).

[140] Section 2, definition of "distinctive".

Even though a trade mark may be registered upon proof of acquired distinctiveness, the effect of the registration is limited by the Act. First, it is provided that no registration of a trade mark prevents the *bona fide* use by a person of his or her own name as a trade name or the *bona fide* use, other than as a trade mark, of any descriptive or geographical expression, in such a manner as to not likely have the effect of depreciating the value of the goodwill attaching to the registered trade mark.[141] Second, the Registrar must, having regard to the evidence produced, restrict the registration to the wares or services in association with which the trade mark is shown to have been so used as to have become distinctive and to the defined territorial area in Canada in which the trade mark has shown to have become distinctive.[142]

An applicant who claims that its trade mark is registrable under subsection 12(2) must file with the Registrar evidence by way of affidavit or statutory declaration establishing the extent to which and the time during which the trade mark has been used in Canada and any other evidence the Registrar may require in support of the claim.[143] The onus of showing that such a mark has acquired distinctiveness or secondary meaning is on the trade mark owner and is categorized as being a heavy burden.[144] However, the standard of proof remains on the balance of probabilities and reference to a heavy burden appears to refer to the exceptional aspect of subsection 12(2).[145]

The evidentiary burden of proving distinctiveness does not require proof of exclusive use of a trade mark since a trade mark that is distinctive to a substantial portion of the relevant market may be registered.[146]

The provisions of subsection 12(2) of the Act do not extend to a trade mark which is the name in any language of the wares or services in connection with which it is used or proposed to be used. Presumably, this type of trade mark is the generic name of the product and is not capable of acquiring distinctiveness. In addition, the subsection does not apply to a trade mark, which is in whole or in part a protected geographical indication, where the

---

[141] Section 20.

[142] Subsection 32(2) of the *Trade-marks Act.*

[143] Subsection 32(1) and see *Standard Coil Products (Can.) Ltd. v. Standard Radio Corp.* (1971), 1 C.P.R. (2d) 155 (Fed. T.D.), affirmed (1976), 26 C.P.R. (2d) 288 (Fed. C.A.).

[144] *Standard Coil Products (Can.) Ltd. v. Standard Radio Corp.* (1971), 1 C.P.R. (2d) 155 (Fed. T.D.), affirmed (1976), 26 C.P.R. (2d) 288 (Fed. C.A.).

[145] *Molson Breweries, a Partnership v. John Labatt Ltd.* (2000), 5 C.P.R. (4th) 180 (Fed. C.A.), leave to appeal refused (2000), 7 C.P.R. (4th) vi (S.C.C.).

[146] *Molson Breweries, a Partnership v. John Labatt Ltd.* (2000), 5 C.P.R. (4th) 180 (Fed. C.A.), leave to appeal refused (2000), 7 C.P.R. (4th) vi (S.C.C.).

trade mark is to be registered in association with a wine or a spirit not originating in a territory indicated by the geographical indication.[147]

If a trade mark has become distinctive at the date of registration, such registration shall not be held invalid merely on the ground that evidence of such distinctiveness was not submitted to the competent authority or tribunal before the grant of such registration.[148] Such proof may be adduced at any time and the registration held valid provided that the evidence is sufficient to show that the trade mark had become distinctive at the date of registration.[149]

The evidence of the respective deponents must be considered in light of the methods that were employed in selecting them so that the court can assess whether or not they are representative.[150] The deponents must not be induced to give their testimony by leading questions or other inappropriate practices.[151] A properly conducted survey may be accepted as evidence of secondary meaning.[152]

The subsection requires only that there be evidence of substantial recognition of the secondary meaning of the trade mark in the territorial area in Canada in issue.[153]

A claim that a mark has become distinctive depends on all the circumstances relating to the mark. Exclusive use of the mark may be compelling evidence but is not an absolute requirement.[154]

e) Names of Wares or Services

A trade mark is not registrable if it is the name in any language of any of the wares or services in association with which it is used or proposed to be used.[155] All languages are to be considered. Registration is denied to such trade marks since they cannot distinguish wares or services of one person from the wares or services of others. Such trade marks differ from trade

---

[147] Subsections 12(1) (c), 12(1)(g) and (h).

[148] Subsection 18(2).

[149] *John Labatt Ltd. v. Carling Breweries Ltd.* (1974), 18 C.P.R. (2d) 15 (Fed. T.D.).

[150] *Robert C. Wian Enterprises Inc. v. Mady* (1965), 46 C.P.R. 147 (Can. Ex. Ct.).

[151] *Canada (Registrar of Trade Marks) v. G.A. Hardie & Co.,* [1949] S.C.R. 483 (S.C.C.).

[152] *Canadian Schenley Distilleries Ltd. v. Canada's Manitoba Distillery Ltd.* (1975), 25 C.P.R. (2d) 1 (Fed. T.D.).

[153] *Trade Mark Examination Manual,* para. IV.10.03.

[154] *Molson Breweries, a Partnership v. John Labatt Ltd.* (2000), 5 C.P.R. (4th) 180 (Fed. C.A.), leave to appeal refused (2000), 7 C.P.R. (4th) vi (S.C.C.).

[155] Subsection 12(1)(c).

marks which are merely descriptive of character or quality or origin in that they are not eligible for registration, even upon proof of secondary meaning.

If only a portion of the trade mark is the name of the wares or services and the remaining portion of the mark contains distinctive matter the Registrar of Trade-marks may require an applicant for registration of the trade mark to disclaim the right to the exclusive use of the portion of the trade mark which is a name.

If a trade mark is allowed to become the name of the wares or services through popular use of the mark as a generic term the registration may be attacked on the basis that the mark is no longer distinctive.[156]

f) Confusing With a Registered Trade Mark

A trade mark is not registrable if it is confusing with a registered trade mark.[157] The word "confusing" when applied as an adjective to a trade mark or trade name is defined to mean a trade mark or trade name, the use of which would cause confusion in the manner and the circumstances described in section 6.[158] Section 6 provides that the use of a trade mark causes confusion with another trade mark if the use of both trade marks in the same area would be likely to lead to the inference that the wares or services associated with those trade marks are manufactured, sold, leased, hired or performed by the same person, whether or not such wares or services are of the same general class.

In determining whether trade marks are confusing, the Court or the Registrar, as the case may be, shall have regard to all of the surrounding circumstances including:

(a)   the inherent distinctiveness of the trade marks and the extent to which they have become known;
(b)   the length of time the trade marks have been in use;
(c)   the nature of the wares, services or business;
(d)   the nature of the trade; and
(e)   the degree of resemblance between the trade marks in appearance or sound or in the ideas suggested by them.[159]

---

[156] *Aladdin Industries Inc. v. Canadian Thermos Products Ltd.,* [1969] Ex. C.R. 80 (Can. Ex. Ct), affirmed (1972), [1974] S.C.R. 845 (S.C.C.).
[157] Subsection 12(1)(d).
[158] Section 2.
[159] Subsection 6(5).

Confusing trade marks are registrable if the applicant is the owner of all such trade marks, which are known as associated trade marks.[160] To be registrable under this exception, the applicant for registration of the confusing trade mark must be the same person as the owner of the registered trade mark. It is not sufficient if they are related companies. [161]

Upon the registration of any trade mark associated with any other registered trade mark a note of the registration of each trade mark will be made on the record of the registration of the other trade mark.[162]

No amendment of the register recording any change in the ownership in the name or address of the owner of any one of a group of associated trade marks will be made unless the Registrar is satisfied that the same change has occurred with respect to all of the trade marks in such group and corresponding entries are made contemporaneously with respect to all such trade marks.[163] The Registrar has a duty to refuse to record any assignment or change relating to only one of the associated trade marks.

g) Prohibited Trade Marks

A trade mark is not registrable if it is a prohibited mark as described in part 7(d) of this chapter.[164]

10. SUMMARY AND CHECKLIST

When commencing the process of selecting, changing or extending a brand name the following matters should be considered.

1. The brand name should symbolize the image and values desired to be associated with the brand.
2. The brand name should assure the customer that the goods or services associated with it will be of the quality or value the consumer has come to expect.
3. The brand name must distinguish the brand owner's goods or services from those of its competitors.

---

[160] Subsection 15(1) and see *Wilkinson Sword (Can.) Ltd. v. Juda* (1966), 51 C.P.R. 55 (Can. Ex. Ct.).

[161] See the definition of "related companies" in section 2 and *Ugine Aciers v. Canada (Registrar of Trade Marks)* (1978), 40 C.P.R. (2d) 28 (Fed. C.A.).

[162] Subsection 15(2).

[163] Subsection 15(3) and see *Philco International Corp. v. Canada (Registrar of Trade Marks)* (1979), 48 C.P.R. (2d) 86 (Fed. T.D.).

[164] Subsections 12(1)(e), (f), (g) and (h) and sections 9, 10, 10.1 and 11.1 to 11.2.

4.   In a global market there are a multitude of linguistic and cultural issues which will affect the choice of a brand name. The pronounceability and the meaning of the brand name in each relevant language must be considered. Similar considerations apply to the design presentation of the brand name.

5.   The brand name should be simple and easy to understand.

6.   The brand name should be easily remembered.

7.   The brand name should be easily readable and pronounceable.

8.   The brand name should be meaningful. A name should communicate positive product attributes and avoid unpleasant connotations.

9.   The proposed brand name must also be legally available in the countries it is proposed to be used. The availability of the mark for use and registration must be assessed separately in each country. Consideration must also be given to the availability of domain names which include the brand name or a substantial part of it.

10.   Carefully consider choosing a coined word as a brand name since considerable financial resources and time may be required before the brand name becomes known.

11.   Carefully consider choosing a brand name which incorporates the brand owner's trade name since this will tie the brand name to the trade name.

12.   Obtaining a trade mark registration will facilitate the protection of the brand name by granting exclusive rights to the trade mark owner and providing for public notice of such rights.

13.   A brand owner should understand how the trade mark system works when selecting a brand name since the decisions made will effect the rights potentially available in the future.

14.   The essence of a protectable trade mark is its distinctiveness. The critical factor is the message actually given to the public.

15.   There are a large number of official marks in Canada whose existence can cause problems for businesses seeking new marks or extending an existing brand name.

16.   The right to registration is not inherent in a trade mark but depends upon compliance with the terms of the *Trade-marks Act*. A number of characteristics may preclude obtaining a registration. A trade mark is not registrable if it is

(a)   primarily merely the name or the surname of an individual who is living or has died within the preceding thirty years;

(b)   whether depicted, written or sounded, either clearly descriptive or deceptively misdescriptive in the English or French language of the character or quality of the wares or services in association with which it is used or proposed to be used or of the conditions of or the persons employed in their production or of their place of origin;

(c)   the name in any language of any of the wares or services in connection with which it is used or proposed to be used;

(d)   confusing with a registered trade mark; or

(e)   a mark, denomination or protected geographical indication whose adoption is prohibited.

Chapter 3: Branding on the Internet

1. INTRODUCTION

The explosion of the internet and the rapid development of online commerce has had a significant impact on branding. As it has developed, the internet has changed from an instrument primarily used to exchange ideas and information to a means to sell goods and services. Notwithstanding some initial turbulence, the internet will continue to play a major role in the world economy.

The importance of brands is heightened on the internet since consumers will be more likely to rely on and trust a strong brand to give them confidence to make online purchases. Where neither face-to-face interaction nor an opportunity to inspect the goods are possible, a trusted brand is vitally important.

During the "dot.com boom", new dot.com companies rushed to build brand awareness in traditional ways. Many dot.com businesses spent more than half of their venture financing on brand development. While such spending was successful for some online businesses such as Amazon.com and America Online, other "dot.com" businesses failed to establish consistency in presenting their wares or services to the public, and were unsuccessful. At the same time established companies and brands attempted to enter the online world with varying degrees of success.

The internet has a number of advantages. First, it offers potential interactivity with consumers on a one-to-one basis. For example, foreign markets or foreign nationals living abroad can be targeted through email communications. More control can be exercised over such interactions than traditional methods of selling goods to the public, which are directed to a mass anonymous audience.

Second, internet businesses have the ability to manage traditional customers and transactions more efficiently. For example, Barnes and Noble and Amazon.com utilize online databases of titles and user-friendly purchasing systems to attract consumers. Once the up-front investment is made, additional products, customization for additional customers and other features can frequently be added or changed without incurring substantial costs.

Third, an online business can take advantage of network effects where the value of the network and the value that each consumer realizes increases disproportionately as more people join it. This is also referred to as viral marketing. Email lists, websites, chat rooms and bulletin boards allow effective communication and marketing with a minimal budget at a much faster rate than conventional methods. For example, Hotmail.com created a subscriber base more rapidly than any company in history and currently is the largest email provider in the world. Their strategy was to give away free email addresses and services but attached a tag to the bottom of every free message stating "Get your private, free email at *http://www.hotmail.com*".

Fourth, companies can use their websites as a communication/marketing vehicle and as a distribution channel. A website can serve as storefront, office and distribution centre in cyberspace. For example, Dell Inc. applied a direct marketing model to the internet with tremendous success. It delivered its products directly to the public through its own distribution channel and avoided the necessity of going through other channels of distribution.

Finally, the internet has significantly expanded the ability of companies to offer loyalty programs to consumers. This is important in encouraging customers to make multiple purchases and establish online customer loyalty.

Notwithstanding these developments and the potential advantages of the internet, most commentators agree that the traditional rules for successfully developing brands are no different in the online world than in the traditional "bricks and mortar" world.[165] Although there is the potential for increased efficiency, luring potential customers to a site, maintaining customer interest and developing customer loyalty are daunting tasks, particularly since the internet itself has vastly increased consumer choice and control. The strong brands that survived the end of the dot.com boom appear to have adopted traditional branding theory and developed differentiated brand names such as AMAZON, LYCOS, GOOGLE and AMERICA ON-LINE.

Online branding strategies will be important to business thinking for years to come. Online businesses will continue to develop internet brands by providing a tailored one-to-one experience to consumers. Such an approach has been followed by Amazon.com and Travelocity.com.

Established bricks and mortar businesses may use the internet to reinforce their brands. By developing a website they add value for their customers by providing information and building a better relationship. Typically, many companies in this position cannot conveniently deliver or distribute

---

[165] See generally *Branding@thedigitalage*, edited by H. Myers and R. Gerstman, (2001).

their product over the internet. American Express, Pepsi and BMW are examples of companies which currently use this approach.

Finally, other businesses have repositioned their brands to include complimentary internet channels. These businesses must be careful to avoid alienating their existing customers or distribution networks. Typical of businesses in this category are large brokerage companies which have traditional direct client relationships but who have since developed online trading capabilities at lower commission levels.

2. BASIC CONCEPTS

a) The Internet

The internet is a global web of interconnecting computer networks. It was originally created in early 1969 under the name ARPANET as a U.S. Department of Defence project. The project was intended to create a global communications network which could provide uninterrupted computer communications during a catastrophe. Since the internet is a web of networks, communications are routed from point to point via many alternative routes.

The internet is accessible to virtually anyone with a computer and a modem. At the end of 2002, it was estimated that the global number of internet users was 655 million.[166] By using the internet individuals can send e-mail, upload and download files, remotely log on to other computers and access the world-wide web. While e-mail and information searches are the most common uses, the online purchase of goods and services is increasing despite consumer concerns with respect to protection of personal data and security of internet transactions.

Websites on the internet are actually files stored on computers acting as servers to which internet access is provided. The pages of the site are written in a format which can be read by internet browsers such as Netscape or Internet Explorer. The most common format is Hypertext Markup Language (HTML). HTML allows hypertext links to be created so that individuals browsing a specific page can jump to another website at the notional click of a button.

When a hypertext link is activated, typically by clicking a mouse, a message is sent to the requested site and a copy of the page is downloaded to the computer of the individual who commenced the process.

---

[166] "E-Commerce and Development Report 2002" of the United Nations Conference on Trade and Development. Nua Internet Surveys, Nua.com report suggests more than 600 million at *http://www.nua.com/surveys*.

HTML provides for hidden text which can be read by browsers or search engines such as Google, Yahoo or Altavista. The hidden text can be stored within the comment lines or meta-tags. The hidden text is normally invisible to individuals who visit the site.

b) The Domain Name System

Domain names are the alpha numeric text strings to the right of the "@" in an e-mail address or immediately following the two slashes in a web address. By convention, the domain name specifies an internet protocol (IP) number consisting of a network address and a host ID on a TCP/IP network. The IP numbers play a critical role in addressing all communications over the internet.

Because the IP numbers are difficult to remember, alpha numeric domain names were introduced as a mnemonic. When an individual types an alpha numeric Uniform Resource Locator (URL) into a web browser, the host computer translates the domain name into an IP number. Since IP numbers can be arbitrarily assigned to domain names, the names can remain constant even when the resources to which they refer change.

The domain naming conventions treat a domain name as having three parts. For example, in the address *www.casselsbrock.com*, the ".com" is the Top Level Domain or TLD, while "casselsbrock" is the Second Level Domain (SLD). Any additional reference is treated as a third or higher level domain.

The legacy root, the most widely used list of TLDs which will actually map to IP numbers, is currently made up of 249 two-letter country code TLDs (ccTLDs), a number of three-letter generic TLDs (gTLDs) currently consisting of .com, .net, .org, .biz and proposed .pro, and a number of four letter TLDs including .arpa, .info, .name, .aero, and .coop. The ccTLDs are primarily derived from the International Organization for Standards (IOS) Standard 3166 and include .ca for Canada and .us for the United States among others.

There have been conflicting views over whether new TLDs should be added to the legacy root. There are also a number of alternative TLDs that are not acknowledged by the majority of domain name servers.

The gTLDs allow anyone from anywhere to register as many available domain names as they wish. For this reason they are sometimes referred to as unrestricted or open domains. Other domains are referred to as restrictive, since a registrant must meet certain requirements. For example, .name is limited to individuals, .pro is limited to accredited lawyers, doctors, accountants and so on. In addition, some ccTLDs are restricted and require a local presence or specific legal documentation in order to register, although many ccTLDs are unrestricted.[167]

The United States government came to control the domain name system because the individuals who developed it depended on government grants. In 1992, Network Solutions Inc., a public company, became responsible for the operation of the system, including registration of domain names in the .com, .net and .org registries. Until 1998, Network Solutions was the sole register and administrator of the commercial gTLDs.

As a result of dissatisfaction with this system, the U.S. Department of Commerce initiated a consultative process that resulted in the creation of the Internet Corporation for Assigned Names and Numbers (ICANN) to manage the internet name and address system. Among other things, ICANN opened up the domain name registration market to competition and implemented a Uniform Dispute Resolution Policy (UDRP) to resolve disputes between competing domain name claimants.

Canada's ccTLD, the .ca domain, was first available in May of 1987. It was initially managed by John Demco of the University of British Columbia but in 1997 the Canadian Internet Registration Authority (CIRA) was created to make the .ca domain more commercial. CIRA is a not-for-profit organization which operates and manages the .ca registry.

3. DOMAIN NAMES

a) Availability

The first step in obtaining domain names is to make an assessment of which gTLD and/or ccTLD is appropriate. Consideration must be given to registering names in multiple languages and for variations which are either used or may be used or which could be used by third parties. Registrations should be obtained to allow for future expansion or to prevent or block third parties from obtaining them. The number of variants in issue, combined with the number of TLDs involved, can make the process both complex and expensive.

Second, if the domain name is not a component of an existing registered trade mark owned by the brand owner, trade mark availability searches should be done to ensure that the use of the domain name will not infringe the rights of existing trade mark owners or the common law rights of others,

---

[167] For a survey on the role of national governments in ccTLDs see Michael Geist, *Governments and Country-Code Top Level Domains: A Global Survey*, Preliminary Report, December 2003 at *http://www.michaelgeist.ca/geistgovernmentcctlds.pdf*.

particularly traders who carry on business on the internet. Since the gTLDs are available to business and individuals around the world and grant exclusive worldwide rights in any registered domain name, in appropriate cases consideration must be given to trade mark rights in more than one country.

The registration system is first-come-first-served and there is no assessment of registrability or entitlement or a process of opposition similar to that which typically applies to trade marks. A name which is not registrable as a trade mark because it is generic or descriptive may still serve as a domain name and the allocation of a domain name is not dependent upon use within a specific territory or limited to specific wares or services. Domain names serve as an address and each name must be unique but very small differences can distinguish one from another within the domain name system.

Typically, there will be a WHOIS search database for each gTLD and ccTLD which can be consulted online to ascertain if a domain name has previously been registered in that TLD. For gTLDs, public availability of WHOIS data is mandated by ICANN through Registrar Accreditation Agreements. These agreements require registrars to collect and maintain accurate and up-to-date contact data from domain name holders. Typically, this is done through a WHOIS service. The situation with respect to ccTLD domains is less certain and there is considerable variation concerning whether a WHOIS function is provided and what information is contained in it.[168]

b) Acquisition and Management

i) Registration

Once it is decided which gTLD(s) and/or ccTLD(s) is appropriate, registration of a domain name may be carried out by submitting an application to the appropriate registrar. Typically, this is done online and it is merely a matter of providing the necessary information that the registrar requires.

Registrants who wish to register in the .com, .org or .net domains or other gTLD domains must do so through a registrar who has been accredited by ICANN. Through its Registrar Accreditation Agreements,[169] ICANN requires that registrars must enter into a written registration agreement with

---

[168] For a list of ccTLD registries see *www.iana.org/cctld/cctld-whois.htm*.
[169] See Registrar Accreditation Agreement at *http://www.icann.org/registrars/ra-agreement*.

an applicant for a domain name which includes provisions dealing with the following matters:

(a) an applicant must provide accurate and reliable contact details and promptly correct and update them during the term of the registration;

(b) that, to the best of the applicant's knowledge and belief, the registration of the domain name or the manner in which it is used will not infringe the legal rights of any third parties;

(c) the willful provision of inaccurate or unreliable information, the willful failure to update information or the failure to respond to registrar inquiries by the registrant for over 15 days shall be a material breach and a basis for cancellation of the registration; and

(d) the registrant agrees that its registration is subject to a mandatory administrative dispute resolution policy.

In order to obtain a registration in the .ca domain, applicants must satisfy the Canadian presence requirements.[170] As with ICANN, an applicant must use a CIRA certified registrar to effect the registration and agree to be subject to the CIRA domain name dispute resolution policy.

ii) Management

There are ongoing domain name management issues. Each registration includes applicable contact information for the registrant, billing, administration and technical matters. If there are multiple domain names and different employees or departments involved within a business, it can be difficult to coordinate the management process. In some cases, third parties such as an advertising agency may register a domain name relating to a promotional event. Because of this, it is prudent to develop a generic name and e-mail address as the standard contact information for all domain name registrations. This will avoid potential problems where employees named in a registration leave the company or their employment is terminated. Similar considerations apply to access codes and account information with registrars.

The importance of developing generic contact information is illustrated in two situations. First, there may be numerous renewal dates for existing domain name registrations. If a renewal notice is not appropriately responded to, a registrar may de-activate the domain in which case it will no

---

[170] See registration rules at *http://www.cira.ca*.

longer resolve to the designated IP address, resulting in blank pages or error messages when customers attempt to browse the site. Further, the de-activated domain name may become available for registration by a third party.

Second, the administrative contact for a domain name frequently has the authority to change any aspect of the domain name record, including the server that the IP address points to. If an individual employee, listed as a domain administrative contact, leaves the company on unfavorable terms, the prospect for problems exists if the employee knows that they can control the relevant domain names.

It can be helpful to have similar domain names consolidated into a single account with a specific registrar as this will assist in management of these domain names. Some registrars will allow customers to assign varying access levels to designated individuals.

It is also important to conduct searches from time to time to ascertain whether domain names have been registered which are similar to or confusing with the domain names being managed.

c) Protecting Domain Names as Trade Marks

A domain name which satisfies the registrability requirements of the *Trade-marks Act*[171] and is used as a trade mark[172] may be protected as a trade mark. [173] In Canada, this means that such trade marks must be registered in association with services.[174] Amazon.com[175] or Yahoo.com are good examples of domain names which are commonly associated with the online services provided by the trade mark owner.

---

[171] See **Chapter 2, part 9** and see *Black v. Molson Canada* (2002), 21 C.P.R. (4th) 52 (Ont. S.C.J.).

[172] See **Chapter 4, part 3.**

[173] *ITV Technologies Inc. v. WIC Television Ltd.* (2003), 29 C.P.R. (4th) 182 (F.C.).

[174] See *Pro-C Ltd. v. Computer City Inc.* (2001), 55 O.R. (3d) 577 (Eng.) (Ont. C.A.), leave to appeal refused (2001), 2001 CarswellOnt 5074 (S.C.C.) concerning use in general. For cases discussing the practice in the U.S. Patent and Trade mark Office, see *In Re Eilberg*, 49 U.S.P.Q.2d 1955 (TTAB 1998); *In Re MediaShare Corp.*, 43 U.S.P.Q.2d 1304 (TTAB 1997).

[175] Where the trade mark includes a reference to a gTLD or ccTLD, the applicant will be required to disclaim the right to the exclusive use apart from the trade mark of these references. See section 35 of the *Trade-marks Act* and **Chapter 4, part 5(d)**.

4. INTERNET CONCERNS

a) Cybersquatting and the UDRP

Cybersquatting occurs when a third party registers a domain name consisting of, or similar to, a brand name to which they have no legitimate claim and later attempts to sell or license the registered domain name to the brand owner. In the classic case, the cybersquatter registers domain names that are similar or identical to a registered trade mark.

Cyberpiracy occurs when a domain name incorporating a variation of a brand name is used on a website to lure traffic from the brand owner's site. A variation, sometimes referred to as typosquatting, occurs when the third party registers a domain name virtually identical to a brand name but misspelt with the intention of getting hits from individuals who inadvertently misspell or mistype the brand name.[176]

Actions brought in the courts have been successful in enjoining this type of activity. For example, in *British Telecom plc v. One In A Million Ltd.*,[177] the defendant systematically registered domain names containing the brand names of well known British companies presumably with the intention of selling them back to the brand owners. The Court found that this constituted trade mark infringement under the relevant U.K. legislation as well as passing off.

In 1999, the World Intellectual Property Organization (WIPO) released a report entitled *The Management of Internet Names and Addresses; Intellectual Property Issues*.[178] The purpose of the report was to provide recommendations to ICANN concerning the implementation of a policy dealing with the conflict between intellectual property owners and the internet and domain names. The report was directed to domain name registers of the gTLDs.

The report contained many recommendations, including a recommendation that domain name registration agreements require that an applicant submit to an administrative dispute resolution policy limited to cases of abusive registration of domain names. This recommendation was imple-

---

[176] See *A & F Trademark, Inc. et al. v. Party Night, Inc.,* (May 28, 2003), Doc. D2003-0172 (WIPO) decided under the UDRP.

[177] [1998] 4 All E.R. 476 (Eng. C.A.) and see *Law Society (British Columbia) v. Canada Domain Name Exchange Corp.* (2002), 22 C.P.R. (4th) 88 (B.C. S.C. [In Chambers]); *Rolls-Royce plc v. Fitzwilliam* (2002), 19 C.P.R. (4th) 1 (Fed. T.D.).

[178] *http://wipo2.wipo.int.*

mented and a Uniform Domain Name Dispute Resolution Policy[179] (UDRP) was approved and adopted on October 24, 1999.

The UDRP policy is incorporated by reference into applicable registration agreements and sets forth the terms and conditions applicable to a dispute between the registrant and a third party relating to the registration and use of a domain name. The UDRP has been adopted by all accredited registrars for domains ending in .com, .net, .org and .biz. It has also been adopted for many ccTLDs.

A registrant is required to submit to a mandatory administrative proceeding in the event that a complainant asserts that:

(a)   the domain name is identical or confusingly similar to a trade mark or service mark in which the complainant has rights;

(b)   the registrant has no rights or legitimate interest in respect of the domain name; and

(c)   the domain name has been registered and is being used in bad faith.

The complainant must prove each of these elements are present.

For the purpose of such proceedings, the following circumstances, in particular but without limitation if found to be present, are evidence of registration and use of a domain name in bad faith:

(a)   circumstances indicating that the registrant has registered or acquired the domain name primarily for the purpose of selling, renting, or otherwise transferring the domain name registration to the complainant, who is the owner of the trademark or service mark or to a competitor of that complainant, for valuable consideration in excess of documented out-of-pocket costs directly related to the domain name; or

(b)   the registrant has registered the domain name in order to prevent the owner of the trademark or service mark from reflecting the mark in a corresponding domain name, provided that the registrant has engaged in a pattern of such conduct; or

(c)   the registrant has registered the domain name primarily for the purpose of disrupting the business of a competitor; or

(d)   by using the domain name, the registrant has intentionally attempted to attract, for commercial gain, internet users to its website or other on-line location, by creating a likelihood of confusion with the complainant's mark as to the source, sponsorship, affil-

---

[179] *http://www.icann.org/dndr/udrp/policy.htm.*

iation, or endorsement of the registrant's website or location or of a product or service on the registrant's website or location.

The complainant selects the arbitrator from among those approved by ICANN by submitting the complaint to a specific service provider. The service provider maintains a publicly available list of panelists and selects the individual panelist who will hear the arbitration unless either of the parties elects to have a three member panel. All fees charged by the service provider are the responsibility of the complainant; if the registrant chooses to expand the number of arbitrators from one to three, the fees will be split evenly.

The remedies available are limited to requiring the cancellation of the registration or the transfer of the registration to the complainant. The existence of the proceedings does not prevent either the registrant or the complainant from submitting the dispute to a court of competent jurisdiction either before or after the mandatory administrative proceeding is initiated.

If it is decided that the domain name should be canceled or transferred, the registrant is given 10 business days before the decision is implemented to commence legal proceedings against the complainant, if so advised. Such proceedings must be instituted either in the jurisdiction in which the registrar is located, provided that the registrant contractually submitted to jurisdiction there, or the location of the registrant as shown in the registrar's WHOIS database.[180]

While most arbitrations are not precedent based, UDRP decisions typically cite other UDRP decisions. This can create some difficulties as there is no statutory right to appeal and there are a multitude of decisions.

The UDRP was intended to apply to the most direct and obvious forms of abusive registration, leaving more difficult cases to the courts. However, the application of the policy has been broadened as UDRP decisions have expanded the definition of bad faith through precedent. First, it has been widely accepted that passive holding of a domain name constitutes bad faith use.[181] Second, false or inaccurate contact information may be proof of bad faith. Finally, some cases have found that anyone who knowingly registers a name that is identical or similar to a trade mark is, by virtue of that fact alone, guilty of bad faith registration and use.[182]

---

[180] *Black v. Molson Canada* (2002), 21 C.P.R. (4th) 52 (Ont. S.C.J.).

[181] *Telstra v. Nuclear Marshmellows*, Doc. D2000-0003 (WIPO). For an annotated version of the UDRP, see *Berkman Centre for Internet & Society UDRP Opinion Guide* at *http://cyber.law.harvard.edu/udrp/opinion/contents.html*.

[182] *Veuve Clicquot Ponsardin, Maison Fondee en 1772 v. The Polygenix Group Co.*, Doc. D2000-0163 (WIPO). This is referred to as opportunistic bad faith.

Concerns have been raised concerning the policy because complainant selection of dispute providers has a tendency to reward providers who deliver name transfers.[183]

While the UDRP has been adopted by all accredited domain name registers for the gTLDs, it has not been adopted by all managers of ccTLDs. The CIRA has developed and adopted its own domain name dispute resolution policy (CDRP)[184] and rules. While the CDRP appears to be have been modeled after the UDRP policy there are significant differences between the two. The application of the CDRP is limited to situations in which a complainant establishes that:

(a)   the registrant's dot-ca domain name is confusingly similar to a mark to which the complainant had rights prior to the date of registration of the domain name and continues to have such rights;

(b)   the registrant has no legitimate interest in the domain name as described in CDRP; and

(c)   the registrant has registered the domain name in bad faith as described in CDRP.

The terms "confusingly similar", "mark" and "rights" are defined in CDRP in a detailed fashion. This is different from the UDRP which is much more open-ended.[185]

The United States enacted the *Anticybersquatting Consumer Protection Act* (ACPA) in late 1999 to enable trade mark owners to enforce trade marks and personality rights against cybersquatters. The ACPA provides for significant protections and broad remedies. There is no Canadian equivalent of this legislation.

---

[183] Michael Geist, *Fair.com? An Examination of the Allegation of Systematic Unfairness in the ICANN UDRP* online at *http.//aix1.uottawa.ca/~geist/geistudrp.pdf* and *FundamentallyFair.com? An Update on Bias Allegations and the ICANN UDRP* online at *http.//www.michaelgeist.ca*. Similar comments have been made about providers under the CDRP policy; see article in the *Toronto Star* by Mr. Geist August 11, 2003, *Fairness demands review of domain-name policy.*

[184] Online at *http://www.cira.ca/en/cat-dpr-policy.html.*

[185] See *Cheap Tickets & Travel Inc. v. Emall.ca Inc.* (2003), 25 C.P.R. (4th) 105 (C.I.R.A.); *Elysium Wealth Management Inc. v. Driscol* (2003), 25 C.P.R. (4th) 120 (C.I.R.A.); *Canadian Broadcasting Corp. v. Quon* (2003), 25 C.P.R. (4th) 519 (C.I.R.A.); *Canada v. Bedford* (2003), 2003 CarswellNat 4194, 27 C.P.R. (4th) 522 (C.I.R.A.); *Trans Union LLC v. 1491070* (2003), 27 C.P.R. (4th) 148 (C.I.R.A.); *The Queen in the right of Alberta v. Advantico Internet Solutions Inc.* (2003), 28 C.P.R. (4th) 108 (C.I.R.A.).

b) Criticism or Gripe Sites

There have been a number of cases both in the courts and under the UDRP involving parody sites or sites for critical commentary. Frequently, a domain name is obtained which consists of the brand owner's trade mark combined with the word "sucks" but other methods are also used.

A related problem is referred to as cybersmearing. This term has been used to describe venomous e-mails and postings on online bulletin boards. Frequently, large corporations are the target of such activities. For example, one company discovered that an anonymous internet user posted information to suggest that the company failed to tell investors about a pending lawsuit and implied upcoming losses of over $300 million.

From a brand owner's point of view, it may be difficult to determine how to react to a parody or criticism site or cybersmearing. Some humorous parodies may pose little threat to a brand. On the other hand, a site disseminating information through the phenomena of viral marketing may do significant damage. In order to determine whether steps should be taken, the following matters will be particularly important: who or what is the target of the parody? What is the intent of the parody? What is the breadth and source of the parody?

Once it is decided that it is necessary to take steps, there are a number of possible courses of action. One method of proceeding is to initiate proceedings for infringement of the brand owner's intellectual property rights. A number of Canadian cases have held that the fact that a defendant has created a parody or a burlesque is not a defence to a claim for copyright infringement[186] and have found infringement if copying or reproduction has occurred.[187] However, the courts have been reluctant to find that such activities constitute trade mark infringement, since typically there is no trade mark use as required by the Act.[188]

The statements contained on the site may be defamatory or actionable as an injurious falsehood. If this is the case, proceedings may be brought in the courts.

---

[186] *Cie générale des etablissements Michelin - Michelin & Cie v. CAW – Canada* (1996), 71 C.P.R. (3d) 348 (Fed. T.D.).

[187] *British Columbia Automobile Assn. v. O.P.E.I.U., Local 378* (2001), 10 C.P.R. (4th) 423 (B.C. S.C.).

[188] *Cie générale des etablissements Michelin - Michelin & Cie v. CAW – Canada* (1996), 71 C.P.R. (3d) 348 (Fed. T.D.) and see *Pro-C Ltd. v. Computer City Inc.* (2001), 55 O.R. (3d) 577 (Eng.) (Ont. C.A.), leave to appeal refused (2001), 2001 CarswellOnt 5074 (S.C.C.) concerning use in general.

A domain name challenge under the UDRP is possible. Unfortunately the effectiveness of such complaints is less than clear; some complaints have been dismissed while some have been allowed.[189]

One method of attempting to prevent such actions is to implement a "blocking" strategy. Under this approach the brand owner purchases domain names that could be misused if they were in the wrong hands. For example, owning the brand name combined with the word "sucks" may make it more difficult to establish a criticism or gripe site.

c) Pop-Up Advertisements and Mouse Trapping

Pop-up advertisements are used to catch consumer's attention. A pop-up advertisement is a window not initiated by a user which appears on the user's computer screen when a site is loaded. A user who clicks on the pop-up graphic will be redirected to another website.[190]

Mouse trapping is an aggressive technique that forces users to remain on a specific website by disabling the functionality of their browser or flooding them with pop-up advertisements. Whenever the user tries to leave the site by using the back, forward or close buttons on the browser display screen a new window is automatically opened that prevents the browser from leaving the site. To exit this loop the user is forced to close the internet connection or to reboot their computer.

---

[189] Dr. Milton Mueller, *Success by Default: A New Profile Of Domain Name Trade Mark Disputes under ICANN's UDRP*, Syracruse University School of Information Studies, June 24, 2002. See *Wal-Mart Stores, Inc. v. wallmartcanadasucks.com and Kenneth J. Harvey* (November 23, 2000), Doc. D2000-1104 (WIPO) and *Lockheed Martin Corporation v. Dan Paris* (January 26, 2001), Doc. D2000-1015 (WIPO), where it was concluded that a word or phrase created by appending "sucks" to a trade mark was not confusingly similar to the trademark itself. However, also see *TPI Holdings, Inc. v. AFX Communications a/k/a/ AFX* (February 2, 2001), Doc. D2000-1472 (WIPO); *The Royal Bank of Scotland Group plc, National Westminster Bank plc a/k/a/ NatWest Bank v. Personal and Pedro Lopez* (May 9, 2003), Doc. D2003-0166 (WIPO); *Bayer Aktiengelsellschaft v. Dangos & Partners* (February 3, 2003), Doc. D2002-1115 (WIPO); and *Diageo plc v. John Zuccarini* (October 22, 2000), Doc. D2000-0996 (WIPO), where it was found that gripe site domain names were confusingly similar to a trade mark owned by the complainant.

[190] U.S. case law on the legality of pop-up advertising is unclear. To date, two cases have found that such advertising was not objectionable: *U-Haul International v. WhenU.Com Inc.*, 279 F.supp.2d 723 (E.D. Virginia); *Wells Fargo & Co. v. WhenU.Com Inc.*, Doc. 03-71906 (E.D. Michigan). However, at least one case found such practice to be objectionable contrary to the *Latham Act: 1-800 Contacts Inc. v. WhenU.Com*, Doc. 02 Civ. 8043 (D.A.B.) (S.D.N.Y.).

In an action brought by the United States Federal Trade Commission, John Zuccarini was enjoined from diverting or obstructing consumers on the internet in this fashion. Zuccarini had been registering internet domain names that were misspellings or versions of legitimate domain names-typosquatting. Once a consumer reached one of these sites they were unable to exit it.[191]

d) Metatags and Keywords

A metatag is a computer code contained on a website which is invisible to an individual but which enables a search engine or a web browser to identify that particular website. In addition, many web pages include keyword summaries of the contents of the site in an effort to increase searchability by search engines.

Keywords are commercially exploited and operate independently of the domain system on the layer above it as an alternative method of accessing a site. For example, they have been incorporated into Microsoft's Internet Explorer to provide a shortcut to a website without having to know the whole address. When the word Ford is typed into such a browser an individual will be re-directed to *www.ford.com*. In addition, various search engines offer website owners the opportunity to register sites or keywords with their search engine.

The owner of a website may attempt to increase traffic to the site by entering into agreements with the operators of various search engines to give the site greater exposure. Because each search engine follows its own rules, a strategy which works for one may diminish results with another.

In addition, an owner can arrange for banner or pop-up advertisements which are triggered by certain key words.[192] A pop-up ad is a window not initiated by the user that appears automatically. If the user clicks on the ad they are typically linked to the advertiser's site.

---

[191] *FTC v. Zuccarini*, Doc. 01-CV-4854, (U.S. District Court for the Eastern District of Pennsylvania).

[192] For a discussion of these concepts in the context of an action for infringement and passing off, see *Reed Executive PLC v. Reed Business Information Limited* (May 20, 2002), (High Court of Justice, Chancery Decision), (March 3, 2004) (Court of Appeal (Civil Division)); *U-Haul International Inc. v. WhenU.com, Inc.*, Doc. Civ-02-1469-A, (U.S. District Court for the Eastern District of Virginia, Alexandra Division); *Wells Fargo & Company v. WhenU.com, Inc.* Doc. Civ-03-71906, 2003 (U.S. District Court for the Eastern District of Michigan, Southern Division); *1-800 Contacts Inc. v. WhenU.Com*, Doc. 02 Civ. 8043 (D.A.B.) (S.D.N.Y.).

The goal of many website owners has been to maximize the ranking of their site in searches carried out on search engines and browser programs. Search engine operators have developed protocols to rank sites for the purpose of searching and will sell rankings guaranteeing that a site will appear first in the top ten when a certain search term is used.[193] Optimization is a trial and error process that requires persistence and a careful monitoring of the results. The teamwork of technical personnel and those involved in the implementation of the branding strategy is required.

A number of disputes have occurred in the U.S. where one party uses the trade name or mark of another party in its metatags to attract business and increase traffic to its web page. Some U.S. cases have found that such activities constitute trade mark infringement under relevant U.S. legislation.[194] However, it has been suggested that there may be cases where such use is a legitimate use.[195]

In the English case of *Reed Executive PLC v. Reed Business Information Limited*,[196] a judge of the High Court of Justice was prepared to accept that an inappropriate metatag reference was trade mark infringement under the wording of the U.K. trade mark legislation and, in addition, constituted passing off. However, the wording of the trade marks legislation in that country is substantially different from the Canadian legislation.

In the Canadian case of *British Columbia Automobile Association v. O.P.E.I.U., Local 378*,[197] which involved a labour dispute, the Court had to determine whether various versions of the defendant's website, some of which included metatags similar to the plaintiff's trade marks, amounted to passing off, among other claims. The Court was not prepared to find the most current website and its metatags constituted passing off, but an earlier

---

[193] Information is typically available at the websites of search engines or other interested parties such as *www.google.com*, *www.searchenginewatch.com*, *www.spider-food.net* and *www.yahoo.com*. The U.S. Federal Trade Commission has asked search engine operators to clearly label advertising-sponsored listings so that consumers may differentiate between paid and unpaid listings. The Commission has also requested that operators that use unpaid inclusion programs offer users a clear description of how the program works. For a case that involved Google, see *Search King, Inc. v. Google Technology*, Doc. CIV-02-1457-M (U.S. District Ct -Western District of Oklahoma 2003).

[194] For a summary of some of these cases, see *British Columbia Automobile Assn. v. O.P.E.I.U., Local 378* (2001), 10 C.P.R. (4th) 423 (B.C. S.C.).

[195] *Promatek Industries Ltd. v. Equitrac Corp.*, 300 F.3d 808 (7th Cir. Ill. 2002).

[196] (May 20, 2002) (High Court of Justice, Chancery Decision).

[197] *British Columbia Automobile Assn. v. O.P.E.I.U., Local 378* (2001), 10 C.P.R. (4th) 423 (B.C. S.C.); *Law Society (British Columbia) v. Canada Domain Name Exchange Corp.*, 2002 BCSC 1249 (B.C. S.C. [In Chambers]).

version of the site was found to be objectionable and its use constituted passing off.

e) Linking and Framing

The concept of linking is fundamental to the internet. Linking occurs when an image or reference on a website is selected, causing that document to be automatically displayed to the selecting party. By taking advantage of the link, the party selecting it does not need to enter a URL or other address and obtains rapid access to the linked information. There are a number of different types of links depending on whether the link is within a specific site or to another site or activated or automatic.

A link is automatic when a code is embedded in the web page which instructs the browser, upon obtaining access to the first site, to automatically download a file from the second site. The information from the second site is presented without the need for further action on the part of the user. A link is user-activated when the user clicks the mouse button over the hyperlink in order to obtain access to the information from the second site. If the linked files are located on another server, the user's browser makes a direct connection to the second server. The user activated link may be made to the home page or a sub-page located in the second site, in which case the end user may have to take further action to access a particular file at that site. The link may also be made directly to a specific file, in which case the user will receive the content represented by that file without the need for further action.[198]

The law concerning linking and more specifically whether it could constitute copyright infringement[199] or trade mark infringement in an appropriate case is unsettled. In addition, it is unclear whether consent is required to establish a link.

Framing is a technique whereby information from another website can be viewed while remaining on the initial website. A computer screen is divided into multiple windows by building frames typically consisting of graphics on which the other website is displayed. The law concerning framing is unsettled.

---

[198] *Society of Composers, Authors & Music Publishers of Canada v. Canadian Assn. of Internet Providers* (1999), (sub nom. *SOCAN Statement of Royalties, Public Performance of Musical Works 1996, 1997, 1998 (Tariff 22, Internet), Re)* 1 C.P.R. (4th) 417 (Copyright Bd.), reversed (2002), 19 C.P.R. (4th) 289 (Fed. C.A.), leave to appeal allowed (2003), 2003 CarswellNat 738 (S.C.C.).

[199] See for example Catherine Bate, *O What a Tangled WorldWide Web We Weave: An Analysis of Linking under Canadian Copyright Law,* (2002) 60:21 University of Toronto Faculty of Law Review.

f) Jurisdictional Issues

The recent development of websites and e-commerce raises a number of issues concerning the jurisdiction of a particular court to deal with disputes relating to these matters. Each court has specific rules for determining its jurisdiction and rules or policies concerning when it will respect the jurisdiction of the courts of other countries.

Traditionally, the jurisdiction of courts has been territorial. The concept of jurisdiction was initially based on the royal prerogative. It was established that rulers only had power within the territorial confines of their respective countries. With some exceptions, jurisdiction is still territorial to this date. This is particularly so with respect to intellectual property rights, including registered trade marks and patents which may only be asserted in the territorial jurisdiction for which they have been obtained.

It has been difficult to apply the concept of jurisdiction to the internet, since, as it is frequently said, the internet knows no boundaries. More specifically, when advertisements or other statements containing representations or referring to trade marks and copyright material are reproduced on a website which is available to consumers, it must be determined which court has jurisdiction with respect to potential disputes. Possible disputes include claims relating to contracts, intellectual property, consumer protection, product liability and defamation among others. When such claims are made relating to material reproduced on a website, the owner of the website needs to know in which jurisdiction such claims may be asserted.

There have been relatively few Canadian cases dealing with such matters. While the general requirement that there be a real and substantial connection with the jurisdiction and the activity in issue has been applied,[200] some Canadian courts have applied the approach that has been developed in American jurisprudence.[201]

---

[200] *Society of Composers, Authors & Music Publishers of Canada v. Canadian Assn. of Internet Providers* (1999), (sub nom. *SOCAN Statement of Royalties, Public Performance of Musical Works 1996, 1997, 1998 (Tariff 22, Internet), Re*) 1 C.P.R. (4th) 417 (Copyright Bd.), reversed (2002), 19 C.P.R. (4th) 289 (Fed. C.A.), leave to appeal allowed (2003), 2003 CarswellNat 738 (S.C.C.); *Morguard Investments Ltd. v. De Savoye* (1990), [1990] 3 S.C.R. 1077 (S.C.C.); *Muscutt v. Courcelles* (2002), 60 O.R. (3d) 20 (Ont. C.A.), additional reasons at (2002), 2002 CarswellOnt 2313 (Ont. C.A.).

[201] *Braintech Inc. v. Kostiuk* (1999), 171 D.L.R. (4th) 46 (B.C. C.A.), leave to appeal refused (2000), 2000 CarswellBC 546 (S.C.C.); *Pro-C Ltd. v. Computer City Inc.* (2000), 7 C.P.R. (4th) 193 (Ont. S.C.J.), additional reasons at (September 12, 2000), Doc. Kitchener 929/98 (Ont. S.C.J.), reversed (2001), 14 C.P.R. (4th) 441 (Ont. C.A.), leave to appeal refused (2001), 2001 CarswellOnt 5074

In the U.S., personal jurisdiction may be founded on either general jurisdiction or specific jurisdiction. General jurisdiction can be found only if the person was domiciled in the jurisdiction or his or her activities were substantial or continuous and systematic.[202] With respect to specific jurisdiction, the courts have adopted a three-part test:

(a)   the non-resident defendant must do some act or consummate some transaction with the forum or perform some act by which he purposely avails himself of the privilege of conducting activities in the forum, thereby invoking the benefits and protection of its laws;

(b)   the claim must be one which arises out of or results from the defendant's forum-related activities; and

(c)   exercise of jurisdiction must be reasonable.[203]

The following observations were made concerning the internet in *Zippo Manufacturing Company v. Zippo DotCom Inc.*,[204] a leading U.S. case:

> A three pronged test has emerged for determining whether the exercise of special personal jurisdiction over a non-resident defendant is appropriate: (1) the defendant must have sufficient "minimum contacts" with the forum state, (2) the claim asserted against the defendant must arise out of those contacts, and (3) the exercise of jurisdiction must be reasonable.
>
> The Constitutional touchstone of the minimum contacts analysis is embodied in the first prong. Whether the defendant purposefully established contacts with the forum state, defendants who reach out beyond one state and create continuing relationships and obligations with the citizens of another state are subject to regulation and sanctions in the other State for consequences of their actions. . .[T]he foreseeability that is critical to the due process analysis is that the defendant's conduct and connection with the forum State are such that he should reasonably expect to be haled into court there. This protects defendants from being forced to answer for their actions in a foreign jurisdiction based on random, fortuitous or attenuated contacts. Jurisdiction is proper, however, where contacts proximately result from actions by the defendant himself that create a 'substantial connection' with the forum State.

(S.C.C.); *Easthaven Ltd. v. Nutrisystems.com Inc.* (2001), 14 C.P.R. (4th) 22 (Ont. S.C.J.).

[202]   *Panavision International v. Toeppen,* 141 F.3d 1316 (9th Cir.) (U.S. Court of Appeals, 9th Circuit 1998); *Easthaven Ltd. v. Nutrisystems.com Inc.* (2001), 14 C.P.R. (4th) 22 (Ont. S.C.J.).

[203]   *Panavision International v. Toeppen,* 141 F.3d 320 (9th Cir.) (U.S. Court of Appeals, 9th Circuit 1998).

[204]   952 F.Supp. 119 (W.D.Pa. 1997) with citations omitted.

[3] Enter the Internet, a global super-network' of over 15,000 computer networks used by over 30 million individuals, corporations, organizations, and educational institutions worldwide. The Internet makes it possible to conduct business throughout the world entirely from a desktop. With this global revolution looming on the horizon, the development of the law concerning the permissible scope of personal jurisdiction based on Internet use is in its infant stages. The cases are scant. *Nevertheless, our review of the available cases and materials reveals that the likelihood that personal jurisdiction can be constitutionally exercised is directly proportionate to the nature and quality of commercial activity that an entity conducts over the Internet. This sliding scale is consistent with well developed personal jurisdiction principles. At one end of the spectrum are situations where a defendant clearly does business over the Internet.* If the defendant enters into contracts with residents of a foreign jurisdiction that involve the knowing and repeated transmission of computer files over the Internet, personal jurisdiction is proper. *At the opposite end are situations where a defendant has simply posted information on an Internet Web site which is accessible to users in foreign jurisdictions. A passive Web site that does little more than make information available to those who are interested in it* and *is not grounds for the exercise personal jurisdiction.* The middle ground is occupied by interactive Web sites where a user can exchange information with the host computer. In these cases, the exercise of jurisdiction is determined by examining the level of interactivity and commercial nature of the exchange of information that occurs on the Web site.

To the extent that a website is interactive and can be accessed by consumers outside of Canada, it is prudent to ensure that it complies with the relevant laws in force in the jurisdictions in which those consumers are physically located. This includes intellectual property laws relating to trade marks and patents, consumer protection legislation, product liability claims and claims for defamation.

Different website owners/operators have dealt with this potential liability in different ways. Some parties have not dealt with the issue at all. Presumably, they feel that if such claims arise, at least in a consumer context, they can be dealt with like any other consumer complaint without the necessity of any special legal response. In addition, to the extent that they are the subsidiaries of U.S. companies, they will not be faced with trade mark problems, since the marks they use have typically been registered in multiple jurisdictions.

On the other hand, other website owners/operators have posted disclaimers and incorporated governing law and jurisdiction clauses in purchase agreements, in an attempt to control the terms and conditions upon which they conduct business through their website. In effect they require consumers who do business with them to accept that the law and/or jurisdiction specified by the website owner/operator will apply.

An Ontario case, *Rudder v. Microsoft Corp.*,[205] dealt with this type of situation. In this case, Microsoft used a "click wrap" subscription agreement which provided that all disputes were governed by the laws of the State of Washington and that the venue for any legal proceedings was in that State (where Microsoft's head office is located). With a "click wrap" agreement, a user is asked to indicate their acceptance to the various terms and conditions by clicking "I agree" or an equivalent. The Court found that these provisions were effective to bar a class action proceeding brought in Ontario for breach of the agreement, because sufficient notice of the provisions was given when subscribers were required to acknowledge acceptance by clicking on an "agree" button at the time the full agreement was displayed.

It remains to be seen whether a "web wrap" agreement would be enforced.[206] Under this type of agreement, the acceptance to the relevant terms and conditions takes place through conduct and typically the visitor's use of the website will be characterized as an indication of their agreement to the posted terms and conditions.

g) Privacy Issues

Concerns about privacy reflect a fundamental assumption that individuals are entitled to keep information about themselves to themselves. Private matters are not public matters. The internet has significantly changed the prospect for intrusions on privacy since it allows organizations to gather significant amounts of personal information about consumers.

In 1980, the Organization for Economic Cooperation and Development (OECD) adopted guidelines on the protection of privacy and transborder flows of personal data. Subsequently, in 1996 the Canadian Standards Association released *A Model Code For The Protection of Personal Information* which was based on the OCED guidelines.

In 1995, the European Union (EU) passed the *Data Protection Directive* which sets out privacy protection rules for personal information held by both government and private-sector entities and was intended to harmonize the data-protection rules in the EU. The directive also established rules designed to ensure that personal information was only transferred to coun-

---

[205] (1999), 2 C.P.R. (4th) 474 (Ont. S.C.J.), additional reasons at (November 12, 1999), Doc. 97-CT-046534CP (Ont. S.C.J.) and see *Kanitz v. Rogers Cable Inc.* (2002), 58 O.R. (3d) 299 (Ont. S.C.J.). Ontario has partially reversed the result of this case; see the Ontario *Consumer Protection Act,* 2002, S.O. 2002, c. 30, Schedule A, subsection 7-8.

[206] See article by Chad Bayne, "Quebec Court Provides Initial Guidance on Enforceability of 'Web-wrap' Agreements", (August 2003), Volume 4, No. 6 *Internet and E-Commerce Law in Canada.*

tries outside the EU where continued privacy protection was guaranteed. The 15 member States of the EU were required to implement the directive into their national laws by October 25, 1998.

In Canada, the *Personal Information Protection and Electronic Documents Act* (PIPEDA)[207] applies to federally regulated private-sector organizations that collect, use or disclose personal information either on paper or in electronic format in the course of their commercial activities. The EU has accepted that PIPEDA provides adequate protection to comply with its directive.

The central purpose of PIPEDA is to limit data collection and disclosure to purposes that a reasonable person would consider appropriate in the circumstances.[208] The guidelines set out in PIPEDA are aimed at fulfilling this goal and, among other things, require that organizations must generally seek consent before gathering personal information and must disclose the purposes for which the information is collected. Collection of personal information must be limited to that actually necessary for the identified purposes and information must not be retained longer than necessary. Organizations are also expected to safeguard the information adequately and to disclose the information to any individual who wants access to data about him or herself.

PIPEDA was brought into force January 1, 2001, but there was a three year grace period for businesses operating solely within a province. As of January 1, 2004, the Act applies to provincially regulated companies not involved in the inter-provincial exchange of data. However, if a particular province has adopted legislation that is substantially similar to PIPEDA, the Governor in Council can exempt an organization, class of organizations and activity or class of activities from the application of part 1 of PIPEDA as regards the collection, use or disclosure of personal information that occurs in that province, if the Governor in Council is satisfied that the province has implemented legislation that is substantially similar to part 1 of PIPEDA.[209]

---

[207] S.C 2000, c. 5.

[208] Section 3.

[209] Paragraph 26(2)(b). Quebec has adopted an *Act respecting the protection of personal information in the private sector*, S.Q. 1993, c. 17. Pursuant to an exemption order dated November 19, 2003, any organization, other than a federal work, undertaking or business, that carries on an enterprise within the meaning of section 1525 of the Civil Code of Québec and to which the above noted Act applies is exempt from the application of part 1 of PIPEDA; SOR/2003-374. Notice has been given by the Governor in Council that it is proposed to make exemption orders exempting any organization, other than a federal work, undertaking or business, to which the *Personal Information Protection Act*, S.A.

The Federal Privacy Commissioner is charged with the enforcement of PIPEDA. The Commissioner receives complaints about non-compliance with PIPEDA and can audit an organization even in the absence of a complaint. The Commissioner's only power in dealing with complaints is to make recommendations and attempt to reach a settlement. However, a complainant may pursue the complaint in the Federal Court.[210]

In order to comply with this legislation, companies must develop specific privacy policies. The policy should be directed to complying with the privacy legislation that applies to personal information collected in the relevant jurisdictions or fair information practices if no such legislation exists. The policy should be displayed in a prominent place on the company's website and should be written in plain language. In general terms, the policy should explain:

(a) what personal information is being collected;

(b) why it is being collected;

(c) how it will be used;

(d) who will have access to it;

(e) how long it will be retained;

(f) who it will be disposed to; and

(g) who to contact for more information about the policy.

Leaving aside these legislative developments, many consumers are reluctant to make purchases on the internet out of fear that the personal information they provide will be misused or compromised. There is a growing trend among businesses engaged in e-commerce to develop privacy policies proactively to protect their reputation. In this regard, a company's reputation for protecting private information remains its strongest suit. In order to survive, a business must have the trust of its customers.

5. SUMMARY AND CHECKLIST

Branding on the internet cannot be ignored. Brand owners must consider the following matters.

1. Most businesses should establish an online branding strategy to take advantage of the internet and to remain competitive.

2003, c. P-6.5 of the Province of Alberta or the *Personal Information Protection Act*, S.B.C. 2003, c. 63 of the Province of British Columbia applies, from the application of Part 1 of PIPEDA; Canada Gazette, Vol. 138, No. 15 - April 10, 2004.

[210] Section 14.

2. The necessary domain names, including variants, must be obtained and registered in the appropriate gTLD(s) or ccTLD(s).
3. Domain names must be coordinated and managed appropriately. Typically, generic contact information should be developed and maintained. It is helpful to have similar domain names consolidated into a single account with a specific registrar.
4. If a domain name satisfies the registrability requirements of the *Trade-marks Act* and is used as a trade mark, consideration should be given to protecting it as a trade mark.
5. Searches should be conducted from time to time to ascertain whether domain names have been registered which are similar or confusing with the domain names being managed.
6. If abusive registrations have been obtained, proceedings may be brought under the UDRP or CDRP. Alternatively, actions for trade mark infringement or passing off are possible.
7. Criticism or gripe sites must be monitored and handled with care.
8. Website optimization should be considered.
9. Linking or framing must be considered on a case by case basis.
10. To the extent that a website is interactive and can be accessed by consumers outside of Canada, it is prudent to ensure that it complies with the relevant laws in force in the jurisdictions in which those consumers are physically located. This includes intellectual property laws relating to trade marks and patents, consumer protection legislation, product liability claims and claims for defamation. Alternatively, a website owner/operator may post disclaimers and incorporate governing law and jurisdiction clauses in purchase agreements in an attempt to control the terms and conditions upon which they conduct business through their website.
11. A privacy policy must be developed and displayed prominently on the brand owner's website.

Chapter 4: Protecting Brand Names—Registration

1. INTRODUCTION

The primary methods of protecting a brand name are by obtaining a registration under the *Trade-marks Act* and by bringing an action in the courts for infringement under the Act or asserting common law claims to enjoin passing off. Obtaining a registration is an effective first step in protecting a brand name as it will assist the owner in asserting rights relating to the registration.

The *Trade-marks Act* provides a public registry system which is national in scope, showing for each registered trade mark: the date of registration; a summary of the application for registration; a summary of all documents deposited with the application or subsequently filed affecting rights to the trade mark; particulars of each renewal and particulars of each change of name and address.[211] The purpose of providing this system is to define and protect the rights of registered trade mark owners.

This registration system co-exists with common law rights relating to trade marks and trade names. Common law rights are acquired through actual use of a mark in association with wares or services. As a common law trade mark becomes known and goodwill is associated with it, the common law trade mark owner will be able to assert claims against others who use confusing common law trade marks in the specific region or area that the common law trade mark owner has built up goodwill. These rights are asserted by bringing an action for passing off in the courts. A common

---

[211] Subsection 26 (2) of the *Trade-marks Act*. This information can be accessed online at *http://strategis.ic.gc.ca/cipo/trademarks/search/tmsearch.do*.

law trade mark owner may also assert its rights by opposing an application for the registration of a trade mark.

The *Trade-marks Act* facilitates the protection of trade marks by providing for public notice of rights and granting exclusive rights to owners. There are a number of benefits associated with obtaining a registration which include:

(a)   A trade mark registration is evidence of the exclusive rights granted under the Act and of the validity of the registered mark.[212]

(b)   The registration of a trade mark confers exclusive rights to the use of the trade mark throughout Canada even though the owner may only be using the mark in a specific area of the country. Such rights may not be available to the owner of a common law trade mark.

(c)   A registration provides a barrier to registration by others of confusing trade marks and is referenced on a searchable register.

(d)   As an application may be filed on the basis of proposed use, the system in effect allows a brand owner to reserve rights in a trade mark which has not been used.[213]

(e)   A registration carries the right to apply for a corresponding registration in other countries that adhere to the Convention of the Union of Paris. The Convention provides for a priority system implemented by national legislation, under which an applicant can rely on its earliest filing date in one country as its filing date in another so long as the application is filed within six months of the applicant's initial filing.[214]

(f)   After five years a registration becomes incontestable against attack on the grounds of previous use or making known unless it is established that the person who adopted the mark did so with knowledge of that previous use or making known.[215]

(g)   The Act facilitates the transfer and licensing of trade marks.[216]

(h)   Registration makes available two statutory causes of action which are not available to common law trade-mark owners: that is, the right to bring proceedings for trade mark infringement and for depreciation of the value of the goodwill attached to a registered trade mark.[217]

---

[212]   See **part 6 of this chapter.**
[213]   See **part 5 of this chapter.**
[214]   See **part 4(b) of this chapter.**
[215]   See **part 6 of this chapter.**
[216]   See **part 7 of this chapter.**
[217]   See **Chapter 5, part 4.**

(i)   Obtaining a registration will assist the owner in using the Trade-marks Opposition Board as a forum for challenging trade mark applications of others.

(j)   The owner of a registered trade mark may bring proceedings in the Federal Court of Canada, which has jurisdiction to grant injunctions with nationwide effect.

A brand owner must understand how the trade mark system works so that it can be used to the maximum extent possible to protect the brand name and related slogans, the product and in some cases product packaging. The potential benefits of the Act need to be carefully considered and implemented in a proactive fashion. Common law trade mark rights may be helpful on a case by case basis.

A brand owner also needs to know what is taking place in the marketplace to ensure that its rights are not being infringed.[218] This means that all employees must be on the lookout on a continuing basis. Consideration should also be given to obtaining the assistance of professional watch service companies, particularly in the context of the internet.

2. ACQUISITION OF RIGHTS

a) Adoption

The Act contemplates that rights in a mark are acquired by adopting it. A trade mark is deemed to be adopted when a person[219] or its predecessor in title commenced to use the trade mark in Canada or made the trade mark known in Canada.[220] If the trade mark has not previously been used or made known by the applicant or its predecessor in title it is deemed to be adopted on the filing of an application for registration of a trade mark in Canada.[221]

An application for a mark may be filed on the basis of

(a)   the use of the trade mark in Canada;

---

[218] See **Chapter 9, part 9**.

[219] The term "person" is defined to include any lawful trade union, any lawful association engaged in trade or business or the promotion thereof and the administrative authority of any country, state, province, municipality or other organized administrative area.

[220] Section 3 of the *Trade-marks Act* and see *Enterprise Rent-A-Car Co. v. Singer* (1998), (sub nom. *Enterprise Car & Truck Rentals Ltd. v. Enterprise Rent-A-Car Co.*) 79 C.P.R. (3d) 45 (Fed. C.A.).

[221] Section 3 of the *Trade-marks Act*.

(b) making the trade mark known in Canada;

(c) registration and use in a country with whom Canada has treaty obligations; or

(d) proposed use.

The ability to file an application on the basis of proposed use is particularly useful since the filing date of the application will be its priority date although it may take considerable time to obtain a registration.

Trade marks which have not previously been used or made known include newly developed brand names applied for on a proposed use basis, or brand names that the owner has caused to be duly registered in its country of origin but not yet used in Canada. Such marks are deemed to be adopted on the filing of an application for registration in Canada.[222]

A brand owner who uses a common law trade mark may only obtain rights in the mark when goodwill or reputation is established in the minds of purchasers by associating the trade mark with the goods or services of the brand owner such that the trade mark is recognized by the purchasers as distinctive of the owner's goods or services.[223]

b) Making Known

As set out above a trade mark is deemed to be adopted when a person or its predecessor in title made the trade mark known in Canada. A trade mark is deemed to be made known in Canada by a person only if it is used by such person in a country of the Paris Union,[224] other than Canada, in association with wares and services and:

(a) such wares are distributed in association with the mark in Canada; or

(b) such wares or services are advertised in association with the mark in

(i) any printed publication circulated in Canada in the ordinary course of commerce among potential dealers in or users of such wares or services, or

---

[222] Section 3 of the *Trade-marks Act*. See **part 4(b) of this chapter** concerning when the foreign filing date may be relied on for this purpose.

[223] *Reckitt & Colman Products Ltd. v. Borden Inc.*, [1990] 1 All E.R. 873 (U.K. H.L.), as adopted by the S.C.C. in *Ciba-Geigy Canada Ltd. v. Apotex Inc.* (1992), 44 C.P.R. (3d) 289 (S.C.C.).

[224] As of October 15, 2003, 164 states, including the United States and the United Kingdom, were party to the convention.

    (ii)   radio broadcasts, as defined in the *Radio Act,* ordinarily received in Canada by potential dealers in or users of such wares or services

and the mark has become well known in Canada by reason of such distribution or advertising.[225]

Use of the trade mark for the purposes of making known must satisfy the requirements of the Act.[226] It is not sufficient to show circulation of printed publications or radio broadcasts by themselves, but that the publications or broadcasts circulated among or were ordinarily received in Canada by potential dealers in or users of such wares or services.[227] The advertisements relied on to show the mark is well known must be substantial and have a significant impact on the Canadian market.[228] In order to become well known in Canada, it may be sufficient to show that a substantial area or part of Canada knows the mark as opposed to the entire country.[229] These requirements are matters of substantive law and not evidence.[230]

Once it has been established that the trade mark has been made known, the party who has done so is entitled to secure registration of the trade mark subject to successful completion of any opposition proceedings.[231]

As a practical matter, reliance on making known will be relatively infrequent if the mark has actually been used in Canada, an application could be filed on this basis and the requirements to show use are less restrictive than the requirements to show making known. In addition, it is more cost effective from the brand owner's point of view to file on the basis of proposed use or a foreign application or registration.

c) Proposed Use

Under the Act it is possible to apply to register a mark before the mark has been actually used. A proposed trade mark is defined to mean a mark

---

[225] Section 5.

[226] *Robert C. Wian Enterprises Inc. v. Mady* (1965), 46 C.P.R. 147 (Can. Ex. Ct.).

[227] *Robert C. Wian Enterprises Inc. v. Mady* (1965), 46 C.P.R. 147 (Can. Ex. Ct.).

[228] *Robert C. Wian Enterprises Inc. v. Mady* (1965), 46 C.P.R. 147 (Can. Ex. Ct.); *Re Andres Wines Ltd. & E. & J. Gallo Winery* (1975), 25 C.P.R. (2d) 126 (Fed. C.A.); *Parker-Knoll Ltd. v. Canada (Registrar of Trade Marks)* (1977), 32 C.P.R. (2d) 148 (Fed. T.D.); *Motel 6 Inc. v. No. 6 Motel Ltd.* (1981), 56 C.P.R. (2d) 44 (Fed. T.D.).

[229] *Valle's Steak House v. Tessier* (1980), 49 C.P.R. (2d) 218 (Fed. T.D.).

[230] *Valle's Steak House v. Tessier* (1980), 49 C.P.R. (2d) 218 (Fed. T.D.); *Motel 6 Inc. v. No. 6 Motel Ltd.* (1981), 56 C.P.R. (2d) 44 (Fed. T.D.).

[231] Section 38.

that is proposed to be used by a person for the purpose of distinguishing or so as to distinguish wares or services manufactured, sold, leased, hired or performed by that person from those manufactured, sold, leased, hired or performed by others.[232] The ability to file an application based on proposed use allows a brand owner to, in effect, reserve a mark without incurring the expense of establishing use in the marketplace. This is particularly helpful.

An application for such a trade mark must contain a statement that the applicant, by itself or through a licensee, or both, intends to use such a trade mark in Canada.[233] Use must commence after filing the application[234] but must occur before a registration may be obtained. A certificate of registration may be obtained after the filing of a declaration that the applicant, a successor in title or a licensee[235] has commenced use of the trade mark in Canada in association with the wares or services specified in the application.[236]

While an application may be filed on the basis of proposed use, the time in which use must occur is limited. After the successful completion of opposition proceedings a notice of allowance will be issued. An application will be deemed to be abandoned unless a declaration of use is filed with the Registrar before the later of (a) six months after the notice of allowance and (b) three years after the date of filing of the application.[237]

If the declaration of use shows use only with respect to some of the wares or services set out in the application, the registration will be limited to these wares or services and not extended to those set out in the application.

---

[232] Section 2.

[233] Subsection 30(e).

[234] *Medtronic Inc. v. Intertronic Systems Ltd.* (1979), 55 C.P.R. (2d) 200 (T.M. Opp. Bd.).

[235] An entity that is licensed by or with the authority of the applicant to use the trade mark, if the applicant has direct or indirect control of the character or quality of the wares or services. See subsection 40(2) and section 50.

[236] Subsection 40(2).

[237] Subsection 40(3). An extension may be sought to extend the three-year period, but the request must be justified by objective reasons. On the expiration of three years from the initial deadline to file a declaration of use set out in the notice of allowance, significant and substantive reasons which clearly justify a further extension must be presented. See *Trade-marks Office Practice Notice* published in the *Trade-marks Journal* No. 2258, February 4, 1998 at page 292 and *A. Lassonde Inc. v. Canada (Registraire des marques de commerce)* (2003),(sub nom. *A. Lassonde Inc. v. (Canada) Registrar of Trade-marks*) 27 C.P.R. (4th) 316 (Fed. T.D.).

d) Trade Marks Registered Abroad

Foreign trade mark owners may take advantage of the provisions of the Act concerning marks which may not satisfy all of the requirements for registrability. Section 14 provides that, notwithstanding section 12, a trade mark that the applicant or applicant's predecessor in title has caused to be duly registered in the country of origin of the applicant is registrable if, in Canada:

(a) it is not confusing with a registered trade mark;
(b) it is not without distinctive character, having regard to all the circumstances of the case, including the length of time during which it has been used in any country;
(c) it is not contrary to morality or public order or of such a nature as to deceive the public; or
(d) it is not a trade mark the adoption of which is prohibited by sections 9 or 10.

In order to comply with the section the foreign registration must exist at least until the date when the Canadian registration is granted. Accordingly, in a case where a registration obtained in the United States was struck out while the Canadian application based on this registration was pending, the Canadian application was not granted.[238]

Section 14 is only available to an applicant with a country of origin that is a member of the Paris Union[239] or a member of the World Trade Organization.[240]

The section extends to foreign applications based on use or proposed use, but a registration must be obtained before the Canadian application will be approved for advertisement.[241] However, the section does not extend to trade marks that have been used but not registered in the country of origin.[242]

---

[238] *Union Carbide Corp. v. W.R. Grace & Co.* (1987), 14 C.P.R. (3d) 337 (Fed. C.A.).

[239] As of March 1999, 153 states, including the United States and the United Kingdom, were party to this convention.

[240] See definition of WTO Member in section 2.

[241] Subsection 30(d) and see *McDonald's Corp. v. Canada (Deputy Attorney-General)* (1977), 31 C.P.R. (2d) 272 (Fed. T.D.).

[242] *Lime Cola Co. v. Coca-Cola Co.*, [1947] Ex. C.R. 180 (Can. Ex. Ct.); *Gottfried Co. v. Comfort Kimona & Dress Manufacturing Co.*, [1948] Ex. C.R. 611 (Can. Ex. Ct.).

Compliance with section 14 relieves the applicant from compliance with the requirements set out in section 12 relating to registrability. For example, a trade mark which is not registrable by virtue of section 12 on the basis that it is clearly misdescriptive may still be registrable under section 14.[243]

The term "distinctive character" means that the trade mark must have the qualities characteristic of a distinctive trade mark and actually distinguish the wares or services of the owner from the wares or services of others or be adapted to distinguish the wares or services of the owner from the wares or services of others.[244] The onus of showing that a descriptive trade mark is not without distinctive character is a heavy one and evidence showing the mark has become distinctive of the applicant in Canada is required.[245]

In order that a trade mark may be registrable under the provisions of section 14, it is necessary that it be substantially the same as the trade mark registered in the country of origin.[246] If the trade mark differs only by elements that do not alter its distinctive character or affect its identity in the form under which it is registered in the country of origin, the mark will be regarded as the trade mark so registered.[247]

If the applicant applies to register the same or substantially the same trade mark in Canada for use in association with the same kind of wares or services within six months from the date of first filing in a country which adheres to the Convention of the Union of Paris, then the date of filing in that country becomes the effective Canadian filing date.[248]

3. TRADE MARK USE

a) The Concept

The concept of use is of fundamental importance under the Act since rights are determined by it. A trade mark is deemed to have been adopted

[243] *Pilkington Brothers (Can.) Ltd. v. International Molded Plastics Inc.* (1957), 27 C.P.R. 79 (Reg. T.M.).

[244] *Imperial Tobacco Co. of Canada v. Philip Morris Inc.* (1976), 27 C.P.R. (2d) 205 (T. M. Bd.).

[245] *Canadian Counsel of Professional Engineers v. Lubrication Engineers, Inc.* (1992), (sub nom. *Lubrication Engineers Inc. v. Canadian Council of Professional Engineers*) 41 C.P.R. (3d) 243 (Fed. C.A.); *Boston Pizza International Inc. v. Boston Chicken Inc.* (2003), 24 C.P.R. (4th) 150 (Fed. C.A.).

[246] *Gottfried Co. v. Comfort Kimona & Dress Manufacturing Co.*, [1948] Ex. C.R. 611 (Can. Ex. Ct.).

[247] Subsection 14(2).

[248] Subsection 34 and see **part 4(b) of this chapter** for all the requirements.

when a person or its predecessor in title commenced to use the trade mark in Canada.[249] Applications are most often based on use or proposed use. A registration gives to the owner the exclusive right to the use of the mark in Canada in respect of the wares or services set out in the registration.[250] Use must be shown in order to maintain a registration which is the subject of section 45 proceedings.[251] A plaintiff must show that it has used its mark and the defendant has used this mark or a confusing mark in order to be successful in an action for infringement.

A brand owner must understand and comply with the requirements relating to trade mark use in order to protect the brand name under the Act. The Act sets specific rules to establish use for wares, services and exported wares[252] which can be restrictive, particularly for wares.

Section 4 provides that a trade mark is deemed to be used in association with wares if, at the time of the transfer of the property in or possession of such wares, in the normal course of trade, it is marked on the wares themselves or on the packages in which they are distributed or it is in any other manner so associated with the wares that notice of the association is then given to the person to whom the property or possession is transferred.

A trade mark is deemed to be used in association with services if it is used or displayed in the performance or advertising of such services.[253]

A trade mark that is marked in Canada on wares or on packages in which they are contained is, when such wares are exported from Canada, deemed to be used in Canada in association with such wares.[254]

The provisions summarized above also incorporate the definition of a trade mark and, in particular, the requirement that the mark be used for the purposes of distinguishing wares or services manufactured, sold, leased, hired or performed by the brand owner from those manufactured, sold, leased, hired or performed by others.[255]

---

[249] Section 3.

[250] Section 19.

[251] See **part 8 of this chapter**.

[252] Section 4 and see *Enterprise Rent-A-Car Co. v. Singer* (1998), (sub nom. *Enterprise Car & Truck Rentals Ltd. v. Enterprise Rent-A-Car Co.*) 79 C.P.R. (3d) 45 (Fed. C.A.).

[253] Subsection 4(2).

[254] Subsection 4(3).

[255] *Clairol International. Corp. v. Thomas Supply & Equipment Co.* (1968), 55 C.P.R. 176 (Can. Ex. Ct.); *British Petroleum Co. v. Bombardier Ltd.* (1973), 10 C.P.R. (2d) 21 (Fed. C.A.); *Canadian Olympic Assn. v. Konica Canada Inc.* (1991), (sub nom. *Assoc. Olympique Canadienne v. Konica Canada Inc.*) 39 C.P.R. (3d) 400 (Fed. C.A.), leave to appeal refused (1992), 41 C.P.R. (3d) v (note) (S.C.C.); *Coca-Cola Ltd. v. Pardhan* (1999), 85 C.P.R. (3d) 489 (Fed. C.A.), leave to appeal refused (2000), 2000 CarswellNat 721 (S.C.C.); but

The use must be a use as a trade mark and not as a mere generic or descriptive term or name.[256] If a trade mark becomes so popular that consumers use the mark as the generic name of the wares or services in issue, the registration may become invalid on the basis that the trade mark is no longer distinctive.[257]

b) Wares

A trade mark is deemed to be used in association with wares if, at the time of the transfer of the property in or possession of such wares in the normal course of trade, it is marked on the wares themselves or on the packages in which they are distributed or it is in any other manner so associated with the wares that notice of the association is then given to the person to whom the property or possession is transferred.[258] As a result of these requirements, the definition is restrictive in nature.

The first requirement under the Act is to show the trade mark in issue was in use at the time of the transfer of the property in or possession of such wares. It has been held that the word "use" is related not only to the words "at the time of the transfer of property or possession", but also to the words "in the normal course of trade" and as such if any part of the chain of sale from manufacturer to consumer takes place in Canada this is sufficient "use" in Canada within the meaning of section 4.[259]

Second, there must be a normal commercial transaction relating to the trade mark in question in order to show "use". The transaction must be a

---

compare with *United Grain Growers Ltd. v. Lang Mitchener* (2001), 12 C.P.R. (4th) 89 (Fed. C.A.), leave to appeal allowed (2001), 2001 CarswellNat 1903 (S.C.C.), which refused to interpret section 45 in a similar fashion.

[256] *Canada (Registrar of Trade Marks) v. Cie internationale pour l'informatique CII Honeywell Bull, S.A.* (1985), 4 C.I.P.R. 309 (Fed. C.A.), reversing (1983), 1 C.I.P.R. 231 (Fed. T.D.).

[257] *Dubiner v. Cheerio Toys & Games Ltd.*, [1966] Ex. C.R. 801 (Can. Ex. Ct.); *Aladdin Industries Inc. v. Canadian Thermos Products Ltd.* (1969), 57 C.P.R. 230 (Can. Ex. Ct.).

[258] Subsection 2 and 4(1); and see *Clairol International. Corp. v. Thomas Supply & Equipment Co.* (1968), 55 C.P.R. 176 (Can. Ex. Ct.); *Union Electric Supply Co. v. Canada (Registrar of Trade Marks)*, [1982] 2 F.C. 263 (Fed. T.D.); *Cie générale des établissements Michelin - Michelin & Cie v. CAW-Canada* (1996), (sub nom. *Cie Générale des Établissements Michelin-Michelin & Cie v. C.A.W. -Canada*) 71 C.P.R. (3d) 348 (Fed. T.D.).

[259] *Manhattan Industries Inc. v. Princeton Manufacturing Ltd.* (1971), 4 C.P.R. (2d) 6 (Fed. T.D.).

bona fide transaction.[260] Token use such as test shipments or sending of samples or the like may not be sufficient to constitute trade mark "use".[261]

Finally, the mark must be associated with the wares such that notice of the association is given to the person to whom the property or possession is transferred. It is sufficient use if the trade mark is placed on the cover or wrapper in which the article is sold,[262] or on a label attached to the goods[263] or associated with them on show cards, display units or delivery vans so long as notice of the association is given at the time of the transfer of the property or possession.[264]

If the mark is not physically on the wares or their packaging, satisfying the requirement may be problematic. For example, the use of a trade mark in news releases, in advertisements, on a letterhead or on envelopes will not be sufficient to constitute use in association with wares.[265]

c) Services

None of the restrictions relating to the use of a mark in association with wares described above apply to the use of a mark with services.[266] In order to establish use in association with services, the mark must be used or displayed in the performance or advertising of such services.[267] Because of the territorial nature of trade marks, the service must be performed in

---

[260] *Molson Cos. v. Halter* (1976), 28 C.P.R. (2d) 158 (Fed. T.D.); *Tubeco Inc. v. Assn. québécoise des fabricants de tuyau de Béton Inc.* (1980), 49 C.P.R. (2d) 228 (Fed. T.D.).

[261] *Ports International Ltd. v. Canada (Registrar of Trade Marks)* (1983), [1984] 2 F.C. 119 (Fed. T.D.); but see *Fetherstonhaugh & Co. v. ConAgra Inc.* (2000), 10 C.P.R. (4th) 542 (T.M. Bd.), reversed (2002), (sub nom. *ConAgra Foods, Inc. v. Fetherstonhaugh & Co.*) 23 C.P.R. (4th) 49 (Fed. T.D.).

[262] *Manhattan Industries Inc. v. Princeton Manufacturing Ltd.* (1971), 4 C.P.R. (2d) 6 (Fed. T.D.).

[263] *Union Electric Supply Co. Ltd. v. Canada (Register of Trade Marks)* (1982), 63 C.P.R. (2d) 56 (Fed. T.D.).

[264] *Gen. Mills Canada Ltd. v. Procter & Gamble Inc.* (1985), 6 C.P.R. (3d) 551 (T.M. Opp. Bd.); *Smith, Kline & French Canada Ltd. v. Apotex Inc.* (1984), 1 C.P.R. (3d) 256 (Fed. C.A.), reversing (1983), 71 C.P.R. (2d) 146 (Fed. T.D.).

[265] *Molson Cos. v. Halter* (1976), 28 C.P.R. (2d) 158 (Fed. T.D.); *Parker-Knoll Ltd. v. Canada (Registrar of Trade Marks)* (1977), 32 C.P.R. (2d) 148 (Fed. T.D.); *Aerosol Fillers Inc. v. Plough (Canada) Ltd.* (1979), 45 C.P.R. (2d) 194 (Fed. T.D.), affirmed (1980), 53 C.P.R. (2d) 62 (Fed. C.A.).

[266] *Gesco Industries Inc v. Sim & McBurney* (2000), 9 C.P.R. (4th) 480 (Fed. C.A.).

[267] *Danjaq Inc. v. Zervas* (1997), (sub nom. *Danjaq, S.A. v. Zervas*) 75 C.P.R. (3d) 295 (Fed. T.D.).

Canada. Use is not established by advertising the trade mark in Canada when the performance of these services takes place elsewhere. [268]

Nothing in the Act restricts services to those that are independently offered to the public or that are not ancillary or connected with wares.[269] For example, when a company makes its coupons available to consumers so they may obtain the company's products at a reduced price this has been held to be use in association with a service.[270]

d) Exported Wares

A trade mark that is marked in Canada on wares or on packages in which they are contained is, when such wares are exported from Canada, deemed to be used in Canada in association with such wares.[271]

e) Deviating Use

A trade mark should be used in the form in which it is registered. The use of a variation of a registered mark may be potential grounds for expungement of the mark.[272] However, this potential result may be avoided by obtaining a separate registration for the variant.

It has been held that the practice of departing from the precise form of a trade mark as registered is an objectionable and dangerous course of action.[273] However, it remains to be seen how significant the deviation must be in order to destroy the validity of the mark. In the leading case *Honey Dew Ltd. v. Rudd*, a registration had been obtained for a design in the shape of a slim penguin but the owner of the mark changed the design to a more corpulent penguin. The registration was attacked on this basis and the case proceeded to the Federal Court of Appeal. The Court found that the use of the corpulent design did not destroy the validity of the registered mark. The Court stated that cautious variations could be made without adverse con-

---

[268] *Porter v. Don the Beachcomber* (1966), 48 C.P.R. 280 (Can. Ex. Ct.); *Marineland Inc. v. Marine Wonderland & Animal Park Ltd.*, [1974] 2 F.C. 558 (Fed. T.D.); *Motel 6 Inc. v. No. 6 Motel Ltd.* (1981), 56 C.P.R. (2d) 44 (Fed. T.D.).

[269] *Gesco Industries Inc v. Sim & McBurney* (2000), 9 C.P.R. (4th) 480 (Fed. C.A.).

[270] *Kraft Ltd. v. Canada (Registrar of Trade marks)* (1984), 1 C.P.R. (3d) 457 (Fed. T.D.).

[271] Subsection 4(3); also see *Phil Borden Ltd. v. UARCO Inc.* (1975), [1976] 1 F.C. 548 (Fed. C.A.); *Coca-Cola Ltd. v. Pardhan* (1999), 85 C.P.R. (3d) 489 (Fed. C.A.), leave to appeal to the S.C.C. refused (2000), 2000 CarswellNat 721 (S.C.C.).

[272] See section 18 and section 45.

[273] *Honey Dew Ltd. v. Rudd* (1928), [1929] Ex. C.R. 83 (Can. Ex. Ct.).

sequences if the same dominant features were maintained and the differences were so unimportant as to not mislead an unaware purchaser of the wares.[274] Maintenance of the same commercial impression is of vital importance.

It has also been decided that the use of a trade mark in conjunction with another trade mark or a prefix may not be use of the trade mark but use of a new mark. For example, use of the composite trade mark CII HONEYWELL BULL did not constitute use of the trade mark BULL.[275] The application of this approach can have unwelcome results, since the brand owner may lose its registered mark and be left with a variant which, in the absence of a registration, may only be protected by common law rights.

4. ENTITLEMENT

The Act sets out a series of rules for determining who is entitled to obtain a registration of a mark. The rules apply in cases of potential or real confusion between the mark applied for and pre-existing rights associated with trade marks, whether registered or not, and trade names.[276] The determination is made as of a priority date which varies depending on the basis on which the application is filed.

a) Marks Which Have Been Used or Made Known in Canada

An applicant who has filed an application for a trade mark that the applicant or its predecessor in title has used or made known in Canada in association with wares or services is entitled (subject to the completion of opposition proceedings) to secure its registration, unless at the date on which the applicant or its predecessor in title first used it or made it known it was confusing with:

---

[274] *Promafil Canada Ltée. v. Munsingwear Inc.* (1992), 44 C.P.R. (3d) 59 (Fed. C.A.), leave to appeal refused (1993), 47 C.P.R. (3d) v (note) (S.C.C.). In addition, any deviation from the form registered must be fully explained and justified; *Saccone & Speed Ltd. v. Canada (Registrar of Trade Marks)* (1982), 67 C.P.R. (2d) 119 (Fed. T.D.) and see *Ivey Lea Shirt Co. v. Muskoka Fine Watercraft & Supply Co.* (2001), (sub. nom. *Ivy Lea Shirt Co. v. 1227624 Ontario Ltd.*) 11 C.P.R. (4th) 489 (Fed. T.D.).

[275] *Canada (Registrar of Trade Marks) v. Cie international pour l'informatique CII Honeywell Bull, S.A.* (1985), 4 C.I.P.R. 309, 4 C.P.R. (3d) 523 (Fed. C.A.), reversing (1983), 1 C.I.P.R. 231 (Fed. T.D.).

[276] A "trade name" is defined in section 2 of the Act to mean the name under which any business is carried on, whether or not it is the name of a corporation, a partnership or an individual.

(a)   a trade mark that has been previously used or made known in Canada;

(b)   a trade mark in respect of which an application for registration had been previously filed; or

(c)   a trade name that had been previously used

by any other person.

The priority date for applications based on use or making known in Canada is the date of first use or making known. This is the sole rule for determining priority for such applications. For example, in disputes between principal and agent or manufacturer and distributor the relevant issue is whether the importer or agent, or the manufacturer or distributor, as the case may be, was the first to use the trade mark in Canada.[277] This in turn will involve a determination of the distinctiveness of the mark.[278]

Use of a trade mark for the purpose of "making known" must be prior to the date of the application for registration. If the applicant or registrant was not the first to use the trade mark or make it known, the application may be opposed or the registration expunged at the suit of the person who first used the trade mark or made it known.[279]

b) Marks Registered and Used Abroad

An applicant who has filed an application for a trade mark that the applicant or the applicant's predecessor in title has duly registered in or for the country of origin of the applicant, and has been used in association with wares or services is entitled, subject to the completion of opposition proceedings, to secure its registration in respect of the wares or services in association with which it is registered in that country and has been used, unless at the date of filing of the application it was confusing with:

(a)   a trade mark that had been previously used in Canada or made known in Canada;

(b)   a trade mark in respect of which an application for registration had been previously filed in Canada; or

---

[277] Subsection 16(1); *Lin Trading Co. v. CBM Kabushiki Kaisha* (1985), (sub nom. *CBM Kabushiki Kaisha v. Lin Trading Co.*) 5 C.P.R. (3d) 27 (T.M. Opp. Bd.), affirmed (1987), 14 C.P.R. (3d) 32 (Fed. T.D.), affirmed (1988), 21 C.P.R. (3d) 417 (Fed. C.A.).

[278] *Royal Doulton Tableware Ltd. v. Cassidy's Ltd. – Cassidy's Ltée* (1984), 1 C.P.R. (3d) 214 (Fed. T.D.); *Lin Trading Co. v. CBM Kabushiki Kaisha, supra.*

[279] Sections 16, 17 and 18.

(c)   a trade name that had been previously used in Canada now

by any other person.[280]

The priority date for applications based on a mark registered and used abroad is the date of the filing of the application. An applicant may rely on its filing date as the date upon which it adopted the mark and is entitled to obtain a registration and priority over another person who has subsequently used or applied for the mark.[281]

If specific requirements, including requirements relating to timely filing, are satisfied, an applicant may rely on its foreign filing date. More specifically, when an application for the registration of a trade mark has been made in any country which adheres to the Convention of the Union of Paris, and an application is subsequently made in Canada for use in association with the same kind of wares or services of the same, or substantially the same trade mark by the same applicant or the applicant's successor in title, the date of filing of the application in the other country is deemed to be the date of filing of the application in Canada, and the applicant is entitled to priority in Canada accordingly, notwithstanding any intervening use in Canada or making known in Canada or any intervening application or registration if:

(a)   the application in Canada is filed within six months from the filing date of the foreign application, which period shall not be extended;
(b)   the applicant or, if the applicant is a transferee, the applicant's predecessor in title who filed the earlier application was at the date of the application a citizen or national of or domiciled in that country or had a real and effective industrial or commercial establishment in that country; and
(c)   the applicant furnishes, in accordance with any request under the Act evidence necessary to establish fully the applicant's right to priority by any other person.[282]

c) Proposed Use Marks

An applicant who has filed an application for a proposed trade mark, is entitled (subject to the completion of opposition proceedings and filing a declaration of use of the trade mark) to secure its registration in respect to

---

[280] Subsection 16(2).
[281] Subsection 16(3) and section 3.
[282] Section 34.

the wares or services specified in the application, unless at the date of the filing of the application it was confusing with:

(a)   a trade mark that had been previously used or made known in Canada;

(b)   a trade mark in respect of which an application for registration had been previously filed; or

(c)   a trade name that had been previously used in Canada,[283]

by any other person.

The priority date for applications based on proposed use in Canada is the date of the filing of the application. An applicant may rely on its filing date as the date upon which it adopted the mark and is entitled to obtain the registration and priority over another person who has subsequently used or applied for the mark.[284]

A certificate of registration cannot be obtained until receipt of a declaration that the applicant, a successor in title or a licensee[285] has commenced the use of the trade mark in Canada in association with the wares or services specified in the application.[286]

5. APPLICATIONS FOR REGISTRATION

a) The Application

Once the brand name has been chosen and any design presentation finalized the process of obtaining a registration can begin. This begins with the filing of an application with the Registrar of Trade-marks. It is prudent to apply for both the brand name and any design presentation separately as this will result in a broader ambit of protection.

An application must contain the following information:

(a)   A statement in ordinary commercial terms of the wares or services in association with which the trade mark has been or is proposed to be used.[287] If the wares or services fall into different general

---

[283] Subsection 16(3).

[284] Subsection 16(3) and section 3.

[285] An entity that is licensed by or with the authority of the applicant to use the trade mark, if the applicant has direct or indirect control of the character or quality of the wares or services. See section 50.

[286] Subsection 40(2).

[287] Subsection 30(a).

categories, they should be grouped by category. Canada does not use any particular system for the classification of wares or services. Many countries, including the United States, are party to the *Arrangement of Nice Concerning the International Classification of Goods and Services* which sets out a system for the classification of goods and services.

(b)   If the trade mark has been used in Canada, the date of first use in Canada for each of the general classes of wares or services described in the application.[288] It is important that this date be accurate since, in the case of conflicting applications, this date will be the applicant's priority date.[289] An applicant may, out of caution, select a date which is later than the actual date of first use,[290] but in such a case it is preferable to state the date is "as early as".

(c)   If the trade mark has been made known in Canada, the date and manner of making known in Canada and the name of any country which adheres to the Convention of the Union of Paris in which the trade mark has been used.[291]

(d)   Particulars of registration and use in a country of the Union are required where this is the basis of the application.[292] Before such an application will be approved for advertisement a certified copy of the registration must be filed.[293]

(e)   In the case of a proposed trade mark, a statement that the applicant, by itself or through a licensee, or by itself and through a licensee, intends to use the trade mark in Canada.[294] Use must occur after the filing of the application. A registration will only issue on receipt of a declaration that the use of the trade mark in Canada, in association with the wares or services specified in the application, has commenced.[295]

(f)   In the case of an application for a certification mark, particulars of the defined standard and a statement that the applicant is not

---

[288] Subsection 30(b). Failure to correctly state the date of first use is not a ground for the expungement of any resulting registration: *Biba Boutique Ltd. v. Dalmys (Can.) Ltd.* (1976), 25 C.P.R. (2d) 278 (Fed. T.D.), but may be a ground of opposition in that the application did not conform with section 30.

[289] Subsection 16(1).

[290] *Marineland Inc. v. Marine Wonderland & Animal Park Ltd.*, [1974] 2 F.C. 558 (Fed. T.D.).

[291] Subsection 30(c).

[292] Subsection 30(d).

[293] Subsection 31(1) and subsection 40(2).

[294] Subsection 30(e).

[295] Subsubsection 40(2).

engaged in the manufacture, sale, leasing or hiring of wares or the performance of services such as those in association with which the certification mark is used.[296]

(g)   The applicant's address in Canada or, if abroad, the applicant's address and the name and address of a Canadian representative.[297]

(h)   Unless the application is for the registration of only a word or words not depicted in special form, a drawing of the trade mark.[298]

(i)   A statement that the applicant is satisfied that it is entitled to use the trade mark in Canada in association with the wares or services described in the application.[299]

While an application may be amended, there are significant limitations on the matters which may be amended.[300]

If colour is a feature of the mark, this claim is included in the application.[301] Colour commonly may form an important aspect of the trade mark and help to make it distinctive.[302] However, colour will not by itself make a trade mark distinctive and there must be some additional independent feature in order to obtain a registration.[303]

b) Examination

Once a duly completed application and the prescribed fee is received by the Registrar, a filing date is attributed to the application.[304] The Trade-marks Office then carries out a search of the register to identify similar or confusing trade marks. The application and search results are passed to an examiner. The application is examined and must be refused if:

---

[296] Subsection 30(6).

[297] Subsection 30(g).

[298] Subsection 30(h).

[299] Subsection 30(i).

[300] See sections 30-33, *Trade-marks Regulations* (1996) SOR/96-195.

[301] See sections 28 of the Trade-marks Regulations.

[302] See *Trade-marks Regulations* (1996), SOR/96-195, section 28; *Smith, Kline & French Canada Ltd., Re* (1987), 12 C.I.P.R. 204, 9 F.T.R. 129 (Fed. T.D.), affirmed (1987), 9 F.T.R. 127 (Fed. T.D.).

[303] *Smith, Kline & French Canada Ltd., Re* (1984), 10 C.P.R. (3d) 246 (Reg. T.M.), reversed (1987), 12 C.I.P.R. 204, 9 F.T.R. 129 (Fed. T.D.), affirmed (1987), 9 F.T.R. 127 (Fed. T.D.); *Novopharm Ltd. v. Bayer Inc.* (2000), 9 C.P.R. (4th) 304 (Fed. C.A.).

[304] Section 25, *Trade-marks Regulations* (1996).

(a)   the application does not comply with the requirements of section 30;[305]

(b)   the trade mark is not registrable;[306] or

(c)   the applicant is not the person entitled to registration of the trade mark because it is confusing with another trade mark for which an application is pending.[307]

The Registrar must not refuse any application without first notifying the applicant of the objections and the reasons for such objections and giving the applicant adequate opportunity to answer the objections.[308] Examiner's reports are issued which satisfy these criteria.

Where the Registrar, by reason of a registered trade mark, is in doubt whether the trade mark claimed is registrable because of potential confusion with a registered mark, the application may be approved for advertisement. However, in such cases the Registrar must, by registered letter, notify the owner of the registered trade mark in issue of the advertisement of the application.[309]

c) Disclaimer

The Registrar may require the applicant to disclaim the right to the exclusive use apart from the trade mark of such portion of the trade mark as is not independently registrable, but such disclaimer does not prejudice or affect the applicant's rights then existing or thereafter arising in the disclaimed matter. In addition, the disclaimer does not prejudice or affect the applicant's right to registration on a subsequent application if the disclaimed matter has then become distinctive of the applicant's wares or services.[310]

A disclaimer of a portion of a trade mark will not assist in overcoming an objection on the basis of confusion with a registered trade mark or

---

[305] Subsection 37(1)(a).

[306] Subsection 37(1)(b) and see **Chapter 2, part 9**.

[307] Subsection 37(1)(c) and see *Unitel International Inc. v. Canada (Registrar of Trade Marks)* (1999), (sub nom. *Unitel International Inc. v. Canada (Registrar of Trade-Marks)*) 86 C.P.R. (3d) 467 (Fed. T.D.), affirmed (2000), 9 C.P.R. (4th) 127 (Fed. C.A.).

[308] Subsection 37(2) and see *Mister Transmission (International) Ltd. v. Registrar of Trade Marks* (1978), [1979] 1 F.C. 787 (Fed. T.D.).

[309] Subsection 37(3).

[310] Section 35.

pending application.[311] A disclaimer of all elements of a trade mark will not be accepted if the trade mark as a whole is not registrable.[312] A disclaimer will not be accepted in relation to a deceptively misdescriptive aspect of a trade mark when the unregistrable matter is a dominant feature of a composite mark.[313] The failure to give a disclaimer is not a ground of opposition.[314]

d) Advertisement

On successful completion of the examination stage, the Registrar is required to advertise the application.[315] The application is advertised in the *Trade-marks Journal* in the manner prescribed in the *Trade-marks Regulations* (1996).[316] Particulars of the application and the trade mark in question are included in the *Trade-marks Journal*.

6. REGISTRATION

a) Allowance

When an application has not been opposed, or it has been opposed and the opposition has been decided in favour of the applicant, the application will be allowed[317] and the mark registered.[318]

When an application for registration of a proposed trade mark is allowed, the Registrar will give notice to the applicant and will register the

---

[311] *Frank W. Horner Ltd. v. Mowatt & Moore Ltd.* (1975), 27 C.P.R. (2d) 124 (Reg. T.M.).

[312] *Molson Cos. v. John Labatt Ltd.* (1981), 58 C.P.R. (2d) 157 (Fed. T.D.).

[313] *Lake Ontario Cement Ltd. v. Canada (Registrar of Trade Marks)* (1976), 31 C.P.R. (2d) 103 (Fed. T. D.).

[314] *Sunny Crunch Foods Ltd. v. Canada (Registrar of Trade Marks)* (1982), 63 C.P.R. (2d) 201 (Fed. C.A.), reversing (1978), (sub nom. *Robin Hood Multifoods Ltd. v. Sunny Crunch Foods Ltd.*) 40 C.P.R. (2d)175 (T.M. Opp. Bd.); *T.G. Bright & Co. v. Andres Wines* (1986), 12 C.P.R. (3d) 1 (Fed. C.A.).

[315] Subsection 37(1); *Trade-marks Regulations* (1996), section 34. The Registrar, after notifying applicant of the advertisement date, can reverse that decision; see *Beaver Knitwear Ltd. v. Canada (Registrar of Trade Marks)* (1986), 11 C.P.R. (3d) 257 (Fed. T.D.).

[316] Sections 15 and 34.

[317] Subsection 39(1).

[318] Subsection 40(1). Unless the mark was filed based on proposed use, there are no other requirements apart from paying the proscribed fee.

trade mark after receiving a declaration that the applicant, its successor in title or licensee[319] has commenced the use of the trade mark in Canada in association with the wares or services specified in the application.[320] If the applicant for a proposed trade mark fails to file a declaration of use before the later of 6 months after the notice by the Registrar and three years after the date of filing of the application in Canada, the application will be deemed to be abandoned.[321]

b) Effect of Registration

Subject to the right to descriptive use under section 20 and other more limited restrictions,[322] the registration of a trade mark in respect of wares or services, unless shown to be invalid, gives to the owner the exclusive right to the use throughout Canada of such trade mark in respect of those wares or services.[323]

A copy of the record of the registration of a trade mark certified by the Registrar is evidence of the facts set out therein and that the person shown as the owner is the registered owner of the trade mark.[324]

A valid registration is required in order to bring an action for infringement under the Act. However, an action for passing off may be brought in the absence of registration, but in such an action the plaintiff will have to prove title and distinctiveness.[325]

c) Marking

The use of a trade mark notice is permissive but prudent. A brand owner should use the notification ™ to identify unregistered trade marks and the copyright symbol ® to identify its registered trade marks. In addition, the brand owner may choose to use a trade mark legend in conjunction with these symbols such as "® a registered trade mark of XYZ Company". The

---

[319] An entity that is licensed by or with the authority of the applicant to use the trade-mark, if the applicant has direct or indirect control of the character or quality of the wares or services. Subsection 40(2) and section 50.

[320] Subsection 40(2).

[321] Subsection 40(3) and see **part 2(c) of this chapter** concerning extensions.

[322] The concurrent right to use a trademark under section 21, the restriction under section 32 of the right to use a *prima facie* unregistrable trade mark and the special provisions of section 67 relating to trade marks in Newfoundland.

[323] Section 19.

[324] Subsection 54(3).

[325] See **Chapter 5, part 5**.

use of such a legend when a trade mark has been licensed combined with a statement that the use is licensed gives rise to a statutory presumption that the use is in fact licensed and under the control of the brand owner.[326]

If the brand name is used in another language or country, the appropriate symbol for that language or country should also be used. However, if the trade mark has not been registered in that country, the symbol ® should not be used in that country.

The use of such notices will have a number of advantageous results. First, third parties will be put on notice of the brand owner's rights. Second, in some cases the use of the notice may assist the brand owner in establishing that the brand name has been used as a trade mark. Third, as set out above, the use of the appropriate legend when a trade mark has been licensed gives rise to a statutory presumption. Finally, it is suggested by some that the use of such notice provides an additional element of confidence for consumers, as they may infer that the names and symbols thus endorsed carry the weight of statutory approval.

d) Invalidity

Section 18 of the Act provides that the registration of the trade mark is invalid if:

(a)   the trade mark was not registrable at the time of registration;[327]

(b)   the trade mark is not distinctive at the time proceedings bringing the validity of the registration into question are commenced;[328]

(c)   the trade mark has been abandoned;[329] or

(d)   subject to section 17 the applicant for registration was not the person entitled to secure the registration.[330]

Under section 18, the onus of proof is on the party seeking to attack the validity of the registration in question.[331]

---

[326] See **part 7(b) of this chapter**.

[327] Subsection 18(1)(a).

[328] Subsection 18(1)(b); also see *Magder v. Breck's Sporting Goods Co.* (1975), [1976] 1 S.C.R. 527 (S.C.C.).

[329] Subsection 18(1)(c).

[330] Subsection 18(1)(c). If a trade mark was distinctive at the date of registration, it cannot be held invalid merely on the ground that no evidence of distinctiveness was submitted prior to such registration: subsection 18(2).

[331] The onus of proving invalidity as a defence to an act for an infringement action is on the defendant: *Parke, Davis & Co. v. Empire Laboratories Ltd.* (1963), [1964] Ex. C.R. 399 (Can. Ex. Ct.), affirmed [1964] S.C.R. 351 (S.C.C.).

Section 17 provides that the only person who may attack a registration on the ground of prior use or prior making known is the person who previously used the trade mark or made it known or their successor in title.[332] In order to expunge an existing registration on this basis the party seeking expungement must establish that they or their predecessor in title:

(a)   used or made known a confusing trade mark or trade name before the relevant priority date for determining entitlement;[333] and

(b)   had not abandoned such confusing trade mark or trade name at the date of advertisement of the application for the trade mark sought to be expunged.[334]

A registration becomes incontestable against attack only on the ground of prior use or making known of a confusing trade mark.[335] Such incontestability applies only in proceedings commenced after the expiration of five years from the date of registration of a trade mark. After this period no registration will be expunged or amended or held invalid on the ground of previous use or making known unless it is established that the person who adopted the registered trade mark in Canada did so with knowledge of that previous use or making known.[336] All other inquiries into the propriety of registration such as registrability, distinctiveness and abandonment may be raised without time limits.[337]

e) Registration of Concurrent Rights

Section 21 of the Act attempts to protect the rights of a person who has, in good faith, used a confusing trade mark or trade name prior to the date of filing of the application for registration of a registered trade mark. In proceedings relating to a registered trade mark which has become incontestable by virtue of the expiration of the five-year period described above, and the Federal Court of Canada considers that it is not contrary to the public interest that the continued use of the confusing trade mark or trade name should be permitted in a defined territorial area concurrently with the

---

[332] Subsection 17(1). This provision also applies to an opposition, see *Robert C. Wian Enterprises Inc. v. Mady* (1965), 46 C.P.R. 147 (Can. Ex. Ct.).

[333] Subsections 16(1), (2) or (3).

[334] Subsection 16(5).

[335] Section 17.

[336] Subsection 17(2); see *Lee v. Michael Segal's Inc.* (1972), 5 C.P.R. (2d) 204 (Fed. T.D.).

[337] *Boston Pizza International Inc. v. Boston Market Corp.* (2003), 26 C.P.R. (4th) 78 (Fed. T.D.).

use of the registered trade mark, the Court may permit the continued use of the unregistered trade mark within that area with an adequate specified distinction from the registered trade mark.[338]

f) Term of Protection and Renewal

A registration of a trade mark is subject to renewal within a period of fifteen years from the day of the registration or last renewal. Unlike other intellectual property rights, such as a patent or copyright, a trade mark registration may be renewed any number of times without limitation.

The Registrar is required to send a notice to the registered owner and its representative for service, if any, stating that if within six months after the date of the notice the prescribed renewal fee is not paid, the registration will be expunged. If the prescribed renewal fee is not paid within the six month period, which may not be extended, the registration will be expunged. If the prescribed fee for a renewal is paid within the time limited for the payment the renewal takes effect as of the day next following the expiration of the period set out above.[339] Apart from payment, there are no other requirements for renewal.

7. ASSIGNMENT AND LICENCES

A brand owner may purchase a brand and become the assignee of the brand name or license others, such as a franchisees, to use the brand name. In both situations, special care must be taken to ensure that the brand name is distinctive of the brand owner.

a) Assignments

Subsection 48(1) of the Act provides that a trade mark, whether registered or unregistered, is transferable, and deemed always to have been transferable, either in connection with or separately from the goodwill of the business, and in respect of either all or some of the wares or services in association with which it has been used.[340] The subsection applies to both registered and unregistered trade marks but not trade names. Trade names

---

[338] Subsection 21(1).

[339] Section 46.

[340] *Cheerio Toys & Games Ltd. v. Dubiner* (1964), 44 C.P.R. 134 (Can. Ex. Ct.), affirmed (1965), [1966] S.C.R. 206 (S.C.C.); *Marchands Ro-Na Inc. v. Tefal S.A.* (1981), 55 C.P.R. (2d) 27 (Fed. T.D.).

presumably may only be transferred with the goodwill of the business they were used in association with.[341]

Subsection 48(2) provides that nothing in subsection 48(1) prevents a trade mark from being held not to be distinctive if, as a result of a transfer, there subsisted rights in two or more persons to the use of confusing trade marks and such rights were exercised by such persons. When determining whether the registration of a trade mark is invalid on the grounds that it is not distinctive, the determination is made at the time of the commencement of the proceedings bringing the validity of the registration into question.[342]

Subsection 48(1) has retroactive effect and validates a trade mark whose validity may have been destroyed through an improper assignment in the past prior to the passing of the Act. After assignment, the trade mark must become distinctive of the new owner and if it does not become distinctive of the new owner, it may be invalid.[343] Care must be taken to ensure that the trade mark distinguishes the wares or services of the assignee from the wares or services of others after assignment.[344] The trade mark must be distinctive of the new registered owner.[345] The assignee must embark on a program of advertising or taking other appropriate steps to bring to the attention of the relevant portion of the public that it is the owner of the mark and the source of the wares or services.

The Act does not permit territorial assignments of trade marks within Canada. If such a course of action were followed, the trade mark would become non-distinctive since, as a result of the transfer, rights in two or more persons to use confusing trade marks would subsist, assuming such rights were exercised by such persons. While the goodwill of the business

---

[341] *Cheerio Toys & Games Ltd. v. Dubiner* (1964), 44 C.P.R. 134 (Can. Ex. Ct.), affirmed (1965), [1966] S.C.R. 206 (S.C.C.).

[342] Subsection 18(1)(b).

[343] See *Wilkinson Sword (Can.) Ltd. v. Juda*, [1968] 2 Ex. C.R.137 (Can. Ex. Ct.); *Magder v. Breck's Sporting Goods Co.* (1975), [1976] 1 S.C.R. 527 (S.C.C.); *Chalet Bar B-Q (Can.) Inc. v. Foodcorp Ltd.* (1981), 55 C.P.R. (2d) 46 (Fed. T.D.), additional reasons at 56 C.P.R. (2d) 14 (Fed. T.D.), reversed (1982), 66 C.P.R. (2d) 56 (Fed. C.A.); *Heinzman v. 751056 Ontario Ltd.* (1990), 34 C.P.R. (3d) 1 (Fed. T.D.).

[344] See *Cheerio Toys & Games Ltd. v. Dubiner* (1964), 44 C.P.R. 134 (Can. Ex. Ct.), affirmed (1965), [1966] S.C.R. 206 (S.C.C.); *Wilkinson Sword (Can.) Ltd. v. Juda*, [1968] 2 Ex. C.R.137 (Can. Ex. Ct.); *Magder v. Breck's Sporting Goods Co.* (1975), [1976] 1 S.C.R. 527 (S.C.C.).

[345] *Wilkinson Sword (Can.) Ltd. v. Juda*, [1968] 2 Ex. C.R.137 (Can. Ex. Ct.) and see **part 7(b) of Chapter 2.**

may be regarded as divisible territorially, for purposes of the Act Canada must be regarded as an indivisible unit.[346]

There are two exceptions to the rule that the use of trade marks cannot be restricted to different parts of Canada. First, under section 21, the Federal Court of Canada may permit concurrent use of trade marks in a defined territorial area.[347] Second, where an unregistrable trade mark is registered on proof of its acquisition of distinctiveness or secondary meaning, the registrar may restrict the registration to the defined territorial area in Canada in which the trade mark is shown to have become distinctive.[348]

Registration is not necessary to make an assignment of a trade mark effective against a third party[349] and is not required to allow an assignee to bring an action for infringement. [350] There is no proscribed form of assignment and in some instances the courts have been prepared to infer an assignment took place without the necessity of a written agreement.[351] In addition, the assignor may be estopped from disputing the validity of a trade mark which has been assigned.[352]

The Registrar is required to register the transfer of any registered trade mark upon being furnished with satisfactory evidence of the transfer and the same information concerning the address of the transferee that would be required in an application by the transferee to register such trade mark.[353] An application for the registration of a trade mark may be amended to change the identity of the applicant after recognition of the transfer by the register.[354]

---

[346] *Great Atlantic & Pacific Tea Co. v. Canada (Registrar of Trade Marks)*, [1945] Ex. C.R. 233 (Can. Ex. Ct.).

[347] *Trade-marks Act*, R.S.C. 1985, c. T-13, section 21 and see **part 6(d) of this chapter**.

[348] Subsection 32(2).

[349] *Star-Kist Foods Inc. v. Canada (Registrar of Trade Marks)* (1985), 4 C.I.P.R. 212 (Fed. T.D.) reversed (1988), 19 C.I.P.R. 60 (Fed. C.A);*White Consolidated Industries Inc. v. Beam of Canada Inc.* (1991), 39 C.P.R. (3d) 94 (Fed. T.D.).

[350] *Wilkinson Sword (Can.) Ltd. v. Juda*, [1968] 2 Ex. C.R.137 (Can. Ex. Ct.).

[351] *Gattuso v. Gattuso Corp.*, [1968] 2 Ex. C.R. 609 (Can. Ex. Ct.); *Philip Morris Inc. v. Imperial Tobacco Ltd.* (1985), 7 C.P.R. (3d) 254 (Fed. T.D.), affirmed (1987), (sub nom. *Philip Morris Inc. v. Imperial Tobacco Ltd. (No. 2)*) 17 C.P.R. (3d) 237 (Fed. C.A.), affirmed (1987), 17 C.P.R. (3d) 289 (Fed. C.A.), leave to appeal refused (1988), (sub nom. *Philip Morris Inc. v. Imperial Tobacco Ltd. (No. 1)*) 19 C.P.R. (3d) vi (note) (S.C.C.); *White Consolidated Industries Inc. v. Beam of Canada Inc.* (1991), 39 C.P.R. (3d) 94 (Fed. T.D.).

[352] *Cheerio Toys & Games Ltd. v. Dubiner*, [1966] S.C.R. 206 (S.C.C.).

[353] Subsection 48(3). *Trade marks-Regulations* (1996), ss. 48-50.

[354] *Trade-marks Regulations* (1996), s. 31(a) and 48.

Where, as the result of an assignment, a trade mark becomes the property of one person for use in association with some of the wares or services specified in the registration and another person for use with other such wares or services and the transfer is registered by the registrar, each person is deemed to be a separate registered owner and to have a separate registration of the trade mark for use in association with the respective wares or services.[355] However, the Registrar will not allow such a partial transfer if the effect of having separate owners would likely cause confusion.

b) Licence

Both at common law and under the earlier statutes, the general rule was that any licensing of a trade mark destroyed its validity.[356] As a result, the Act was amended to make provision for licensing trade marks through a system of permitted use. The registered owner could permit the use of a registered trade mark by other persons subject to control by the owner. The registered user system was repealed and licences were allowed in 1993.

Section 50 now provides that, for the purposes of the Act, if an entity is licensed by or with the authority of the owner of a trade mark to use the trade mark in a country and the owner has, under the licence, direct or indirect control of the character or quality of the wares or services, then the use, advertisement or display of the trade mark in that country as or in a trade mark, trade name or otherwise by that entity has, and is deemed always to have had, the same effect as such a use, advertisement or display of the trade mark in that country by the owner. The section applies retroactively.[357]

Under the section the use of the mark is deemed to be use by the owner, presumably to ensure that the distinctiveness of the mark is not affected by the licence. However, this deemed use is only for the purpose of the Act and the trade mark owner is not deemed to have sold the goods or provided the services for other purposes.[358]

The Act does not contain any limitation concerning the form of the applicable licence other than it must be with the authority of the owner of a trade mark, who must have under the licence direct or indirect control of the character or quality of the licensed wares or services.

Control by the trade mark owner of the character or quality of the licensed wares or services is of fundamental importance since a licence

---

[355] *Trade-marks Regulations* (1996), s. 50.

[356] *Bowden Wire Ltd. v. Bowden Brake Co. Ltd.* (1913), 31 R.P.C. 385 (U.K. H.L.).

[357] *Eli Lilly & Co. v. Novapharm Ltd.* (2000), 10 C.P.R. (4th) 10 (Fed. C.A.), leave to appeal refused (2001), 275 N.R. 200 (note) (S.C.C.).

[358] *Mister Transmission(International) Ltd. v. Registrar of Trade Marks* (1978), 42 C.P.R. (2d) 123 (Fed. T.D.).

without adequate control may result in the invalidity of the mark.[359] For the purposes of the Act, to the extent that public notice is given of the fact that the use of a trade mark is a licensed use and of the identity of the owner, it is presumed, unless the contrary is proven, that the use is licensed by the owner of the trade mark and the character or quality of the wares or services is under the control of the owner.[360] This is a rebuttable presumption.

The ambit of the section is broad. The section is not limited to trade mark use as described in section 4, but extends to "the use, advertisement or display of the trade mark ...or in a trade mark, trade name or otherwise".

While a related company may control another—for example, a parent and wholly owned subsidiary—the courts do not accept that such control is sufficient for the purposes of section 50. Even in a parent subsidiary relationship, there must be evidence of a licence agreement and control of the character or quality of the licensed wares or services.[361]

Subject to any agreement between the owner of a trade mark and a licensee, the licensee may call on the owner to bring proceedings for infringement, and, if the owner refuses or neglects to do so within two months after being so called on, the licensee may institute proceedings for infringement in the licensee's own name as if the licensee were the owner, making the owner a defendant.[362]

8. EXPUNGEMENT FOR NON-USE

a) Section 45

If a trade mark is not in use or the actual mark used deviates substantially from the form registered,[363] summary proceedings may be instituted to expunge the registration.

The Registrar, at the written request made after three years from the date of the registration by any person who pays the prescribed fee, shall, unless the Registrar sees good reason to the contrary, give notice to the registered owner requiring the registered owner to furnish within three months an affidavit or statutory declaration showing with respect to each of the wares or services specified in the registration, whether the trade mark

---

[359] See **Chapter 9, part 5**.

[360] Subsection 50(2).

[361] *MCI Communications Corp. v. MCI Multinet Communications Inc.* (1995), 61 C.P.R. (3d) 245 (T.M. Opp. Bd.); *Cheung Kong (Holdings) Ltd. v. Living Realty Inc.* (1999), 4 C.P.R. (4th) 71 (Fed. T.D.).

[362] Subsection 50(3).

[363] See **part 3(e) of this chapter**.

was in use in Canada at any time during the three year period immediately proceeding the date of the notice and, if not, the date when it was last so in use and the reason for the absence of such use since such date.[364] The request can be made by any person. [365] There is no special form prescribed for the request. The Registrar may also at any time give such notice on his own initiative.

The purpose of this section is to provide a summary procedure for trimming the register of "dead wood"[366] which may preclude new applications. The section is intended to provide a summary procedure[367] and not to create or rescind substantive rights.[368] Proceeding under the section is not an alternative to initiating proceedings in the Federal Court seeking expungement.

In order to ensure the summary nature of the proceeding, a requesting party cannot file evidence before the Registrar or on an appeal from the decision of the Registrar.[369] In addition, cross examination on the affidavit or statutory declaration of the registered owner is not allowed.[370]

b) Evidence

The registered owner has three months within which to furnish an affidavit or statutory declaration showing, with respect to each of the wares or services specified in the registration, whether the trade mark is in use in Canada.[371] The Registrar may extend the time for furnishing the affidavit or statutory declaration.[372]

Sections 45 does not prohibit the filing of more than one affidavit nor is a registrant prohibited from filing affidavits sworn by third parties.[373]

---

[364] Section 45.

[365] *Rogers, Bereskin & Parr v. Canada (Registrar of Trade Marks)* (1986), 9 C.P.R. (3d) 260 (Fed. T.D.).

[366] *Aerosol Fillers Inc. v. Plough (Canada) Ltd.* (1979), 45 C.P.R. (2d) 194 (Fed. T.D.), affirmed (1980), 53 C.P.R. (2d) 62 (Fed. C.A.).

[367] *Anheuser-Busch Inc. v. Carling O'Keefe Breweries of Canada Ltd.* (1982), [1983] 2 F.C. 71 (Fed. C.A.).

[368] *Rogers, Bereskin & Parr v. Canada (Registrar of Trade Marks)* (1986), 9 C.P.R. (3d) 260 (Fed. T.D.).

[369] *Aerosol Fillers Inc. v. Plough (Canada) Ltd.* (1979), 45 C.P.R. (2d) 194 (Fed. T.D.), affirmed (1980), 53 C.P.R. (2d) 62 (Fed. C.A.).

[370] *Aerosol Fillers Inc. v. Plough (Canada) Ltd.* (1979), 45 C.P.R. (2d) 194 (Fed. T.D.), affirmed (1980), 53 C.P.R. (2d) 62 (Fed. C.A.).

[371] Subsection 45(1).

[372] Section 47.

[373] *Canada (Registraire des marques de commerce) c. Harris Knitting Mills Ltd.* (1985), 5 C.I.P.R. 53 (Fed. C.A.).

Section 45 requires an affidavit or statutory declaration not merely stating but "showing" sufficient facts so as to demonstrate trade mark use[374] within the meaning of the definition of a "trade-mark" in section 2 and of "use" in section 4 of the Act.[375] The evidence must also describe the nature of the business and the normal course of trade of the owner of the trade mark.[376]

Where the evidence shows the trade mark is being used only in respect to some of the wares or services specified in the registration, the registration should be amended and not expunged.[377]

The use shown in the evidence must be use of the trade mark as registered and not some other mark.[378] However, deviating use, if fully explained and justified, may be sufficient.[379]

The use must be "in a normal course of trade" as opposed to a fictitious or colourable use.[380] Ambiguities in section 45 evidence must be interpreted against the registrant.[381]

---

[374] *Aerosol Fillers Inc. v. Plough (Canada) Ltd.* (1979), 45 C.P.R. (2d) 194 (Fed. T.D.), affirmed (1980), 53 C.P.R. (2d) 62 (Fed. C.A.); *John Labatt Ltd. v. Rainier Brewing Co.* (1982), 68 C.P.R. (2d) 266 (Fed. T.D.), reversed (1984), 2 C.I.P.R. 22 (Fed. C.A.); and see *United Grain Growers Ltd. v. Lang Michener* (2001), 12 C.P.R. (4th) 89 (Fed. C.A.).

[375] See **part 3 of this chapter**.

[376] *S.C. Johnson & Son Inc. v. Canada (Registrar of Trade Marks)* (1981), 55 C.P.R. (2d) 34 (Fed. T.D.); *Sim & McBurney v. Majdell Manufacturing Co.* (1986), 11 C.P.R. (3d) 306 (Fed. T.D.).

[377] *John Labatt Ltd. v. Rainier Brewing Co.* (1982), 68 C.P.R. (2d) 266 (Fed. T.D.), reversed (1984), 2 C.I.P.R. 22 (Fed. C.A.).

[378] *Canada (Registrar of Trade Marks) v. Cie international pour l'informatique CII Honeywell Bull, S.A.* (1985), 4 C.I.P.R. 309, 4 C.P.R. (3d) 523 (Fed. C.A.), reversing (1983), 1 C.I.P.R. 231 (Fed. T.D.); *Rogers, Bereskin & Parr v. Canada (Registrar of Trade Marks)* (1986), 9 C.P.R. (3d) 260 (Fed. T.D.).

[379] See cases noted in **part 3(e)**.

[380] *Porter v. Don The Beachcomber*, [1966] Ex. C.R. 982 (Can. Ex. Ct.); *Molson Cos. v. Halter* (1976), 28 C.P.R. (2d) 158 (Fed. T.D.); *American Distilling Co. v. Canadian Schenley Distilleries Ltd.* (1977), 38 C.P.R. (2d) 60 (Fed. T.D.); *Aerosol Fillers Inc. v. Plough (Canada) Ltd.* (1979), 45 C.P.R. (2d) 194 (Fed. T.D.), affirmed (1980), 53 C.P.R. (2d) 62 (Fed. C.A.); *Ports International Ltd. v. Canada (Registrar of Trade Marks)* (1983), [1984] 2 F.C. 119 (Fed. T.D.); *Phillip Morris Inc. v. Imperial Tobacco* (1987), 13 C.P.R. (3d) 289 (Fed. T.D.); *Gowling Lafleur Henderson LLP v. Supertex Industrial S.A. de CV* (2002), 26 C.P.R. (4th) 251 (T.M. Bd).

[381] *Aerosol Fillers Inc. v. Plough (Canada) Ltd.* (1979), 45 C.P.R. (2d) 194 (Fed. T.D.), affirmed (1980), 53 C.P.R. (2d) 62 (Fed. C.A.).

c) Absence of Use

Where by reason of the evidence furnished or the failure to furnish such evidence, it appears to the Registrar that the trade mark, either with respect to all of the wares or services specified in the registration, or with respect to any of the wares or services, is not in use in Canada, and that the absence of use has not been due to special circumstances[382] that excuse the absence of use, the registration of the trade mark is liable to be expunged or amended accordingly.[383]

It is difficult to state precisely what circumstances will excuse the absence of use of a trade mark. The duration of the absence of use and the likelihood it will last a prolonged period are important factors. However, circumstances may excuse the absence of use for a brief period of time without excusing a prolonged absence of use. It is also essential to know to what extent the absence of use relates solely to a deliberate decision on the part of the owner of the trade mark rather than to obstacles beyond the control of the owner. It will be more difficult to justify absence of use due solely to a deliberate decision by the owner of the trade mark.[384] The onus is on the registered owner to establish that the mark has not been abandoned or that there are special circumstances justifying non-use.

d) The Decision

The Registrar may hear representations made by or on behalf of the registered owner of the trade mark, and by or on behalf of the person who has requested that notice be given. The parties are given the opportunity to make representations in writing, or orally, or both.

When the Registrar reaches a decision as to whether the registration of the trade mark should be expunged or amended, notice of the decision with

---

[382] *Benson & Hedges (Canada) Ltd. v. Labatt's Ltd.* (1980), 48 C.P.R. (2d) 33 (Fed. T.D.), affirmed (1983), 75 C.P.R. (2d) 287 (Fed. C.A.); *George Weston Ltd. v. Sterling & Affiliates* (1984), 3 C.P.R. (3d) 527 (Fed. T.D.); *Canada (Registraire des marques de commerce) c. Harris Knitting Mills Ltd.* (1985), 5 C.I.P.R. 53 (Fed. C.A.); *Professional Gardener Co. v. Canada (Registrar of Trade Marks)* (1985), 5 C.I.P.R. 314 (Fed. T.D.).

[383] *Canada (Registraire des marques de commerce) c. Harris Knitting Mills Ltd.* (1982), 66 C.P.R. (2d) 158 (Fed. T.D.), reversed (1985), 5 C.I.P.R. 53 (Fed. C.A.).

[384] *John Labatt Ltd. v. Cotton Club Bottling Co.* (1976), 25 C.P.R. (2d) 115 (Fed. T.D.), *Canada (Registraire des marques de commerce) c. Harris Knitting Mills Ltd.* (1982), 66 C.P.R. (2d) 158 (Fed. T.D.), reversed (1985), 5 C.I.P.R. 53 (Fed. C.A.); *NTD Apparel Inc. v. Ryan* (2003), 27 C.P.R. (4th) 73 (Fed. T.D.).

the reasons therefore must be given to the registered owner and to the person at whose request the notice was given.[385]

The decision must relate only to the matters listed in section 45 and finally determines nothing else.[386] The Registrar must act in accordance with this decision if no appeal is initiated within the time limited by the Act or, if an appeal is taken, must act in accordance with the final judgment given on such appeal.[387]

e) Appeal

The Registrar's decision is final, subject to appeal to the Federal Court.[388] The appeal must be initiated within two months from the date of dispatch of the decision by the Registrar or within such further time as the Court may allow.[389]

On appeal, evidence in addition to that which was before the Registrar may be adduced[390] and the Court may exercise any discretion vested in the Registrar.[391] Only the registered owner may adduce additional evidence and the requesting party may not submit evidence.[392]

9. EXPUNGEMENT BY THE FEDERAL COURT

Interested parties can attack the registration of a trade mark in the Federal Court. Third parties who allege they have a prior right to a mark but who did not institute opposition proceedings or defendants in actions for infringement frequently assert such claims.

---

[385] Subsection 45(4).

[386] *Broderick & Bascom Rope Co. v. Canada (Registrar of Trade Marks)* (1970), 62 C.P.R. 268 (Can. Ex. Ct.), leave to appeal refused [1971] S.C.R. ix (S.C.C.); *United Grain Growers v. Lang Mitchener* (2001), 12 C.P.R. (4th) 89 (Fed. C.A.), leave to appeal allowed (2001), 2001 CarswellNat 1903 (S.C.C.).

[387] Subsection 45(5). Section 61 provides that the judgment on the appeal is filed with the Registrar.

[388] Subsection 56(1).

[389] Subsection 56(5); *Roebuck v. Canada (Registrar of Trade Marks)* (1987), 15 C.P.R. (3d) 113 (Fed. T.D.).

[390] Subsection 56(5) and see *Austin Nichols & Co. v. Cinnabon Inc.* (1998), 82 C.P.R. (3d) 513 (Fed. C.A.).

[391] *Aerosol Fillers Inc. v. Plough (Canada) Ltd.* (1979), 45 C.P.R. (2d) 194 (Fed. T.D.), affirmed (1980), 53 C.P.R. (2d) 62 (Fed. C.A.).

[392] *Aerosol Fillers Inc. v. Plough (Canada) Ltd.* (1979), 45 C.P.R. (2d) 194 (Fed. T.D.), affirmed (1980), 53 C.P.R. (2d) 62 (Fed. C.A.).

a) Jurisdiction

The Federal Court has exclusive original jurisdiction, on the application of any person interested[393] to order that any entry in the register be struck out or amended on the ground that at the date of such application the entry as it appears on the register does not accurately express or define the existing rights of the person appearing to be the registered owner of the mark. A prior decision of the Registrar under section 45 is not a bar to such an application.[394]

Jurisdiction over the register is exclusively in the Federal Court and on appeal to the Supreme Court of Canada.[395] The courts of the provinces may have jurisdiction in actions for infringement, but are without jurisdiction to direct that the registration of a trade mark be expunged or amended.[396]

An application for expungement is made to the Federal Court[397] either by the filing of an application,[398] by counterclaim in an action for infringement of the trade mark, or by statement of claim in an action claiming additional relief under the Act. [399]

An application is heard and determined on evidence introduced by affidavit unless the Court otherwise directs.[400] However, the proceedings are not interlocutory and affidavits must be confined to facts within the personal knowledge of the deponent.[401] Affidavits should comply with the usual rules of evidence.

In such proceedings, the Court may order that any procedure permitted by its rules and practice be made available to the parties, including the introduction of oral evidence generally or in respect of one or more issues specified in the order.[402]

---

[393] Subsection 57(1).

[394] *Noxzema Chemical Co. v. Sheran Manufacturing* (1968), 55 C.P.R. 147 (Can. Ex. Ct.); *Saxon Industries Inc. v. Aldo Ippolito & Co.* (1982), 66 C.P.R. (2d) 79 (Fed. T.D.); *Long v. Pacific Northwest Enterprises Inc.*, [1985] 2 F.C. 534 (Fed. T.D.).

[395] And see section 20 of the *Federal Courts Act*, R.S.C. 1985, c. F-7 as amended; *Canadian Shredded Wheat Co. v. Kellogg Co.* (1938), [1939] Ex. C.R. 58 (Can. Ex. Ct.), affirmed (1939), [1939] S.C.R. 329 (S.C.C.).

[396] *Canadian Shredded Wheat Co. Ltd. v. Kellogg Co. of Canada Ltd. et al.*, [1936] O.W.N. 199 (Ont. H.C.).

[397] Subsection 57(1).

[398] See part 5 of the *Federal Court Rules, 1998,* SOR/98-106.

[399] Section 58.

[400] Subsection 59(3).

[401] *P.S. Part Source Inc. v. Canadian Tire Corp.* (2001), (sub nom. *P.S. Partsource Inc. v. Canadian Tire Corp.*) 11 C.P.R. (4th) 386 (Fed. C.A.).

[402] Subsection 59(3).

In matters concerning the register, the Court should not only determine the claims between the parties, but also look to the preservation of the "purity of the register"[403] and the public interest.[404]

b) Person Interested

The Act provides that the term "person interested" includes any person who is affected, or reasonably apprehends that he may be affected by any entry in the register, or by any act or omission or contemplated act or omission under or contrary to the Act, and includes the Attorney General of Canada.[405]

In order to be a "person interested" an applicant must be affected or reasonably apprehend that they may be affected by an entry in the register.[406] For example, where a person has previously used the registered trade mark and whose application for a trade mark has been barred by the registration,[407] who has been sued or threatened with infringement[408] or whose agent or distributor has wrongfully obtained the registration in issue,[409] have been found to be "a person interested".

---

[403] *Battle Pharmaceuticals v. British Drug Houses Ltd.*, [1944] Ex. C.R. 239 (Can. Ex. Ct.), affirmed [1946] S.C.R. 50 (S.C.C.); *General Motors Corp. v. Bellows*, [1949] S.C.R. 678 (S.C.C.); *Aladdin Industries Inc. v. Canadian Thermos Products Ltd.* (1969), 57 C.P.R. 230 (Ex. Ct.), affirmed (1972), 6 C.P.R. (2d) 1 (S.C.C.).

[404] *British Drug Houses, Ltd. v. Battle Pharmaceuticals*, [1944] Ex. C.R. 239 (Can. Ex. Ct.), affirmed (1945), [1946] S.C.R. 50 (S.C.C.); *Aladdin Industries Inc. v. Canadian Thermos Products Ltd.* (1969), 57 C.P.R. 230 (Can. Ex. Ct.), affirmed (1972), 6 C.P.R. (2d) 1 (S.C.C.).

[405] Section 2. See *Aladdin Industries Inc. v. Canadian Thermos Products Ltd.* (1969), 57 C.P.R. 230 (Can. Ex. Ct.), affirmed (1972), 6 C.P.R. (2d) 1 (S.C.C.).

[406] *Coronet Wallpaper (Ontario) Ltd. v. Wall Paper Manufacturers Ltd.* (1983), 77 C.P.R. (2d) 282 (Fed. T.D.); *Rentokil Group Ltd. v. Barrigar & Oyen* (1983), 75 C.P.R. (2d) 10 (Fed. T.D.).

[407] *Sequa Chemicals Inc. v. United Colour & Chemicals Ltd.* (1992), 44 C.P.R. (3d) 371 (Fed. T.D.).

[408] *Havana House Cigar & Tobacco Merchants Ltd. v. Skyway Cigar Store* (1998), 81 C.P.R. (3d) 203 (Fed. T.D.), reversed (1999), 3 C.P.R. (4th) 501 (Fed. C.A.).

[409] *Citrus Growers Assn. Ltd. v. William D. Branson Ltd.* (1990), 36 C.P.R. (3d) 434 (Fed. T.D.).

c) Limitations

No registration of a trade mark shall be expunged or amended or held invalid on the ground of any previous use or making known of a confusing trade mark or trade name by a person other than the applicant for such registration or his predecessor in title, except at the instance of such other person or his successor in title.[410] The burden lies on such other person or their successor to establish that they had not abandoned such confusing trade mark or trade name at the date of advertisement of the applicant's application.[411]

In proceedings commenced after the expiry of five years from the date of registration of a trade mark, no registration shall be expunged, amended or held invalid on the ground of the previous use or making known, unless it is established that the person who adopted the registered trade mark in Canada did so with knowledge of such previous use or making known.[412] Apart from this limitation, the *Trade-marks Act* does not prescribe a limitation period for bringing an application to expunge a registered trade mark.[413]

No person is entitled to institute any proceeding in the Federal Court calling into question any decision given by the Registrar of which such person had express notice and from which they had a right to appeal.[414]

d) Grounds for Expungement

i) Section 18

Section 18 sets out the grounds under which the validity of a registration of a trade mark may be questioned. The registration of a trade mark is invalid if:

(a)   the trade mark was not registerable at the date of registration;

(b)   the trade mark is not distinctive at the time proceedings bringing the validity of the registration into question are commenced; or

(c)   the trade mark has been abandoned and

---

[410] Subsection 17(1) and see *Robert C. Wian Enterprises Inc. v. Mady* (1965), 46 C.P.R. 147 (Can. Ex. Ct.).

[411] Subsection 17(1).

[412] Subsection17(2).

[413] *Boston Pizza International Inc. v. Boston Market Corp.* (2003), 27 C.P.R. (4th) 52 (Fed. T.D.).

[414] Subsection 57(2).

(d)   subject to section 17, the applicant for registration was not the person entitled to secure the registration.

The burden of proof in proceedings for expungement lies on the party seeking to expunge or amend.[415] Where a mark has stood unchallenged on the register for many years, it should not be expunged where grave commercial injustice would result.[416] Acquiescence or laches may be advanced as a defence.[417]

ii) Not Registerable

If the trade mark was not registerable at the date of its registration, such registration is invalid and may be expunged.[418] On an application to expunge based on this ground evidence must be presented to overcome the provisions of subsection 54(3), which provides that the certificate of registration is evidence of the facts set out in it. [419] The registration is considered to be *prima facie* valid.

---

[415] *General Motors Corp. v. Bellows*, [1947] Ex. C.R. 568 (Can. Ex. Ct.), affirmed [1949] S.C.R. 678 (S.C.C.); *Building Products Ltd. v. B.P. Canada Ltd.* (1961), 36 C.P.R. 121 (Can. Ex. Ct.); *Cheerio Toys & Games Ltd. v. Dubiner* (1964), 44 C.P.R. 134 (Can. Ex. Ct.), affirmed (1965), [1966] S.C.R. 206 (S.C.C.).

[416] *Pepsi-Cola Co. v. Coca-Cola Co.*, [1938] Ex. C.R. 263 (Can. Ex. Ct.), affirmed on this issue (1939), [1940] S.C.R. 17 (S.C.C.), affirmed without dealing with this point [1942] 2 W.W.R. 257 (Canada P.C.).

[417] *Carling O'Keefe Breweries of Canada Ltd. v. Anheuser-Busch Inc.* (1982), (Fed. T.D.), reversed in part on other grounds (1986), 10 C.P.R. (3d) 433 (Fed. C.A.).

[418] Subsection 18(1)(a); also see **Chapter 2, part 9** and *Adidas (Canada) Ltd. v. Colins Inc.* (1978), 38 C.P.R. (2d) 145; *Carling O'Keefe Breweries of Canada Ltd. v. Anheuser-Busch Inc.* (1982), (Fed. T.D.), reversed in part on other grounds (1986), 10 C.P.R. (3d) 433 (Fed. C.A.); *Jordan & Ste-Michelle Cellars Ltd. v. Gillespies & Co.* (1985), 6 C.P.R. (3d) 377 (Fed. T.D.).

[419] *W.J. Hughes & Sons "Corn Flower" Ltd. v. Morawiec* (1970), 62 C.P.R. 21 (Can. Ex. Ct.); *Chateau-Gai Wines Ltd. v. Canada (Attorney General)*, [1970] Ex. C.R. 366 (Can. Ex. Ct.); *Mr. P's Mastertune Ignition Services Ltd. v. Tune Masters Inc.* (1984), 82 C.P.R. (2d) 128 (Fed. T.D.); *Professional Publishing Associates Ltd. v. Toronto Parent Magazine Inc.* (1986), 9 C.P.R. (3d) 207 (Fed. T.D.); *Rainsoft Water Conditioning Co. v. Rainsoft (Regina) Ltd.* (1987), 12 C.I.P.R. 193 (Fed. T.D.).

iii) Not Distinctive

If a trade mark is not distinctive at the time proceedings bringing the validity of the registration into question are commenced, its registration is invalid.[420]

Section 18(2) of the Act provides that no registration of a trade mark that has been so used in Canada by the registrant or his predecessor in title so as to become distinctive at the date of registration shall be held invalid merely on the ground that evidence of such distinctiveness was not submitted to the Registrar before the grant of such registration.

iv) Abandonment

The registration of a trade mark is invalid if the trade mark has been abandoned.[421] Whether a trade mark has been abandoned is a question of fact which must be decided in each case after taking into consideration all of the surrounding circumstances. The onus of proving abandonment is on the party asserting such claim.[422]

Non use of a trade mark by itself is not sufficient to establish abandonment[423] and there must be an intention to abandon.[424] Intention may be inferred from long disuse[425] or from the adoption of a new mark to replace

---

[420] Subsection 18(1)(b); also see **Chapter 2, part 7(b)**; *Santana Jeans Ltd. v. Manager Clothing Inc.* (1993), 52 C.P.R. (3d) 472 (Fed. T.D.); *Consorzio del Prosciutto di Parma v. Maple Leaf Meats Inc.* (2001), 11 C.P.R. (4th) 48 (Fed. T.D.); *Boston Pizza International Inc. v. Boston Chicken Inc.* (2002), 24 C.P.R. (4th) 150 (Fed. C.A.) and see case comment by Bradley J. Freeman "Expungement of Foreign Registered Trade-marks in Canada", *Boston Pizza International Inc. v. Boston Chicken Inc.* (2003), 17 I.P.J. 97.

[421] Subsection 18(1)(c).

[422] *Union Electric Supply Co. v. Canada (Registrar of Trade Marks) (No. 2)* (1982), 63 C.P.R. (2d) 179 (Fed. T.D.); *Burroughs Wellcom Inc. v. Kirby, Shapiro, Eades & Cohen* (1983), 73 C.P.R. (2d) 13 (Fed. T.D.); *Road Runner Trailer Manufacturing Ltd. v. Road Runner Trailer Co.* (1984), 1 C.P.R. (3d) 443 (Fed. T.D.).

[423] *Coronet-Werke Heinrich Schlerf GmbH v. Produits Ménagers Coronet Inc.* (1984), 4 C.P.R. (3d) 108 (T.M. Opp. Bd.), reversed in part (1986), 10 C.P.R. (3d) 482 (Fed. T.D.); *Saccone & Speed Ltd. v. Canada (Registrar of Trade Marks)* (1982), 67 C.P.R. (2d) 119 (Fed. T.D.).

[424] *Dastous v. Matthews-Wells Co.* (1949), [1950] S.C.R. 261 (S.C.C.); *Stampede Wrestling Corp. v. Whalen* (1986), 47 Alta. L.R. (2d) 363 (Fed. T.D.).

[425] *Bundey American Corporation v. No-Frills Car & Truck Rental Inc.* (2001), 16 C.P.R. (4th) 68 (Fed. T.D.).

an unused mark.[426] The intention with which abandonment is concerned is that of using the mark in connection with a particular ware or service.[427]

v) Entitlement

An applicant for registration was not the person entitled to secure the registration if:

(a)   they did not satisfy the requirements of section 16;[428]

(b)   the registration was obtained by the inclusion of a materially false statement of use that was fundamental to the registration, in which case it is not necessary to show either fraud or intent to deceive; [429] or

(c)   the registration was obtained on the basis of a fraudulent misrepresentation[430] or in fraud of the rights of the true owner.[431]

10. SUMMARY AND CHECKLIST

To ensure that a brand name is protected the following matters must be considered.

1.   The primary methods of protecting a brand name are by obtaining a registration under the *Trade-marks Act* and by bringing an action in the courts for infringement under the Act or asserting common law claims to enjoin passing off.

2.   Common law rights are acquired through actual use of a mark in association with wares or services. As a common law trade mark becomes known and goodwill is associated with it, the common law trade mark

---

[426] *Dastous v. Matthews-Wells Co.* (1949), [1950] S.C.R. 261 (S.C.C.).

[427] *Dastous v. Matthews-Wells Co.* (1949), [1950] S.C.R. 261 (S.C.C.).

[428] See **part 4 of this chapter** and section 17 and subsection 18(1).

[429] *Unitel Communications Inc. v. Bell Canada* (1995), 61 C.P.R. (3d) 12 (Fed. T.D.); *WCC Containers Sales Limited v. Haul-All Equipment Ltd.* (2003), 28 C.P.R. (4th) 175 (F.C.).

[430] *Bonus Foods Ltd. v. Essex Packers Ltd.* (1964), 43 C.P.R. 165 (Can. Ex Ct.); *Biba Boutique Ltd. v. Dalmys (Can.) Ltd.* (1976), 25 C.P.R. (2d) 278 (Fed. T.D.); *WCC Containers Sales Limited v. Haul-All Equipment Ltd.* (2003), 28 C.P.R. (4th) 175 (F.C.).

[431] As to the expungement of a trade mark registered by an agent on the ground of prior use of the principal, see *Turban Brand Products Ltd. v. Khan* (1980), 51 C.P.R. (2d) 71 (Fed. T.D.); *Wilhelm Layher GmbH v. Anthes Industries Inc.* (1986), 8 C.P.R. (3d) 187 (Fed. T.D.); and see subsection 17(2).

owner will be able to assert claims against others who use confusing common law trade marks in the specific region or area that the common law trade mark owner has built up goodwill. These rights are asserted by bringing an action for passing off in the courts.

3. The *Trade-marks Act* facilitates the protection of a trade mark by providing for public notice of rights and granting exclusive rights to the owner. There are significant benefits associated with obtaining a registration.

4. A brand owner must understand how the trade mark system works so that it can be used to the maximum extent possible to protect the brand name and related slogans, the product and, in some cases, product packaging. The potential benefits of the Act need to be carefully considered and implemented in a proactive fashion. Common law trade mark rights may be helpful on a case by case basis.

5. Rights in a trade mark are acquired by "adopting" it. A trade mark is deemed to be adopted when a person (or its predecessor in title) commenced to use the trade mark in Canada or made the trade mark known in Canada. If the trade mark has not previously been used or made it known it is deemed to be adopted on the filing of an application for registration of a trade mark in Canada.

6. The concept of "use" is of fundamental importance under the Act since rights are determined by it. A brand owner must understand and comply with the requirements relating to trade mark "use" in order to protect the brand name under the Act. The Act contains specific rules to establish "use" for wares, services and exported wares which can be restrictive particularly for wares.

7. Once a brand name has been chosen and any design presentation finalized an application can be filed with the Registrar of Trade-marks.

8. If specific requirements, including a requirement to file within six months from the filing date of the foreign application, are satisfied a foreign trade mark owner may rely on its foreign filing date. In addition, such owners may take advantage of the provisions of the Act concerning marks which may not satisfy all of the requirements for registrability.

9. The Act sets out a series of rules for determining who is entitled to obtain a registration of a mark. The rules apply in cases of potential or real confusion between the mark applied for and pre-existing rights associated with trade marks, whether registered or not, and trade names. The determination is made as of a priority date which varies depending on the basis on which the application is filed.

10. Subject to limited exceptions, the registration of a trade mark in respect of any wares or services, unless shown to be invalid, gives to the owner the exclusive right to the use throughout Canada of such trade mark in respect of such wares or services.

11. A trade mark should be used in the form in which it is registered. The use of a variation of a registered mark may be potential grounds for expungement of the mark. However, this potential result may be avoided by obtaining a separate registration for the variant.

12. A brand owner should use the notation™ to identify its unregistered trade marks and the symbol ® to identify its registered trade marks. In addition, a trade mark legend may be used as well. The use of such notices will have a number of advantageous results.

13. A registration of a trade mark is subject to renewal within fifteen years from the day of the registration or last renewal. Unlike other intellectual property rights, such as a patent or copyright, a trade mark registration may be renewed any number of times without limitation.

14. A brand owner may purchase a brand and become the assignee of the brand name or license others, such as a franchisees, to use a brand name. In both situations special care must be taken to ensure that the brand name continues to be distinctive of the brand owner.

15. If a trade mark is not in use or the actual mark used deviates substantially from the form registered, summary proceedings may be instituted to expunge the registration.

16. Interested parties can attack the registration of a trade mark in the Federal Court. Third parties who allege they have a prior right to a mark but who did not institute opposition proceedings or defendants in actions for infringement frequently assert such claims.

Chapter 5: Protecting Brand Names—Enforcement

1. INTRODUCTION

As we have seen, a brand name may be protected by obtaining a trade mark registration. A brand name may also be protected, directly or indirectly, by taking action to enforce the rights associated with it against a competitor or other third party. Rights may be asserted directly when a competitor or potential competitor uses a confusing brand name or makes a misrepresentation leading or likely to lead the public to believe that the wares or services offered by it are the wares and services of the brand owner. The owner of a registered trade mark can bring an action in the courts for trade mark infringement or, if a registration has not been obtained, an action for passing off may be brought. Rights may be asserted indirectly when a third party's attempt to obtain a trade mark registration is scrutinized in the context of a trade mark opposition.

If a brand owner does not take appropriate steps to ensure that competitors do not use trade marks or trade names which are confusingly similar to its brand name, the distinctiveness of the brand name may be diminished.

2. CONFUSING TRADE MARKS

Section 6 of the *Trade-marks Act* sets out statutory criteria for determining when trade marks and trade names are confusing. These criteria must be considered in the following situations, among others:

(a) When an assessment is made concerning whether a proposed mark is potentially available for use.[432]

(b) In the prosecution of a trade mark application where a Trade-marks Examiner has issued an office action asserting that the

---

[432] See **Chapter 2, part 8**.

subject matter of the application is confusing with a registered mark or a pending application which is entitled to priority;

(c) In opposition proceedings, where the opponent takes the position that the applicant's trade mark is not registrable or the applicant is not the person entitled to registration in that the trade mark applied for is confusing with a registered trade mark;[433]

(d) In an action for infringement, where the plaintiff asserts that the defendant is selling, distributing or advertising wares or services in association with a confusing trade mark or trade name;

(e) In proceedings seeking the expungement of a registered trade mark where the party seeking expungement has taken the position that the trade mark is invalid on the ground of the previous use or making known of a confusing trade mark or a trade name.

The application of the statutory criteria remains the same in all instances, but the party bearing the onus of proof will vary depending on the proceedings. In opposition proceedings, the onus is on the applicant of the mark to establish the absence of a reasonable prospect of confusion.[434] In an action for infringement or an action or proceeding seeking expungement, the onus of proof is on the party raising the issue to show a reasonable probability of confusion.

a) The Statutory Criteria

Under the Act, the use of a trade mark causes confusion with another trade mark if the use of both marks in the same area would be likely to lead to the inference that the wares or services associated with such trade marks are manufactured, sold, leased, hired or performed by the same person,[435] whether or not such wares or services are of the same general class.[436] The use of a trade mark causes confusion with a trade name and the use of a

---

[433] See **part 3 of this chapter**.

[434] *Berry Bros. & Rudd Ltd. v. Planta Tabak-Manufaktur Dr. Manfred Oberman* (1979), 47 C.P.R. (2d) 205 (T.M. Opp. Bd.), reversed (1980), 53 C.P.R. (2d) 130 (Fed. T.D.).

[435] Subsection 6(2) and see *Bonus Foods Ltd. v. Essex Packers Ltd.* (1964), 43 C.P.R. 165 (Can. Ex. Ct.); *Benson & Hedges (Canada) Ltd. v. St. Regis Tobacco Corp.* (1968), [1969] 57 C.P.R. 1 (S.C.C.).

[436] *United Artists Pictures Inc. v. Pink Panther Beauty Corp.* (1998), (sub nom. *United Artists Corp. v. Pink Panther Beauty Corp.*) 80 C.P.R. (3d) 247 (Fed. C.A.).

trade name causes confusion with a trade mark under corresponding conditions.[437]

In determining whether trade marks or trade names are confusing, the Court or the Registrar, as the case may be, must have regard to all of the surrounding circumstances, including:

(a) the inherent distinctiveness of the trade marks or trade names and the extent to which they have become known;
(b) the length of time the trade marks or trade names have been in use;
(c) the nature of the wares, services or business;
(d) the nature of the trade; and
(e) the degree of resemblance between the trade marks or trade names in appearance or sound or in the ideas suggested by them.[438]

The items listed above are not exhaustive.[439]

To determine whether two trade marks are confusing, the Court or the Registrar, must make a determination of the effect of the marks on those persons who normally make up the market. This does not mean a rash, careless or unobservant purchaser, or a person of higher education, possessed of expert qualifications. Rather, it is the average person endowed with average intelligence acting with ordinary caution.[440] The issue must be determined as a matter of first impression, taking into consideration imperfect recollection and careless pronunciation.[441]

The risk of confusion for the average anglophone consumer or the average francophone consumer or in special circumstances the average

[437] Subsections 6(3) and (4).
[438] Subsection 6(5).
[439] *Cochrane-Dunlop Hardware Ltd. v. Capital Diversified Industries Ltd.* (1976), 30 C.P.R. (2d) 176 (Ont. C.A.); *Carling O'Keefe Breweries of Canada Ltd. v. Anheuser-Busch Inc.* (1982), (sub nom. *Carling O'Keefe Breweries of Can. Ltd. v. Anheuser-Busch Inc. (No. 1)*) 68 C.P.R. (2d) 1 (Fed. T.D.), reversed in part (1986), 10 C.P.R. (3d) 433 (Fed. C.A.); *Mr. Submarine Ltd. v. Amandista Investments Ltd.* (1986), 9 C.I.P.R. 164 (Fed. T.D.), reversed (1987), 19 C.P.R. (3d) 3 (Fed. C.A.); *United Artists Pictures Inc. v. Pink Panther Beauty Corp.* (1998), (sub nom. *United Artists Corp. v. Pink Panther Beauty Corp.*) 80 C.P.R. (3d) 247 (Fed. C.A.).
[440] *Canadian Schenley Distilleries Ltd. v. Canada's Manitoba Distillery Ltd.* (1975), 25 C.P.R. (2d) 1 (Fed. T.D.); *Canada Post Corp. v. Micropost Corp.* (1998), 84 C.P.R. (3d) 225 (Fed. T.D.); *Hudson's Bay Co. v. Baylor University* (2000), (sub nom. *Baylor University v. Hudson's Bay Co.*) 8 C.P.R. (4th) 64 (Fed. C.A.).
[441] *Sealy Sleep Products Ltd. v. Simpson's-Sears Ltd.* (1960), 33 C.P.R. 129 (Can. Ex. Ct.).

bilingual consumer should be considered. The perspective of the average bilingual consumer is only considered where a trade mark consists of unusual or distinct words which might create confusion for someone who knew what they meant in both English and French.[442]

Each of the statutory criteria need not be given equal weight.[443] Typically, the degree of resemblance between the trade marks in appearance, sound or in ideas suggested by them is the dominant factor.[444]

The trade marks or trade names in question must be considered in their entirety. It is not a correct approach to put the trade marks side-by-side and make a careful comparison in order to observe similarities and differences.[445] The question to be considered is whether the use of the trade mark as a whole leads to the inference that the wares or services are manufactured or performed by the same person.

The determination of whether two trade marks or trade names are confusing involves the exercise of personal judgment in light of all the evidence with particular regard to the surrounding circumstances as set out in subsection 6(5) of the Act. This is a judicial determination of a question of fact, not the exercise of discretion.[446]

Each case depends on its own facts, and previous decisions are helpful only in so far as they illustrate the application of the principles set out in the Act.[447]

---

[442] *Pierre Fabre Médicament c. SmithKline Beecham Corp.* (2001), (sub nom. *Smithkline Beecham Corporation v. Pierre Fabre Medicament*) 11 C.P.R. (4th) 1 (Fed. C.A.).

[443] *Miss Universe Inc. v. Bohna* (1994), 58 C.P.R. (3d) 381 (Fed. C.A.).

[444] *Beverley Bedding & Upholstery Co. v. Regal Bedding & Upholstering Ltd.* (1980), 47 C.P.R. (2d) 145 (Fed. T.D.), affirmed (1982), 60 C.P.R. (2d) 70 (Fed. C.A.).

[445] *Henkel Kommanditgesellschaft auf Aktien v. Super Dragon Import Export Inc.* (1984), 3 C.I.P.R. 286 (Fed. T.D.), affirmed (1986), 12 C.P.R. (3d) 110 (Fed. C.A.); *Simmons Ltd. v. A to Z Comfort Beddings Ltd.* (1991), (sub nom. *Park Avenue Furniture Corp. v. Wickes/Simmons Bedding Ltd.*) 37 C.P.R. (3d) 413 (Fed. C.A.); *Molson Co. v. John Labatt Ltd./John Labatt Ltée* (1994), (sub nom. *Molson Cos. Ltd. v. Labatt (John) Ltd.*) 58 C.P.R. (3d) 527 (Fed. C.A.).

[446] See *Pepsi-Cola Co. v. Coca-Cola Co.*, [1938] Ex. C.R. 263 (Can. Ex. Ct.) at 288, reversed (1939), [1940] S.C.R. 17 (S.C.C.), affirmed [1942] 2 W.W.R. 257 (Canada P.C.); *Benson & Hedges (Canada) Ltd. v. St. Regis Tobacco Corp.* (1968), [1969] 57 C.P.R. 1 (S.C.C.).

[447] *Cochrane-Dunlop Hardware Ltd. v. Capital Diversified Industries Ltd.* (1976), 30 C.P.R. (2d) 176 (Ont. C.A.).

b) Inherent Distinctiveness

The first circumstance to be considered in determining whether trade marks or trade names are confusing is the inherent distinctiveness of the trade marks or trade names and the extent to which they have become known.[448] Strong marks, like KODAK or other invented words tend to be more inherently distinctive then weak marks such as PACIFIC COFFEE or PREMIUM SODA, either because of common use or being tinged with a geographic or descriptive character. The extent of protection available to a trade mark will vary, other things being equal, on the degree of distinctiveness of the trade mark.[449]

If other competitors are using trade marks somewhat similar to the trade mark in issue, this will be relevant to the degree of distinctiveness of the trade mark.[450] Where a trade mark consists of words which are common and which are also contained in a number of other trade marks in use in the same market, it will be less distinctive and entitled to less protection than in the case of a strong mark.[451]

The use of a trade mark by several traders in the same field may cause the mark to become non-distinctive and not entitled to protection.[452] However, a new combination of words or designs, each of which is itself common to the trade, may constitute a distinctive combination when looked at as a

---

[448] *United Artists Pictures Inc. v. Pink Panther Beauty Corp.* (1998), (sub nom. *United Artists Corp. v. Pink Panther Beauty Corp.*) 80 C.P.R. (3d) 247 (Fed. C.A.) at 259, leave to appeal allowed (1998), 235 N.R. 399 (note) (S.C.C.).

[449] *General Motors Corp. v. Bellows*, [1947] Ex. C.R. 568 (Can. Ex. Ct.) at 574, affirmed [1949] S.C.R. 678 (S.C.C.) at 691; *Ultravite Laboratories Ltd. v. Whitehall Laboratories Ltd.* (1965), 44 C.P.R. 189 (S.C.C.); *La Maur Inc. v. Prodon Industries Ltd.* (1969), 59 C.P.R. 127 (Can. Ex. Ct.), affirmed [1971] S.C.R. 973 (S.C.C.).

[450] *Dastous v. Matthews-Wells Co.* (1949), [1950] S.C.R. 261 (S.C.C.) at 276; *Haw Par Bros. International Ltd. v. Canada (Registrar of Trade Marks)* (1979), 48 C.P.R. (2d) 65 (Fed. T.D.); *Sunshine Biscuits Inc. v. Corporate Foods Ltd.* (1982), 61 C.P.R. (2d) 53 (Fed. T.D.); *Chalet Bar B-Q (Can.) Inc. v. Foodcorp Ltd.* (1981), 55 C.P.R. (2d) 46 (Fed. T.D.), additional reasons at (1981), 56 C.P.R. (2d) 14 (Fed. T.D.); *Caricline Ventures Ltd. v. ZZTY Holdings Ltd.* (2001), 16 C.P.R. (4th) 484 (Fed. T.D.), affirmed (2002), 22 C.P.R. (4th) 321 (Fed. C.A.).

[451] *Maximum Nutrition Ltd. v. Kellogg Salada Canada Inc.* (1992), (sub nom. *Kellogg Salada Canada Inc. v. Maximum Nutrition Ltd.*) 43 C.P.R. (3d) 349 (Fed. C.A.); *Molson Co. v. John Labatt Ltd./John Labatt Ltée* (1994), (sub nom. *Molson Cos. Ltd. v. Labatt (John) Ltd.*) 58 C.P.R. (3d) 527 (Fed. C.A.).

[452] *Pepsi-Cola Co. v. Coca-Cola Co.* (1939), [1940] S.C.R. 17 (S.C.C.), affirmed [1942] 2 W.W.R. 257 (Canada P.C.).

whole.[453] Such a trade mark does not lie in each of the particular components, but in the combination of them. It is the commercial impression produced by the mark as a whole that must be considered.

If the owner of a trade mark allows it to be used as the name of the wares or services in question it may lose its distinctiveness and become generic.[454]

A mark, which is not inherently distinctive, may acquire distinctiveness through extensive use in the marketplace which makes the mark known to purchasers of the wares or services in issue.[455]

c) Duration of Use

The second circumstance to be considered in determining whether trade marks or trade names are confusing is the length of time they have been in use.[456] Where both trade marks have been used for a considerable period of time in the same area without evidence of actual confusion, it may be inferred that confusion is unlikely to occur in the future.[457]

---

[453] *Pepsi-Cola Co. v. Coca-Cola Co.*, [1938] Ex. C.R. 263 (Can. Ex. Ct.) at 288, reversed (1939), [1940] S.C.R. 17 (S.C.C.), affirmed [1942] 2 W.W.R. 257 (Canada P.C.); *Yamaska Garments Ltd. v. Canada (Registrar of Trade Marks)*, [1945] Ex. C.R. 223 (Can. Ex. Ct.); *Kimberly-Clark of Canada Ltd. v. Molnlycke AB* (1982), 61 C.P.R. (2d) 42 (Fed. T.D.); *Molson Co. v. Carling O'Keefe Breweries of Canada Ltd.* (1979), 53 C.P.R. (2d) 198 (T.M. Opp. Bd.), affirmed (1981), 55 C.P.R. (2d) 15 (Fed. T.D.).

[454] *Cheerio Toys & Games Ltd. v. Dubiner* (1964), 44 C.P.R. 134 (Can. Ex. Ct.), affirmed (1965), [1966] S.C.R. 206 (S.C.C.).

[455] *United Artists Pictures Inc. v. Pink Panther Beauty Corp.* (1998), (sub nom. *United Artists Corp. v. Pink Panther Beauty Corp.*) 80 C.P.R. (3d) 247 (Fed. C.A.).

[456] Subsection 6(5)(b).

[457] *Hudson's Bay Co. v. Baylor University* (2000), (sub nom. *Baylor University v. Hudson's Bay Co.*) 8 C.P.R. (4th) 64 (Fed. C.A.); *Christian Dior S.A. v. Dion Neckwear Ltd.* (1996), 71 C.P.R. (3d) 268 (T.M. Opp. Bd.), affirmed (2000), (sub nom. *Dion Neckwear Ltd. v. Christian Dior, S.A.*) 5 C.P.R. (4th) 304 (Fed. T.D.), reversed (2002), (sub nom. *Dion Neckwear Ltd. v. Christian Dior, S.A.*) 20 C.P.R. (4th) 155 (Fed. C.A.); *Toys "R" Us (Canada) Ltd. v. Manjel Inc.* (2003), (sub nom. *Toys "R" Us (Canada) Ltd. v. Manjel Inc.*) 24 C.P.R. (4th) 449 (Fed. T.D.); see *Kellogg Canada Inc. v. Weetabix of Canada Ltd.* (2002), 20 C.P.R. (4th) 17 (Fed. T.D.) concerning co-existence in other jurisdictions.

d) The Nature of the Wares, Services or Business

The third circumstance to be considered in determining whether trade marks or trade names are confusing is the nature of the wares, services or business.[458] This circumstance is particularly influenced by the reputation or goodwill associated with the trade marks in issue.[459]

Where, by virtue of the goodwill associated with it a trade mark has become famous, it is entitled to a broader range of protection and the distinction between the wares associated with the respective trade marks should receive less emphasis. However, there must be a connection or similarity in the products or services in issue. Where there is no such connection it is very difficult to justify the extension of property rights into areas of commerce that do not remotely affect the trade mark owner. Only in exceptional circumstances, if ever, should this be the case.[460]

If the trade mark is inherently weak the fact that the wares, services or businesses are different may be sufficient to avoid the likelihood of confusion.[461]

The fact that the wares or services are cheap or expensive or purchased hastily or after careful consideration must be considered.[462] If the wares or

---

[458] Subsection 6(5)(c); *Oshawa Holdings Ltd. v. Fjord Pacific Marine Industries Ltd.* (1980), 47 C.P.R. (2d) 86 (Fed. T.D.), affirmed (1981), 36 N.R. 71 (Fed. C.A.); *Mr. Submarine v. Amandista Investments Ltd.* (1987), 19 C.P.R. (3d) 3 (Fed. C.A.); *United Artists Pictures Inc. v. Pink Panther Beauty Corp.* (1998), (sub nom. *United Artists Corp. v. Pink Panther Beauty Corp.*) 80 C.P.R. (3d) 247 (Fed. C.A.).

[459] *Boy Scouts of Canada v. Alfred Sternjakob GmbH & Co. KG* (1984), 2 C.P.R. (3d) 407 (Fed. T.D.).

[460] *United Artists Pictures Inc. v. Pink Panther Beauty Corp.* (1998), (sub nom. *United Artists Corp. v. Pink Panther Beauty Corp.*) 80 C.P.R. (3d) 247 (Fed. C.A.); *Toyota Jidosha Kabushiki Kaisha v. Lexus Foods Inc.* (2000), 9 C.P.R. (4th) 297 (Fed. C.A.); *Advance Magazine Publishers Inc. v. Masco Building Products Corp.* (1999), 86 C.P.R. (3d) 207 (Fed. T.D.).

[461] *Playboy Enterprises Inc. v. Germain* (1978), 39 C.P.R. (2d) 32 (Fed. T.D.), affirmed (1979), 43 C.P.R. (2d) 271 (Fed. C.A.); *Oshawa Group Ltd. v. Creative Resources Co.* (1979), 47 C.P.R. (2d) 115 (Fed. T.D.), reversed (1982), 61 C.P.R. (2d) 29 (Fed. C.A.); *Coronet-Werke Heinrich Schlerf GmbH v. Produits Ménagers Coronet Inc.* (1984), 4 C.P.R. (3d) 108 (T.M. Opp. Bd.), reversed in part (1986), 10 C.P.R. (3d) 482 (Fed. T.D.); *Polysar Ltd. v. Gesco Distributing Ltd.* (1985), 6 C.P.R. (3d) 289 (Fed. T.D.), reversing (1981), 67 C.P.R. (2d) 232 (T.M. Opp. Bd.); *Clorox Co. v. Sears Canada Inc.*, 33 C.P.R. (3d) 48 (T.M. Opp. Bd.), reversed (1992), 41 C.P.R. (3d) 483 (Fed. T.D.), affirmed (1993), 49 C.P.R. (3d) 217 (Fed. C.A.).

[462] *General Motors Corp. v. Bellows*, [1947] Ex. C.R. 568 (Can. Ex. Ct.) at 576, affirmed [1949] S.C.R. 678 (S.C.C.) at 691.

services are expensive and call for a high degree of selection and discrimination on the part of the purchaser, minor differences between marks will be sufficient to distinguish them.[463]

e) Nature of the Trade

The fourth circumstance to be considered in determining whether trade marks or trade names are confusing is the nature of the trade.[464] Matters to be considered include: the customs and usage of the trade, the nature of the markets, the channels of distribution, and the way in which the trade marks are used.[465]

An attempt must be made to determine the attitude of the average reasonable person, or person of ordinary intelligence, who is purchasing the wares or services in question.[466] The reaction of an unwary or hurried purchaser or the foolish or unobservant person should not be considered unless there are special circumstances.[467]

The trade marks are to be compared as used in business and as they will be recalled by imperfect recollection.[468] They should not to be viewed as samples presented, side by side, for critical examination.[469]

Potential confusion is lessened where the purchasers are professionals, acting in the course of their business, who are likely to exercise more care

---

[463] *General Motors Corp. v. Bellows*, [1947] Ex. C.R. 568 (Can. Ex. Ct.) at 576, affirmed [1949] S.C.R. 678 (S.C.C.).

[464] Subsection 6(5)(d).

[465] *Pepsi-Cola Co. v. Coca-Cola Co.,* [1938] Ex. C.R. 263 (Can. Ex. Ct.) at 288, reversed on other grounds (1939), [1940] S.C.R. 17 (S.C.C.), affirmed [1942] 2 W.W.R. 257 (Canada P.C.); *Battle Pharmaceuticals v. British Drug Houses Ltd.*, [1944] Ex. C.R. 239 (Can. Ex. Ct.), affirmed (1945), [1946] S.C.R. 50 (S.C.C.); *Dastous v. Matthews-Wells Co.* (1949), [1950] S.C.R. 261 (S.C.C.) at 276; *United Artists Pictures Inc. v. Pink Panther Beauty Corp.* (1998), (sub nom. *United Artists Corp. v. Pink Panther Beauty Corp.*) 80 C.P.R. (3d) 247 (Fed. C.A.).

[466] *Canadian Schenley Distilleries Ltd. v. Canada's Manitoba Distillery Ltd.* (1975), 25 C.P.R. (2d) 1 (Fed. T.D.).

[467] *Michelin & Cie v. Astro Tire & Rubber Co. of Canada* (1982), 69 C.P.R. (2d) 260 (Fed. T.D.).

[468] *Battle Pharmaceuticals v. British Drug Houses Ltd.*, [1944] Ex. C.R. 239 (Can. Ex. Ct.), affirmed (1945), [1946] S.C.R. 50 (S.C.C.).

[469] *Pepsi-Cola Co. v. Coca-Cola Co.,* [1942] 2 W.W.R. 257 (Canada P.C.); *Hughes v. Sherriff*, [1950] O.R. 206 (Can. Ex. Ct.), affirmed (1950), 12 C.P.R. 79 (Ont. C.A.).

in making a purchase.[470] Similar considerations may apply to the wholesale trade as opposed to the retail trade.[471] However, the question is not whether the parties in issue sell their products in the same channels but whether they are entitled to do so.[472]

The fact that the premises of the parties are close together increases the prospect of confusion.[473]

f) Degree of Resemblance

The fifth circumstance to be considered in determining whether trade marks or trade names are confusing is the degree of resemblance between the trade marks or trade names in appearance or sound, or in the ideas suggested by them.[474]

i) Appearance

If the trade marks and the wares are identical, it is not necessary to consider the other factors set out in section 6 in order to conclude the marks in issue are confusing.[475]

While the trade marks must be assessed in their entirety and not dissected or subjected to meticulous examination, it is still possible to focus on particular features of the mark which may have a determinative influence on the perception of purchasers.[476]

---

[470] *Ortho Pharmaceutical Corp. v. Mowatt & Moore Ltd.* (1972), 6 C.P.R. (2d) 161 (Fed. T.D.); *United Artists Pictures Inc. v. Pink Panther Beauty Corp.* (1998), (sub nom. *United Artists Corp. v. Pink Panther Beauty Corp.*) 80 C.P.R. (3d) 247 (Fed. C.A.).

[471] *Dastous v. Matthews-Wells Co.* (1947), 8 C.P.R. 2 (Can. Ex. Ct.) per Cameron J., reversed on other grounds (1949), [1950] S.C.R. 261 (S.C.C.).

[472] *Clorox Co. v. E.I. Du Pont de Nemours & Co.* (1995), 64 C.P.R. (3d) 79 (Fed. T.D.); *United Artists Pictures Inc. v. Pink Panther Beauty Corp.* (1998), (sub nom. *United Artists Corp. v. Pink Panther Beauty Corp.*) 80 C.P.R. (3d) 247 (Fed. C.A.).

[473] *Cartem Inc. v. Souhaits Renaissance Inc.* (1982), 60 C.P.R. (2d) 1 (Fed. T.D.).

[474] Subsection 6(5)(e).

[475] *Pepsi-Cola Co. v. Coca-Cola Co.*, [1938] Ex. C.R. 263 (Can. Ex. Ct.) at 270, reversed (1939), [1940] S.C.R. 17 (S.C.C.), affirmed [1942] 2 W.W.R. 257 (Canada P.C.); *W.J. Hughes & Sons "Corn Flower" Ltd. v. Morawiec* (1970), 62 C.P.R. 21 (Can. Ex. Ct.).

[476] *United Artists Pictures Inc. v. Pink Panther Beauty Corp.* (1998), (sub nom. *United Artists Corp. v. Pink Panther Beauty Corp.*) 80 C.P.R. (3d) 247 (Fed. C.A.) at p. 262.

If a prefix or suffix is added to the aggrieved party's mark, it is important to remember that the words must not be subjected either to a side-by-side comparison or to a meticulous individual analysis.[477]

State of the Registrar evidence may be considered and the presence of a common element may have an important bearing on the issue of confusion. If the marks possess little or no inherent distinctiveness, in that a prefix is common to the trade, small differences are sufficient to distinguish one mark from another.[478]

ii) Sound

The degree of resemblance of the marks as sounded must be considered.[479] The words may be quite different in appearance and yet the sound may be so similar that confusion is unavoidable.[480] This is particularly so when the wares or services are ordered by telephone.[481] Evidence of pronunciation is admissible in French or English.[482]

Allowance should also be made for the difficulty in pronouncing foreign

---

[477] *Sealy Sleep Products Ltd. v. Simpson's-Sears Ltd.* (1960), 33 C.P.R. 129 (Can. Ex. Ct.); *Seven-Up Co. v. Heavey,* [1964] Ex. C.R. 922 (Can. Ex. Ct.), affirmed (1965), 42 C.P.R. 1n (S.C.C.).

[478] *Simmons Ltd. v. A to Z Comfort Beddings Ltd.* (1991), (sub nom. *Park Avenue Furniture Corp. v. Wickes/Simmons Bedding Ltd.*) 37 C.P.R. (3d) 413 (Fed. C.A.); *Maximum Nutrition Ltd. v. Kellogg Salada Canada Inc.* (1992), (sub nom. *Kellogg Salada Canada Inc. v. Maximum Nutrition Ltd.*) 43 C.P.R. (3d) 349 (Fed. C.A.).

[479] Subsection 6(5)(e).

[480] *Battle Pharmaceuticals v. British Drug Houses Ltd.,* [1944] Ex. C.R. 239 (Can. Ex. Ct.), affirmed (1945), [1946] S.C.R. 50 (S.C.C.); *Ultravite Laboratories Ltd. v. Whitehall Laboratories Ltd.,* [1964] Ex. C.R. 913 (Can. Ex. Ct.), reversed [1965] S.C.R. 734 (S.C.C.); *Choice Hotels International Inc. v. Hotels Confortel Inc.* (1996), 67 C.P.R. (3d) 340 (Fed. T.D.), affirmed (2000), (sub nom. *Choice Hotels International Inc. v. Hotels Confortel Inc.*) 12 C.P.R. (4th) 101 (Fed. C.A.).

[481] *Mead Johnson & Co. v. G.D. Searle & Co.* (1967), 65 D.L.R. (2d) 56 (Can. Ex. Ct.).

[482] *Rouet Ltée v. Roi Hosiery Co.,* [1964] Ex. C.R. 285 (Can. Ex. Ct.); *Imperial Oil Ltd. v. Superamerica Stations Inc.* (1965), 47 C.P.R. 57 (Can. Ex. Ct.); *Ethicon Inc. v. Cyanamid of Canada Ltd.* (1977), 35 C.P.R. (2d) 126 (Fed. T.D.); *Ridout Wines Ltd. v. T.G. Bright & Co.* (1982), 67 C.P.R. (2d) 227 (T.M. Opp. Bd.).

words,[483] the habit of emphasizing particular parts of words,[484] for slurring of prefixes, for mispronunciation and careless pronunciation.[485]

When the first or main part of a word mark is the more emphatic or distinctive part it may be relatively unimportant that the two marks in question exhibit different suffixes.[486]

iii) Idea

Similarity of idea is a factor if it is reasonably apparent to the average purchaser.[487]

3. OPPOSITION PROCEEDINGS

a) Instituting an Opposition

A brand owner must vigilantly monitor the marketplace to ensure that the distinctiveness of its brand name is not being diminished by the use of other brand names which are potentially confusing with it. One way this can be done is to monitor the applications which are advertised in the *Trade-marks Journal*,[488] which is available online.[489] Trade mark opposition proceedings can be an effective tool to protect the distinctiveness of a brand against encroachment by third parties. However, if there are concerns with respect to the validity of a registration to be relied upon by an opponent, it may not be wise to institute a trade mark opposition which will expose the

---

[483] *Rubenstein v. Canada (Registrar of Trade Marks)*, [1952] Ex. C.R. 275 (Can. Ex. Ct.).

[484] *Rouet Ltée v. Roi Hosiery Co.*, [1964] Ex. C.R. 285 (Can. Ex. Ct.); *Imperial Oil Ltd. v. Superamerica Stations Inc.* (1965), 47 C.P.R. 57 (Can. Ex. Ct.).

[485] *Rouet Ltée v. Roi Hosiery Co.*, [1964] Ex. C.R. 285 (Can. Ex. Ct.); *Benson & Hedges (Can.) Ltd. v. Rothmans of Pall Mall Canada Ltd.* (1980), 61 C.P.R. (2d) 177 (T.M. Opp. Bd.).

[486] *Sealy Sleep Products Ltd. v. Simpson's-Sears Ltd.* (1960), 33 C.P.R. 129 (Can. Ex. Ct.); *Pepsi-Cola Co. v. Coca-Cola Co.*, [1938] Ex. C.R. 263 (Can. Ex. Ct.) at 271, reversed (1939), [1940] S.C.R. 17 (S.C.C.), affirmed [1942] 2 W.W.R. 257 (Canada P.C.).

[487] *Kimberly-Clark of Canada Ltd. v. Molnlycke AB* (1982), 61 C.P.R. (2d) 42 (Fed. T.D.); *Michelin & Cie v. Astro Tire & Rubber Co. of Canada* (1981), 67 C.P.R. (2d) 254 (T.M. Opp. Bd.), affirmed (1982), 69 C.P.R. (2d) 260 (Fed. T.D.).

[488] With the assistance of an appropriate service provider, trade mark applications may also be monitored as of their filing date.

[489] *http://napoleon.ic.gc.ca/cipo/tradejournal.nsf/$$View-Template+for+TMJournal+English?OpenForm.*

registration to scrutiny. It is also prudent to carry out searches of other marks owned or applied for by the applicant since they may affect the opposition.

Within two months from the advertisement of an application, any person may, upon payment of the prescribed fee, file a statement of opposition in duplicate with the Registrar.[490] A proposed opponent need not show that they would be adversely affected by registration.[491] The effect of commencing an opposition is to bring the prosecution of the opposed application to a halt until the opposition is concluded.

An extension of the time to file the statement of opposition may be requested before or, in some cases, after the expiration of this time limit.[492] An extension applied for after the expiration of the time limit or the time extended by the Registrar will not be granted unless the Registrar is satisfied that the failure to do the act or apply for the extension within that time or the extended time was not reasonably avoidable.[493]

The Registrar may not extend the time for filing a statement of opposition with respect to any application that has been allowed.[494] However, where an application has been allowed without considering a previously filed request for an extension of time to file a statement of opposition, the Registrar may withdraw the application from allowance at any time before issuing a certificate of registration and, in accordance with the Act extend the time for filing a statement of opposition.[495]

An opposition may be based on any of the following grounds:[496]

    (a)   The application does not comply with the requirements of section 30.[497] Typically, this will include grounds such as the applicant did not use the mark from the date alleged[498] or the applicant could

---

[490] Subsection 38(1).

[491] *Parlam Corp. v. Ciba Co.* (1961), 36 C.P.R. 78 (Can. Ex. Ct.); *Centennial Grocery Brokers Ltd. v. Canada (Registrar of Trade Marks),* [1972] F.C. 257 (Fed. T.D.).

[492] Where in opposition proceedings any extension of time is granted to any party, the Registrar may thereafter grant any reasonable extension of time to any other party in which to take any subsequent step. *Trade-marks Regulations* (1996), section 47.

[493] Subsection 47(2) and see *Fjord Pacific Marine Industries Ltd. v. Canada (Registrar of Trade Marks),* [1975] F.C. 536 (Fed. T.D.).

[494] Subsection 39(2).

[495] Subsection 39(3).

[496] Subsection 38(2).

[497] Subsection 38(2)(a). See **part 5 of Chapter 4.**

[498] *Canadian Schenley Distilleries Ltd. v. Canada's Manitoba Distillery Ltd.* (1975), 25 C.P.R. (2d) 1 (Fed. T.D.).

not have been satisfied it was entitled to use the mark.[499] The date for determining compliance with section 30 is the date of filing of the application.

(b) The trade mark is not registrable.[500] The date for determining grounds relating to registrability is the hearing date.[501]

(c) The applicant is not the person entitled to registration.[502] The dates for determining grounds relating to entitlement are set out in section 16; if the application is based on use, the date of first use; if the application is based on registration and use abroad, the filing date; and if the application is based on proposed use, the filing date.

(d) The trade mark is not distinctive.[503] The date for determining this ground is the date of filing the statement of opposition.[504]

It is prudent to consider that a statement of opposition is similar to a statement of claim in proceedings in the courts. In a statement of opposition, the opponent is required to set forth the grounds of opposition in sufficient detail to enable the applicant to reply.[505] In two recent cases, the Federal Court of Appeal has stated that it would be preferable to make a determination of whether there is sufficient detail on an interlocutory basis,[506] but

---

[499] *Sapodilla Co. v. Bristol-Myers Co.* (1974), 15 C.P.R. (2d) 152 (Reg. T.M.); *Jones v. Dragon Tales Production Inc.* (2002), 27 C.P.R. (4th) 369 (T.M. Opp. Bd.).

[500] Subsection 38(2)(b), and see **part 9 of Chapter 2**.

[501] *Canadian Olympic Assn./Assoc. Olympique Canadienne v. Olympus Optical Co.* (1991), (sub nom. *Canadian Olympic Assn. v. Olympus Optical Co.*) 38 C.P.R. (3d) 1 (Fed. C.A.); *Simmons Ltd. v. A to Z Comfort Beddings Ltd.* (1991), (sub nom. *Park Avenue Furniture Corp. v. Wickes/Simmons Bedding Ltd.*) 37 C.P.R. (3d) 413 (Fed. C.A.); *Canadian Council of Professional Engineers v. Lubrication Engineers Inc.*, (sub nom. *Lubrication Engineers Inc. v. Canadian Council of Professional Engineers*) 41 C.P.R. (3d) 243 (Fed. C.A.).

[502] Subsection 38(2)(c) and see **part 4 of Chapter 4**.

[503] Subsection 38(2)(d) and see **part 7(b) of Chapter 2** and see *Muffin Houses Inc. v. Muffin House Bakery Ltd.* (1985), 4 C.P.R. (3d) 272 (T.M. Opp. Bd.); *Big Apple Ltd. v. BAB Holdings Inc.* (2000), 8 C.P.R. (4th) 252 (T.M. Opp. Bd.), affirmed (2002), (sub nom. *BAB Holdings Inc. v. Big Apple Ltd.*) 16 C.P.R. (4th) 427 (Fed. T.D.).

[504] *Andres Wines Ltd. v. E. & J. Gallo Winery* (1975), [1976] 2 F.C. 3 (Fed. C.A.).

[505] Subsection 38(3)(a).

[506] *Novopharm Ltd. v. CIBA-Geigy Canada Ltd.* (2001), (sub nom. *Novopharm Ltd v. Ciba-Geigy Canada Ltd.*) 15 C.P.R. (4th) 327 (Fed. C.A.); *Novopharm Ltd. v. Astra AB* (2002), (sub nom. *Novopharm Ltd. v. AstraZeneca AB*) 21 C.P.R. (4th) 289 (Fed. C.A.).

it remains to be seen whether the Opposition Board will entertain such a motion. In determining whether the statement of opposition sets out sufficient details or material facts to enable the applicant to reply, at the hearing stage regard must be had to the evidence filed as well as the statement of opposition. [507]

The statement of opposition must also set out the address of the opponent in Canada or the address of its principal office or place of business abroad and the name and address in Canada of some person upon whom service may be made. [508]

If the Registrar considers that the opposition does not raise a substantial issue for decision, the statement of opposition will be rejected and notice of decision given to the opponent. [509] The words "substantial issue" are not equivalent to the words "substantial likelihood that the opponent will succeed". [510] This section is directed at frivolous oppositions only. [511] An arguable case is sufficient and no evidence should be considered. [512]

If the Registrar considers that the opposition raises a substantial issue for decision, a copy of the statement of opposition must be forwarded to the applicant. [513] Within one month thereafter the applicant must file a counter statement with the Registrar and serve a copy upon the opponent setting out the grounds on which the applicant relies to support its application. [514] If the

---

[507] See *Novopharm Ltd. v. CIBA-Geigy Canada Ltd.* (2001), (sub nom. *Novopharm Ltd v. Ciba-Geigy Canada Ltd.*) 15 C.P.R. (4th) 327 (Fed. C.A.); *Novopharm Ltd. v. Astra AB* (2002), (sub nom. *Novopharm Ltd. v. AstraZeneca AB*) 21 C.P.R. (4th) 289 (Fed. C.A.).

[508] Subsection 38(3)(b).

[509] Subsection 38(4); and see *Canadian Tampax Corp. v. Canada (Registrar of Trade Marks)* (1975), 24 C.P.R. (2d) 187 (Fed. T.D.); *Pepsico Inc. v. Canada (Registrar of Trade Marks)* (1975), [1976] 1 F.C. 202 (Fed. T.D.); *Koffler Stores Ltd. v. Canada (Registrar of Trade Marks)*, [1976] 2 F.C. 685 (Fed. T.D.); *Société des produits Marnier-Lapostolle v. Robert Macnish & Co.* (1977), [1978] 1 F.C. 504 (Fed. T.D.).

[510] *Pepsico Inc. v. Canada (Registrar of Trade Marks)* (1975), [1976] 1 F.C. 202 (Fed. T.D.).

[511] *Canadian Tampax Corp. v. Canada (Registrar of Trade Marks)* (1975), 24 C.P.R. (2d) 187 (Fed. T.D.).

[512] *Koffler Stores Ltd. v. Canada (Registrar of Trade Marks)*, [1976] 2 F.C. 685 (Fed. T.D.).

[513] Subsection 38(5).

[514] *Trade-marks Regulations* (1996), section 39 and form 9; service may be made either personally or by registered mail: *Trade-marks Regulations* (1996), section 37.

applicant does not file and serve a counter statement in a timely fashion, the applicant is deemed to have abandoned the application.[515]

No amendment to a statement of opposition or counter statement shall be allowed except with leave of the Registrar upon such terms as he or she may think fit.[516] The practice of the Trade-marks Opposition Board is to only grant leave if it is in the interest of justice to do so having regard to all the surrounding circumstances including:

(a)   the stage the proceedings have reached;
(b)   the reasons advanced as to why the ground was not initially raised;
(c)   the importance of the amendment sought; and
(d)   the prejudice to be suffered by the other party.

Such a decision is not appealable other than in the frame work of the final decision relating to the opposition.[517]

The Trade-marks Opposition Board has no jurisdiction to grant a stay of proceedings on the ground of pending litigation,[518] but the Federal Court (Trial Division) may do so.[519]

b) Evidence

Both the opponent and the applicant are given an opportunity, in the manner prescribed, to submit the evidence upon which they rely and to be heard by the Registrar if they so desire.[520] Within one month after the service of the counter statement, the opponent must file with the Registrar such evidence, by way of affidavit or statutory declaration or certified copies of documents or entries relating to the register,[521] the opponent is relying on to support the opposition or a statement that the opponent does not wish to submit evidence and serve the applicant with a copy of such evidence or

---

[515] Subsection 38(6).

[516] *Trade-marks Regulations* (1996), section 40.

[517] *Nabisco Brands Ltd./Nabisco Brands Ltée v. Perfection Foods Ltd.* (1985), 8 C.I.P.R. 133 (T.M. Opp. Bd.), affirmed (1986), (sub nom. *Nabisco Brands Ltd. v. Perfection Foods Ltd.*) 12 C.P.R. (3d) 456 (Fed. T.D.).

[518] *Anheuser-Busch Inc. v. Carling O'Keefe Breweries of Canada Ltd.* (1982), 45 N.R. 126 (Fed. C.A.).

[519] *Figgie International Inc. v. Citywide Machine Wholesale Inc.* (1993), 50 C.P.R. (3d) 89 (Fed. T.D.); *Royal Bank v. Canadian Imperial Bank of Commerce* (1994), 57 C.P.R. (3d) 483 (Fed. T.D.).

[520] Subsection 38(7).

[521] See section 54.

statement.[522] The opposition will be deemed to have been withdrawn if the opponent does not submit either evidence or the statement.[523]

If such evidence or statement is filed and served, the applicant has a similar time within which to file and serve evidence in support of its application or a statement that it desires to adduce no evidence and shall serve upon the opponent a copy of such evidence or statement, as the case may be.[524] The application will be deemed to have been abandoned if the applicant does not submit either evidence or the statement.[525]

Within one month after service upon the opponent of the applicant's evidence, the opponent may file with the Registrar evidence strictly confined to matters in reply and serve the applicant with a copy of such evidence or statement.[526]

No further evidence may be adduced by any party except with leave of the Registrar upon such terms as he or she may think fit.[527]

In opposition proceedings, the onus of proof is on the applicant to satisfy the Registrar that the trade mark ought to be registered.[528] This is a constant onus and includes the onus, where appropriate, of showing that confusion is unlikely. The Registrar must be satisfied that, on the balance of probabilities that the applied for mark is unlikely to create confusion; the Registrar need not be satisfied beyond doubt that confusion is unlikely.[529] The opponent may present evidence in support of the grounds of the opposition

---

[522] *Trade-marks Regulations* (1996), section 41.
[523] Subsection 38(7.1).
[524] *Trade-marks Regulations* (1996), section 42.
[525] Subsection 38(7.2).
[526] *Trade-marks Regulations* (1996), section 43; see *Trade-marks Regulations* (1996), subsections 44 and 45 for further provisions as to evidence, cross-examination on affidavits, filing and service of exhibits.
[527] *Trade-marks Regulations* (1996), subsection 44(2).
[528] *Oshawa Group Ltd. v. Creative Resources Co.* (1982), 61 C.P.R. (2d) 29 (Fed. C.A.), reversing (1979), 47 C.P.R. (2d) 115 (Fed. T.D.), which affirmed 37 C.P.R. (2d) 21 (T.M. Opp. Bd.); *Coronet-Werke Heinrich Schlerf GmbH v. Produits Ménagers Coronet Inc.* (1984), 4 C.P.R. (3d) 108 (T.M. Opp. Bd.), reversed in part (1986), 10 C.P.R. (3d) 482 (Fed. T.D.); *United Artists Pictures Inc. v. Pink Panther Beauty Corp.* (1998), (sub nom. *United Artists Corp. v. Pink Panther Beauty Corp.*) 80 C.P.R. (3d) 247 (Fed. C.A.).
[529] *Christian Dior S.A. v. Dion Neckwear Ltd.* (1996), 71 C.P.R. (3d) 268 (T.M. Opp. Bd.), affirmed (2000), (sub nom. *Dion Neckwear Ltd. v. Christian Dior, S.A.*) 5 C.P.R. (4th) 304 (Fed. T.D.), reversed (2002), (sub nom. *Dion Neckwear Ltd. v. Christian Dior, S.A.*) 20 C.P.R. (4th) 155 (Fed. C.A.).

raised and bears the burden of proof with respect to such grounds.[530] Once an applicant has filed some evidence which may point to the unlikelihood of confusion the opponent should carefully consider filing evidence in reply.[531]

All evidence, with the exception of certified copies, must be presented by affidavit or statutory declaration, which are filed. It is prudent to ensure that such material complies with the Federal Court Rules, 1998.[532]

At any time before notice requiring filing of argument, the Registrar may, on the application of any party and on such terms as may be directed, order the cross examination under oath of any affiant or declarant on their affidavit or declaration.[533] If an affiant or declarant fails to attend for cross examination, the affidavit or declaration shall not be part of the evidence.[534]

c) The Hearing

Not less than 14 days after completion of the evidence, the Registrar shall give the parties written notice that they may within one month after the date of such notice file written argument.[535] No written argument shall be filed after the expiration of the one month period except with leave of the Registrar.[536] A copy of any argument filed is forwarded by the Registrar to every other party.[537]

Any party who desires to present oral argument to the Registrar must give written notice and the Registrar shall send the parties written notice setting out a hearing date.[538]

After considering the evidence and representations of the opponent and the applicant, the Registrar shall refuse the application or reject the oppo-

---

[530] *British American Bank Note Co. v. Bank of America National Trust & Saving Assn.* (1980), 62 C.P.R. (2d) 120 (T.M. Opp. Bd.); *Wool Bureau of Canada Ltd. v. Queenswear (Can.) Ltd.* (1980), 47 C.P.R. (2d) 11 (Fed. T.D.).

[531] *Christian Dior S.A. v. Dion Neckwear Ltd.* (1996), 71 C.P.R. (3d) 268 (T.M. Opp. Bd.), affirmed (2000), (sub nom. *Dion Neckwear Ltd. v. Christian Dior, S.A.*) 5 C.P.R. (4th) 304 (Fed. T.D.), reversed (2002), (sub nom. *Dion Neckwear Ltd. v. Christian Dior, S.A.*) 20 C.P.R. (4th) 155 (Fed. C.A.).

[532] SOR/98-106.

[533] *Trade-marks Regulations* (1996), subsection 44(2).

[534] *Trade-marks Regulations* (1996), subsection 44(5).

[535] *Trade-marks Regulations* (1996), subsection 46(1).

[536] *Trade-marks Regulations* (1996), subsection 46(2).

[537] *Trade-marks Regulations* (1996), subsection 46(3).

[538] *Trade-marks Regulations* (1996), subsection 46(4).

sition and notify the parties of the decision and the reasons for the decision.[539] The Registrar may not take up considerations not raised in a statement of opposition. If matters not raised by the opponent in its statement of opposition are considered, the hearing officer exceeds his or her jurisdiction, since these matters are strictly and technically beyond the powers conferred by the Act.[540]

d) Appeal

An appeal lies from a decision of the Registrar to the Federal Court[541] within two months from the date upon which notice of decision was dispatched by the registrar or such further time as the court may allow, either before or after the expiry of the two months.[542] An appeal is available only with respect to a "final decision", which effectively disposes of the particular proceeding, and not from an "interlocutory" decision.[543]

The appeal is made by way of notice of appeal filed with the Registrar and the Federal Court.[544] The notice of appeal must be filed with the court and the Registrar and sent by registered mail to the registered owner of any trade mark that has been referred to by the Registrar in the decision complained of and to every other person who was entitled to notice of such decision.[545]

The appeal is not restricted to the record before the Registrar and evidence in addition to that adduced before the Registrar may be adduced.[546] The Court may exercise any discretion vested in the Registrar.[547]

---

[539] Subsection 38(8); *Hardee's Food Systems Inc. v. Hardee Farms International Ltd.* (1982), 63 C.P.R. (2d) 86 (Fed. T.D.).

[540] *Imperial Developments Ltd. v. Imperial Oil Ltd.* (1984), 79 C.P.R. (2d) 12 (Fed. T.D.).

[541] As to procedure, see *Federal Court Rules*, 1998, rule 300.

[542] *Trade-marks Act*, subsection 56(1).

[543] *Anheuser-Busch Inc. v. Carling O'Keefe Breweries of Canada Ltd.* (1982), 45 N.R. 126 (Fed. C.A.); *Centennial Packers Ltd. v. Canada Packers Inc.* (1986), 13 C.P.R. (3d) 187 (Fed. T.D.).

[544] Subsection 56(2). Appeals from the Registrar of Trade-marks have been assigned to the Trial Division of the Federal Court and are initiated by notice of application (see *Federal Court Rules*, 1998, rule 300 (d)), with the result that a further appeal lies to the Federal Court of Appeal as of right. *Andres Wines Ltd. v. E. & J. Gallo Winery* (1975), [1976] 2 F.C. 3 (Fed. C.A.).

[545] Subsection 56(3).

[546] Subsection 56(5). Part 5 of the *Federal Court Rules*, 1998, applies. By virtue of section 60 of the Act, when an appeal has been made, the Registrar must, on the request of any of the parties, transmit all documents on file relating to the matters

The Registrar's expertise must be given some deference. In the absence of additional evidence, decisions of the Registrar, whether of fact, law or discretion, within the Registrar's area of expertise, are to be reviewed on the standard of reasonableness. Where additional evidence is adduced that would have materially affected the Registrar's findings of fact or the exercise of discretion, the judge hearing the appeal must come to his or her own conclusion as to the correctness of the Registrar's decision.[548] The appeal is from the Registrar's decision and not from the reasons on which it is based.[549]

A certified copy of every judgment or order of the Federal Court or the Supreme Court of Canada relating to any trade mark on the register must be filed with the Registrar.[550]

The appeal is the only method of seeking judicial intervention available to an applicant who has been denied registration or an opponent who has failed in opposing the registration of the trade mark. Such a person cannot subsequently apply for expungement under section 57, since no person is entitled to institute under that section any proceeding calling into question a decision given by the Registrar of which such person had express notice and from which they had a right to appeal.[551]

4. INFRINGEMENT

a) The Concept

Section 19 provides that the registration of a trade mark in respect of any wares or services, unless shown to be invalid, gives to the owner the

---

in question. See *Austin Nichols & Co. v. Cinnabon Inc.* (1997), 76 C.P.R. (3d) 45 (Fed. T.D.), affirmed (1998), 82 C.P.R. (3d) 513 (Fed. C.A.).

[547] Subsection 56(5); see *John Haig & Co. v. Haig Beverages Ltd.* (1975), 24 C.P.R. (2d) 66 (Fed. T.D.); *Calona Wines Ltd. v. Bay-Charles Restaurant Ltd.* (1980), 51 C.P.R. (2d) 19 (Fed. T.D.); *Ralston Purina Co. v. Chappell* (1980), 50 C.P.R. (2d) 177 (Fed. T.D.); *Beverley Bedding & Upholstery Co. v. Regal Bedding & Upholstering Ltd.* (1982), 133 D.L.R. (3d) 255 (Fed. C.A.), affirming (1980), 110 D.L.R. (3d) 189 (Fed. T.D.).

[548] *Molson Breweries, A Partnership v. John Labatt Ltd.* (2002), 5 C.P.R. (4th) 180 (Fed. C.A.).

[549] See *Sealy Sleep Products Ltd. v. Simpson's-Sears Ltd.* (1960), 33 C.P.R. 129 (Can. Ex. Ct.).

[550] Section 61.

[551] Subsection 57(2).

exclusive right to the use throughout Canada of such trade mark in respect of such wares or services.[552]

Under section 20, a registered trade mark owner's right to the exclusive use of a trade mark is deemed to be infringed by a person not entitled to its use who sells, distributes or advertises wares or services in association with a confusing trade mark or trade name. Section 6 of the Act, which has been previously discussed, sets out the matters to be considered in making a determination as to whether trade marks or trade names are confusing.[553]

Under section 20, the owner of a registered trade mark may bring proceedings for infringement with respect to any confusing trade mark or trade name in relation to any wares or services, unlike section 19 which is limited to use of the registered owner's trade mark only in association with the wares and services set out in the registration.[554]

Under sections 19 or 20, the plaintiff must establish that the defendant has used the mark in issue as a trade mark. This means the defendant's use of the mark must satisfy the requirements of the definition of a trade mark or trade name set out in section 2 for the purpose of distinguishing ... wares or services ... and as required by section 4 in association with wares or services.[555]

The extent of section 20 has been restricted by providing that no registration of a trade mark prevents a person from making:

(a)   any *bona fide* use of his or her personal name as a trade name; or

(b)   any *bona fide* use, other than as a trade mark:

(i)   of the geographical name of their place of business, or

(ii)   of any accurate description of the character or quality of their wares or services,

in such a manner as is not likely to have the effect of depreciating the value of the goodwill attaching to the registered trade mark.[556]

---

[552] Section 19. The section is subject to the statutory limitations concerning the territorial ambit of protection set out in section 21, (concurrent rights), section 32, (limitations to registrations under subsection 12(2) and 13) and section 67 (Newfoundland).

[553] See **part 2 of this chapter**.

[554] Section 6. *Canadian Council of Blue Cross Plans v. Blue Cross Beauty Products Inc.*, [1971] F.C. 543, 3 C.P.R. (2d) 223 (Fed. T.D.).

[555] See **part 3 of Chapter 4**. Also see *Cie générale des établissements Michelin - Michelin & Cie v. CAW-Canada* (1996), (sub nom. *Cie Générale des Établis-sements Michelin-Michelin & Cie v. C.A.W.-Canada*) 71 C.P.R. (3d) 348 (Fed. T.D.); *Pepper King Ltd. v. Sunfresh Ltd* (2000), 8 C.P.R. (4th) 485 (Fed. T.D.).

[556] *Bonus Foods Ltd. v. Essex Packers Ltd.* (1964), 43 C.P.R. 165 (Can. Ex. Ct.).

In order to take advantage of the restriction, the defendant's use must not likely have the affect of depreciating the value of the goodwill attached to the plaintiff's trade mark. If purchasers are confused by reason of such use this will depreciate the value of the goodwill attaching to the mark.[557] The defendant must also show that it was acting in good faith. It has been held that the restriction applies only to personal names and not corporate names.[558]

Depreciation of the value of the goodwill attached to the trade mark occurs when there is a reduction of the esteem in which the mark itself is held, or through the direct persuasion and enticing of customers who would otherwise be expected to buy or continue to buy goods bearing the trade mark.[559]

The definition of a trade mark includes a distinguishing guise and an action may be brought for the infringement of a distinguishing guise pursuant to sections 19 and 20. In the case of infringement of a trade mark consisting of a distinguishing guise, appeal to the eye will be particularly important in determining whether infringement has occurred.

A registered trade mark is *prima facie* valid and the burden of proving invalidity is on the defendant who raises this issue.[560] If a registration is found to be invalid, there will be no finding of infringement.[561] However, the plaintiff may still succeed with a claim for passing off at common law or under the Act on the same facts if such cause of action was pleaded.[562]

An action for infringement is based on the rights granted by the Act. Such an action differs from the common law or statutory action for passing off in at least two ways:

(a)   infringement is concerned only with one method of passing off, namely by the use of a registered trade mark and a confusing trade mark;

(b)   once a trade mark is shown to be confusing, the defendant cannot

---

[557] *Johnson & Johnson Ltd. v. Philippe-Charles Ltd.* (1974), 18 C.P.R. (2d) 40 (Fed. T.D.); *Pepper King Ltd. v. Sunfresh Ltd.* (2000), 8 C.P.R. (4th) 485 (Fed. T.D.).

[558] *Kayser-Roth Canada (1969) Ltd. v. Fascination Lingerie Inc.*, [1971] F.C. 84 (Fed. T.D.); *Visa International Service Assn. v. Visa Motel Corp.* (1984), 1 C.P.R. (3d) 109 (B.C. C.A.).

[559] *Clairol International Corp. v. Thomas Supply & Equipment Co.*, [1968] 2 Ex. C.R. 552 (Can. Ex. Ct.).

[560] *Parke, Davis & Co. v. Empire Laboratories Ltd.* (1963), 41 C.P.R. 121 (Can. Ex. Ct.), affirmed [1964] S.C.R. 351 (S.C.C.).

[561] *Parke, Davis & Co. v. Empire Laboratories Ltd.* (1963), [1964] Ex. C.R. 399 (Can. Ex. Ct.), affirmed [1964] S.C.R. 351 (S.C.C.).

[562] *Parke, Davis & Co. v. Empire Laboratories Ltd., ante.*

avoid infringement by showing added matter distinguishes its wares or services from those of the trade mark owner.

In addition, the plaintiff in an action for passing off must establish goodwill in the trading indicia it seeks to protect.[563] In an action for the infringement, the plaintiff is entitled to rely on the registration as evidence of ownership. Pursuant to subsection 54(3), a certified copy of a registration is evidence of ownership.[564]

Goods which are introduced into the stream of commerce by the trade mark owner are not infringing because they arrive in a geographical market where the trade mark owner does not wish them to be distributed, whether imported[565] or exported.[566] Frequently, this type of goods are referred to as "grey market" goods.

b) Depreciating the Value of the Goodwill Attached to a Trade Mark

Section 19 provides for an exclusive right which is defined by the mark as registered. Section 20 extends the right to activities which cause confusion. Section 22 extends the rights available under the Act to activities which likely have the effect of depreciating the value of the goodwill attached to the mark.[567]

Section 22 provides that no person shall use a trade mark registered by any person in a manner likely to have the effect of depreciating the value of the goodwill attaching thereto.[568] The rights set out in this section are subject to a discretionary power vested in the court to decline to order the recovery of damages or profits, and permit the defendant to continue to sell wares marked with such trade mark that were in its possession or under its

---

[563] See **part 5 of this chapter**.

[564] See **part 5(c) of this chapter** for a discussion of what must be shown in a passing off context.

[565] *Smith & Nephew Inc. v. Glen Oak Inc.* (1996), 68 C.P.R. (3d) 153 (Fed. C.A.), leave to appeal to S.C.C. refused (1997), [1996] S.C.C.A. No. 433 (S.C.C.).

[566] *Coca-Cola Ltd. v. Pardhan* (1999), 85 C.P.R. (3d) 489 (Fed. C.A.), leave to appeal to S.C.C. refused (2000), 2000 CarswellNat 721 . See *Re Stewart House Publishing Inc.* (2003), 24 C.P.R. (4th) 488 (Ont. S.C.J.), appeal dismissed (2003), 24 C.P.R. (4th) 494 (Ont. C.A.), where a sale by a trustee in bankruptcy was not interfered with.

[567] *Mr. Submarine Ltd. v. Amandista Investments Ltd.* (1986), 9 C.I.P.R. 164 (Fed. T.D.), reversed (1987), 19 C.P.R. (3d) 3 (Fed. C.A.).

[568] *Syntex Inc. v. Apotex Inc.* (1984), 1 C.P.R. (3d) 145 (Fed. C.A.), reversing (1982), 69 C.P.R. (2d) 264 (Fed. T.D.).

control at the time notice was given to it that the owner of the registered trade mark complained of such use.[569]

For the purpose of this section, goodwill is the reputation that has been built up by the owner of the trade mark identified with the wares or services in question.[570] The reduction of the esteem in which the wares or services are held constitutes depreciation of the goodwill. In addition, the direct persuasion and enticing of customers who would otherwise be expected to buy or continue to buy wares bearing the trade mark constitutes depreciation.[571]

It has been held that the verb "use" in section 22 is to be interpreted by reference to the definition of the noun "use" in section 2 and 4. The effect of this is to confine the application and the prohibition of section 22 to a use which any person may make, in association with goods or services within the meaning of section 4 of another's registered trade mark, in such a manner as to depreciate the value of the goodwill attaching thereto. In the leading case considering the section it was found that the presence of the plaintiff's trade marks on the defendant's packages was use within the meaning of section 22, but that their presence on the defendant's brochures was not within it.[572]

Confusion is not the test to be used under section 22. The test is the likelihood of depreciating the value of the goodwill attached to a trade mark. Such a result would not necessarily flow from confusion and might occur without confusion being present.[573]

---

[569] Subsection 22(2) and see *Clairol International Corp. v. Thomas Supply & Equipment Co.* (1968), 55 C.P.R. 176 (Can. Ex. Ct.).

[570] *Clairol International Corp. v. Thomas Supply & Equipment Co.* (1968), 55 C.P.R. 176 (Can. Ex. Ct.); *S.C. Johnson & Son Ltd. v. Marketing International Ltd.* (1977), 32 C.P.R. (2d) 15 (Fed. T.D.); *Cie générale des établissements Michelin - Michelin & Cie v. CAW-Canada* (1996), (sub nom. *Cie Générale des Établissements Michelin-Michelin & Cie v. C.A.W. -Canada*) 71 C.P.R. (3d) 348 (Fed. T.D.).

[571] *Clairol International Corp. v. Thomas Supply & Equipment Co.* (1968), 55 C.P.R. 176 (Can. Ex. Ct.).

[572] *Clairol International Corp. v. Thomas Supply & Equipment Co.* (1968), 55 C.P.R. 176 (Can. Ex. Ct.) and see *Cie générale des établissements Michelin - Michelin & Cie v. CAW-Canada* (1996), (sub nom. *Cie Générale des Établissements Michelin-Michelin & Cie v. C.A.W. -Canada*) 71 C.P.R. (3d) 348 (Fed. T.D.) and see **Chapter 8, part 6(b)** for additional discussion of "use".

[573] *Source Perrier S.A. v. Fira-Less Marketing Co.* (1983), 70 C.P.R. (2d) 61 (Fed. T.D.).

Evidence of confusion or depreciation of the value of goodwill in a foreign jurisdiction is not evidence of confusion or depreciation of the value of goodwill in Canada.[574]

5. COMMON LAW RIGHTS — PASSING OFF

a) Basis of the Action

The essence of a passing off action is a misrepresentation and resultant confusion in the minds of the public which causes or is likely to cause damage to the plaintiff. The foundation of such an action is the existence of a property right in the goodwill and reputation associated with a trade name or business.[575]

The law of passing off can be summarized simply as no one may pass off their goods as those of another. Three elements must be proven in order to succeed. First, the plaintiff must establish the existence of goodwill in a particular trading *indicia*, whether a trade mark, trade name or other distinguishing feature, which indicates to the relevant public that the wares or services offered for sale in association with that indicia originate from, or are associated with, the plaintiff. In this manner the plaintiff's indicia is recognized by the public as distinctive specifically of the plaintiff's goods and services. The *indicia* or "get-up" may include a brand name (in this context referred to as a common law trade mark) or a trade description or individual features of labeling or packaging in which the goods are offered to the public. It is the external appearance of the goods in the form in which they are likely to be seen prior to purchase.[576]

Second, the plaintiff must demonstrate a misrepresentation by the defendant to the public (whether or not intentional) leading or likely to lead the public to believe that the goods or services offered by the defendant are the goods and services of the plaintiff.

Third, the plaintiff must demonstrate that it has suffered or that it will likely suffer damage by reason of the erroneous belief engendered by the

---

[574] *Coca-Cola Ltd. v. Pardhan* (1999), 85 C.P.R. (3d) 489 (Fed. C.A.).

[575] *Walt Disney Productions v. Triple Five Corp.* (1994), 53 C.P.R. (3d) 129 (Alta. C.A.).

[576] *Ciba-Geigy Canada Ltd. v. Apotex Inc.* (1992), 44 C.P.R. (3d) 289 (S.C.C.) at 301; *Toys "R" Us (Canada) Ltd. v. Manjel Inc.* (2003), (sub nom. *Toys "R" Us (Canada) Ltd. v. Manjel Inc.*) 24 C.P.R. (4th) 449 (Fed. T.D.) and see *Sydneywide Distributors Pty. Ltd. v. Red Bull Australia Pty. Ltd.*, [2002] FCAFC 157 (F.C.A.), where the court considered the gestalt related to the plaintiff's energy drink.

defendant's misrepresentation that the source of the defendant's goods or services is the same as the source as those offered by the plaintiff.[577]

Originally, passing off was similar to the tort of deceit and required a misrepresentation concerning the origin of the goods, which was calculated to deceive purchasers and divert business from the plaintiff to the defendant.[578]

The role played by the tort of passing off in the common law has expanded to take into account the changing commercial realities in the present day community. The simple wrong of selling one's goods deceitfully as those of another is not now the core of the action. It is the protection of the community from the consequential damage of unfair competition or unfair trading.[579] In a recent United Kingdom case, the tort was applied to a false endorsement. [580]

The original formulation of the tort included, as a constitutive element, the requirement that the misrepresentation be likely to cause confusion in the minds of consumers between the defendant's goods and those of the plaintiff. Under the present formulation the tort is based on misappropriation of goodwill and confusion is not necessarily required.[581] The original formulation of the tort also required some correspondence between the categories of wares and services dealt with by the respective parties, or some reasonable similarity between the classes of business conducted by the parties.[582] This is no longer the case as a misrepresentation is the operative ingredient and a common field of activity is not strictly necessary.[583]

---

[577] *Reckitt & Colman Products Ltd. v. Borden Inc.,* [1990] 1 All E.R. 873 (U.K. H.L.); *Ciba-Geigy Canada Ltd. v. Apotex Inc.* (1992), 44 C.P.R. (3d) 289 (S.C.C.).

[578] *Oxford Pendaflex Canada Ltd. v. Korr Marketing Ltd.* (1982), 64 C.P.R. (2d) 1, 134 D.L.R. (3d) 271 (S.C.C.).

[579] *Consumers Distributing Co. v. Seiko Time Canada Ltd.* (1984), [1984] 1 S.C.R. 583 (S.C.C.).

[580] *Irvine v. Talksport Ltd.,* [2002] All E.R. 414 (Eng. Ch. Div.), affirmed [2003] All E.R. 881 (U.K. C.A.).

[581] *Consumers Distributing Co. v. Seiko Time Canada Ltd.* (1984), (sub nom. *Seiko Time Canada Ltd. v. Consumers Distributing Co.*) 10 D.L.R. (4th) 161 (S.C.C.); *J. Bollinger v. Costa Brava Wine Co.,* [1959] 3 All E.R. 800 (Eng. Ch. Div.).

[582] *Manchester Brewery Co. v. North Cheshire & Manchester Brewery Co.,* [1898] 1 Ch. 539 (Eng. C.A.), affirmed (1898), (sub. nom *North Cheshire & Manchester Brewery v. Manchester Brewery Co.*) [1899] A.C. 83 (U.K. H.L.); *Eno v. Dunn* (1890), 15 App. Cas. 252 (U.K. H.L.); *Noshery Ltd. v. Penthouse Motor Inn Ltd.* (1969), 61 C.P.R. 207 (Ont. H.C.).

[583] *E.W.B. Vennootschap v. J. Townend & Sons (Hull) Ltd.,* [1979] A.C. 731 (U.K. H.L.).

An action for passing off is different than an action for infringement of a registered trade mark. In an action for infringement, if the trade mark is used, added matter intended to show the true origin of the goods will not affect the issue before the court.[584] In an action for passing off, the defendant may avoid liability if it can be shown that the added matter is sufficient to distinguish the defendant's goods from those of the plaintiff.[585]

A plaintiff may be unsuccessful in bringing an action for infringement on the basis that the registration is invalid, but might still succeed with an action for passing off on the same evidence if pleaded. [586]

b) Subsection 7(b) and (c) of the *Trade-marks Act*

These sections contain a statutory codification of the tort of passing off. They provide that no person shall:

(a)   direct public attention to his wares, services or business in such a way as to cause or be likely to cause confusion in Canada, at the time he commenced so to direct attention to them, between his wares, services or business, and the wares, services or business of another;[587]

(b)   pass off other wares or services as and for those ordered or requested.[588]

The concept of precluding the directing of public attention to wares, services or a business in such a way as to cause or be likely to cause confusion appears to equate, in general terms, to the deception of the public due to a

---

[584] *Saville Perfumery Co. v. June Perfect Ltd.* (1941), 58 R.P.C. 147 (U.K. H.L.) at 162.

[585] *Reckitt & Colman Products Ltd. v. Borden Inc.*, [1990] 1 All E.R. 873 (U.K. H.L.); *Carling O'Keefe Breweries of Canada Ltd. v. Anheuser-Busch Inc.* (1982), (sub nom. *Carling O'Keefe Breweries of Can. Ltd. v. Anheuser-Busch Inc. (No. 1)*) 68 C.P.R. (2d) 1 (Fed. T.D.), reversed in part on other grounds (1986), 10 C.P.R. (3d) 433 (Fed. C.A.).

[586] *Tommy Hilfiger Licensing Inc. v. International Clothiers Inc.* (2003), 29 C.P.R. (4th) 39 (F.C.).

[587] See *Top Notch Construction Ltd. v. Top-Notch Oilfield Services Ltd.* (2001), 13 C.P.R. (4th) 515 (Fed. T.D.).

[588] The common law prohibition against passing off also applies to cases involving services: see *Office Cleaning Services Ltd. v. Westminster Office Cleaning Assn.* (1944), 61 R.P.C. 133 (Eng. C.A.), affirmed *Office Cleaning Services Ltd. v. Westminster Window & General Cleaners Ltd.* (1945), 63 R.P.C. 39 (U.K. H.L.); *Francis, Day & Hunter Ltd. v. Twentieth Century Fox Corp.* (1939), [1939] 4 All E.R. 192 (Ontario P.C.) at 199.

misrepresentation.[589] The reference to the time at which public attention is directed does not have a direct equivalent in common law test.[590]

Under section 7(b) of the Act, there is no requirement that the plaintiff and defendant be competitors.[591]

While the provisions of section 6 of the Act specifying when trade marks or trade names are confusing are not strictly applicable, it is useful to consider the matters set out in that section in applying section 7(b).[592]

Subsection 7(b) has been found to be constitutionally valid federal legislation by the Federal Court of Appeal, in that it is said to round out the regulatory scheme prescribed by parliament in the exercise of its legislative power in relation to patents, copyrights, trade marks and trade names.[593] Subsection 7(c) should be treated in the same fashion as subsection 7(b).

c) Reputation or Goodwill

It is essential for a plaintiff in any action for passing off to satisfy the court of the existence of goodwill in a particular trading indicia, whether a brand name, trade name or other distinguishing feature, which indicates to the relevant public that the wares or services offered for sale in association with that indicia originate from, or are associated with the plaintiff. In this manner the plaintiff's *indicia* is recognized by the public as distinctive of the plaintiff's goods and services.[594] Goodwill in this context has been

---

[589] *Kirkbi AG v. Ritvik Holdings Inc. / Gestions Ritvik Inc.* (2002), (sub nom. *Kirkbi AG v. Ritvik Holdings Inc.*) 20 C.P.R. (4th) 224 (Fed. T.D.), affirmed 2003 FCA 297 (F.C.A.), leave to appeal allowed (2004), 2004 CarswellNat 1211 (S.C.C.).

[590] *Kirkbi AG v. Ritvik Holdings Inc. / Gestions Ritvik Inc.* (2002), (sub nom. *Kirkbi AG v. Ritvik Holdings Inc.*) 20 C.P.R. (4th) 224 (Fed. T.D.), affirmed 2003 FCA 297 (F.C.A.), leave to appeal allowed (2004), 2004 CarswellNat 1211 (S.C.C.).

[591] *Building Products Ltd. v. B.P. Canada Ltd.* (1961), 36 C.P.R. 121 (Can. Ex. Ct.).

[592] *Aluminum Co. v. Tisco Home Building Products (Ontario) Ltd.* (1977), 33 C.P.R. (2d) 145 (Fed. T.D.); *Asbjorn Horgard A/S v. Gibbs/Nortac Industries Ltd.* (1987), 14 C.P.R. (3d) 314 (Fed. C.A.).

[593] *Aluminum Co. v. Tisco Home Building Products (Ontario) Ltd.* (1977), 33 C.P.R. (2d) 145 (Fed. T.D.); *Asbjorn Horgard A/S v. Gibbs/Nortac Industries Ltd.* (1987), 14 C.P.R. (3d) 314 (Fed. C.A.).

[594] *Oxford Pendaflex Canada Ltd. v. Korr Marketing Ltd.* (1982), 64 C.P.R. (2d) 1, 134 D.L.R. (3d) 271 (S.C.C.); *Reckitt & Colman Products Ltd. v. Borden Inc.,* [1990] 1 All E.R. 873 (U.K. H.L.); *Ciba-Geigy Canada Ltd. v. Apotex Inc.* (1992), 44 C.P.R. (3d) 289 (S.C.C.).

defined as the benefit and advantage of the good name, reputation and connection to a business that brings in business.[595]

It is not necessary that the plaintiff show it is the sole source of the goods in question or even that consumers know the plaintiff's name.[596] For example, purchasers may not know the name of the manufacturer of the wares in question, since the wares need not be manufactured by the plaintiff but may be purchased, imported or otherwise acquired by it.

Further, it is not necessary that a person be carrying on business in Canada in order to have goodwill or a reputation which may be protected by way of an action for passing off.[597]

d) Misrepresentation

As previously set out, the plaintiff must show that the defendant has made a misrepresentation. An action for passing off is not confined to any particular means of misrepresentation. Even though no direct misrepresentation has been made, it will be inferred in appropriate factual situations. The following matters have been held sufficient to constitute passing off:

(a)   direct substitution of wares or services in response to orders;[598]

(b)   imitating trade names, trade marks, or get-up;[599]

(c)   representing wares, services or a business as being those of a rival trader;

(d)   the doing of anything which would lead customers to think that there is a connection between the plaintiff's wares, services, or business and the wares, services or business of the defendant, where such a connection does not exist.[600]

Proof of the use of a word or device or one of the essential particulars by which the plaintiff's products or business is characterized does not suffice to establish the cause of action. The plaintiff must demonstrate a misrepresentation by the defendant to the public (whether or not intentional)

---

[595] *Asbjorn Horgard A/S v. Gibbs/Nortac Industries Ltd.* (1987), 14 C.P.R. (3d) 314 (Fed. C.A.).

[596] *Oxford Pendalex Canada Ltd. v. Korr Marketing Ltd., ante.*

[597] *Orkin Exterminating Co. v. Pestco Co. of Canada* (1984), 47 O.R. (2d) 265 (Ont. H.C.), affirmed (1985), 50 O.R. (2d) 726 (Ont. C.A.); *Walt Disney Productions v. Triple Five Corp.* (1994), 53 C.P.R. (3d) 129 (Alta. C.A.).

[598] Subsection 7(c).

[599] Subsection 7(b) and see *A.G. Spalding & Brothers v. A.W. Gamage Ltd.* (1915), 32 R.P.C. 273 (U.K. H.L.).

[600] *Borthwick v. Evening Post* (1888), 37 Ch. D. 449 (Eng. Ch. Div.).

leading or likely to lead the public to believe that the goods or services offered by the defendant are the goods and services of the plaintiff. The burden of satisfying the Court rests on the plaintiff.

Proof of intention to deceive is not necessary,[601] but it will be considered by the Court as strong evidence that the defendant's acts affect the plaintiff's trade.[602] If the Court is convinced that the defendant intended to deceive, it will be more likely to find that it succeeded in its object.[603]

It is important to note whether a defendant has copied additional matter or accompanying *indicia* in which the plaintiff has no goodwill. The courts have referred to such matters as "badges of fraud".[604]

The facts must be weighed in relation to an ordinary member of the public or an average customer who will take ordinary care in purchasing the goods they require.[605] If persons of average intelligence have actually been confused, this may be of assistance to the court in deciding whether an actionable misrepresentation has been made.

e) Damage

The plaintiff must show that it has suffered or that it will likely suffer damage as a result of the defendant's activities.[606]

---

[601] *Consumers Distributing Co. v. Seiko Time Canada Ltd.* (1984), [1984] 1 S.C.R. 583 (S.C.C.).

[602] *Cadbury Schweppes Property Ltd. v. Pub Squash Co. Property,* [1981] 1 All E.R. 213 (P.C.); see also *Old Dutch Foods Ltd. v. W.H. Malkin Ltd.* (1969), 58 C.P.R. 146 (Can. Ex. Ct.).

[603] *Anheuser-Busch Inc. v. Canada Bud Breweries Ltd.,* [1933] O.R. 75 (Ont. S.C.); *Caron Ltée v. United States Dungaree Seafarers Ltd.,* [1978] 4 W.W.R. 681 (B.C. S.C.).

[604] *British Telecom plc. v. One in a Million Ltd.,* [1998] 4 All E.R. 476 (Eng. C.A.); *Hughes v. Sherriff,* [1950] O.R. 206 (Can. Ex. Ct.), affirmed [1950] O.W.N. 483 (Ont. C.A.).

[605] *Ciba-Geigy Canada Ltd. v. Apotex Inc.* (1992), 44 C.P.R. (3d) 289 (S.C.C.) at 301.

[606] *Reckitt & Colman Products Ltd. v. Borden Inc.,* [1990] 1 All E.R. 873 (U.K. H.L.); *Ciba-Geigy Canada Ltd. v. Apotex Inc.* (1992), 44 C.P.R. (3d) 289 (S.C.C.).

f) Defences

i) Plaintiff's Own Wares

It is not actionable to use the plaintiff's name or mark in connection with wares which are in fact the plaintiff's.[607] However, actionable passing off may occur if a product of inferior or deteriorated quality is sold as and for the plaintiff's better class product[608] or the plaintiff's wares are sold in an altered form as and for the original product.[609]

ii) Descriptive Trade Marks

A descriptive word or mark is not usually capable of being protected by an action for passing off unless it can be shown that the descriptive word or mark has acquired a secondary meaning.[610] If a word that is *prima facie* descriptive acquires by use and reputation a secondary and distinctive meaning, its use by one trader may be protected.[611] The onus of proving the acquisition of a secondary meaning is a heavy one[612] and is on the plaintiff.[613] If, in addition to being descriptive, the word is also the name of the goods

---

[607] *Consumers Distributing Co. v. Seiko Time Canada Ltd.* (1984), [1984] 1 S.C.R. 583 (S.C.C.); *A.G. Spalding & Brothers v. A.W. Gamage Ltd.* (1915), 32 R.P.C. 273 (U.K. H.L.).

[608] *A.G. Spalding & Brothers v. A.W. Gamage Ltd.* (1915), 32 R.P.C. 273 (U.K. H.L.) at 284; *Gillette Safety Razor Co. v. Franks* (1924), 41 R.P.C. 499; *Gillette Safety Razor Co. v. Diamond Edge Ltd.* (1926), 43 R.P.C. 310; *A.C. Spark Plug Co. v. Canadian Spark Plug Service* (1934), [1935] Ex. C.R. 57 (Can. Ex. Ct.) at 64; *Hoover Ltd. v. Air-Way Ltd.* (1936), 53 R.P.C. 399; *Du Pont of Canada Ltd. v. Nomad Trading Co.* (1968), 55 C.P.R. 97 (Que. S.C.).

[609] *Westinghouse Brake & Saxby Signal Co. v. Varsity Eliminator Co.* (1935), 52 R.P.C. 295.

[610] *Standard Industries Ltd. v. Rosen* (1954), 24 C.P.R. 41 (Ont. S.C.); *Silhouette Products Ltd. v. Prodon Industries Ltd.* (1965), 47 C.P.R. 183 (Can. Ex. Ct.), affirmed (1967), 51 C.P.R. 304n (S.C.C.).

[611] *Frank Reddaway & Co. v. George Banham & Co.* (1895), [1896] A.C. 199 (U.K. H.L.) at 210 which considered the term "camel hair belting".

[612] *Canadian Shredded Wheat Co. v. Kellogg Co.* (1938), 55 R.P.C. 125 (Ontario P.C.) at 142.

[613] *Canadian Shredded Wheat Co. v. Kellogg Co.*, [1936] O.R. 613 (Ont. C.A.), affirmed [1938] 1 All E.R. 618 (Ontario P.C.); *Parke, Davis & Co. v. Empire Laboratories Ltd.* (1963), 41 C.P.R. 121 (Can. Ex. Ct.), affirmed (1964), 43 C.P.R. 1 (S.C.C.).

themselves, it will be extremely difficult for the word to acquire a secondary and distinctive meaning.[614]

In an action involving a descriptive word, small differences should be sufficient to avoid a misrepresentation. [615] While the use by a defendant of a descriptive word may not be actionable in itself, the cumulative effect of the use of that word with other features of get-up may be sufficient to make out a case.

It is a question of fact whether a descriptive word is used as a trade mark or is merely the name of the type of article.[616] If the word is the name of the type of goods in issue it will be generic and extremely difficult to protect.[617] The conduct of the owner is a relevant consideration in this determination.[618]

iii) Geographical Words

In the absence of evidence that a word has acquired a secondary meaning, every person is at liberty to use the name of the locality where their wares are produced or business is carried on.[619] Confusion by itself is not enough in such a case to establish a cause of action for passing off.[620] However, if the word has acquired a secondary meaning, the fact that the word is the name of the locality where the wares were produced or the business is carried on, is not a defence.[621]

iv) Loss of Distinctiveness

Just as non-distinctive words or marks may acquire distinctiveness, distinctive words or marks, or marks that have become distinctive, may lose

---

[614] *Canadian Shredded Wheat Co. v. Kellogg Co., ante.*

[615] *Office Cleaning Services Ltd. v. Westminster Office Cleaning Assn.* (1944), 61 R.P.C. 133 (Eng. C.A.), affirmed *Office Cleaning Services Ltd. v. Westminster Window & General Cleaners Ltd.* (1945), 63 R.P.C. 39 (U.K. H.L.); *Westfair Foods Ltd. v. Jim Pattison Industries Ltd.* (1989), 26 C.P.R. (3d) 28 (B.C. S.C.), affirmed (1990), 30 C.P.R. (3d) 174 (B.C. C.A.).

[616] *Burberrys v. J.C. Cording & Co.* (1909), 26 R.P.C. 639 (Eng. Ch. Div.).

[617] *Linoleum Manufacturing Co. v. Nairn* (1878), 7 Ch. D. 834 (Eng. Ch. Div.).

[618] *Cheerio Toys & Games Ltd. v. Dubiner* (1964), 44 C.P.R. 134 (Can. Ex. Ct.), affirmed (1965), [1966] S.C.R. 206, 48 C.P.R. 226 (S.C.C.).

[619] *Grand Hotel Co. of Caledonia Springs v. Wilson,* [1904] A.C. 103 (Ontario P.C.); *Hopton Wood Stone Firms Ltd. v. Gething* (1910), 27 R.P.C. 605.

[620] *Steinberg v. Belgium Glove & Hosiery Co.* (1953), 19 C.P.R. 56 (Can. Ex. Ct.).

[621] *Montgomery v. Thompson,* [1891] A.C. 217 (U.K. H.L.). In the case of infringement of a registered trade mark, see subsection 20(b)(i) of the *Trade-marks Act.*

that distinctiveness and become part of the public domain.[622] If it is shown that a word or mark, which at one time was distinctive, has become common to the trade, this will be a defence.

v) Use of a Registered Trade Mark

If the activities complained of by the plaintiff relate to the defendant's use of a registered trade mark, the existence of the registration will be a defence to a claim for passing off.[623]

6. SUMMARY AND CHECKLIST

A brand name may be protected by taking action to enforce the rights associated with it against a competitor or other third party. The following matters should be considered.

1. A brand owner may assert its rights directly when a competitor or potential competitor uses a confusing brand name or makes a misrepresentation leading or likely to lead the public to believe that the goods or services offered by it are the goods and services of the brand owner. The owner of a registered trade mark can bring an action in the courts for trade mark infringement or if a registration has not been obtained an action for passing off may be brought.
2. Rights may be asserted indirectly when a third party's attempt to obtain a trade registration is scrutinized in the context of a trade mark opposition.
3. If a brand owner does not take appropriate steps to ensure that competitors do not use trade marks or trade names which are confusingly similar to its brand name the distinctiveness of the brand name may be put at risk. A brand owner must vigilantly monitor the marketplace to ensure that the distinctiveness of its brand name is not being diminished by the use of other brand names which are potentially confusing with

---

[622] *Cheerio Toys & Games Ltd. v. Dubiner* (1964), 44 C.P.R. 134 (Can. Ex. Ct.), affirmed (1965), [1966] S.C.R. 206, 48 C.P.R. 226 (S.C.C.).

[623] *Molson Canada v. Oland Breweries Ltd./Brasseries Oland Ltée* (2002), (sub nom. *Molson Canada v. Oland Breweries Ltd.*) 19 C.P.R. (4th) 201 (Ont. C.A.); *Jonathan, Boutique Pour Hommes Inc. v. Jay-Gur International Inc.* (2003), 23 C.P.R. (4th) 492 (Fed. T.D.); *Cheerio Toys & Games Ltd. v. Dubiner* (1964), 44 C.P.R. 134 (Can. Ex. Ct.), affirmed (1965), [1966] S.C.R. 206, 48 C.P.R. 226 (S.C.C.).

it. One way this can be done is to monitor the applications which are advertised in the *Trade-marks Journal*.

4. The registration of a trade mark in respect of any wares or services, unless shown to be invalid, gives to the owner the exclusive right to the use throughout Canada of such trade mark in respect of such wares or services.

5. The owner of a registered trade mark may bring proceedings for infringement with respect to a confusing trade mark or trade name in relation to any wares or services. However, no registration prevents a person from making:

   (a)   any *bona fide* use of his personal name as a trade name; or

   (b)   any *bona fide* use, other than as a trade mark:

      (i)   of the geographical name of his place of business, or

      (ii) of any accurate description of the character or quality of his wares or services

   in such a manner as is not likely to have the effect of depreciating the value of the goodwill attaching to the registered trade mark.

6. No person shall use a trade mark registered by any person in a manner likely to have the effect of depreciating the value of the goodwill attaching thereto.

7. Under the *Trade-marks Act*, the use of a trade mark causes confusion with another trade mark if the use of both marks in the same area would be likely to lead to the inference that the wares or services associated with such trade marks are manufactured, sold, leased, hired or performed by the same person, whether or not such wares or services are of the same general class.

8. In determining whether trade marks or trade names are confusing, the Court or the Registrar, as the case may be, must have regard to all of the surrounding circumstances, including:

   (a)   the inherent distinctiveness of the trade marks or trade names and the extent to which they have become known;

   (b)   the length of time the trade marks or trade names have been in use;

   (c)   the nature of the wares, services or business;

   (d)   the nature of the trade; and

   (e)   the degree of resemblance between the trade marks or trade names in appearance or sound or in the ideas suggested by them.

9. Within two months from the advertisement of an application for a trade mark any person may, upon payment of the prescribed fee, file a statement of opposition with the Registrar. A proposed opponent need not show that they would be adversely affected by registration. The effect of commencing an opposition is to bring the prosecution of the opposed application to a halt until the opposition is concluded.

10. The essence of a passing off action is a misrepresentation and resultant confusion in the minds of the public which causes or is likely to cause damage to the plaintiff. The foundation of such an action is the existence of a property right in the goodwill and reputation associated with a trade name or business.

11. The Act contains a statutory codification of the tort of passing off. It provides that no person shall:

   (a)   direct public attention to his wares, services or business in such a way as to cause or be likely to cause confusion in Canada, at the time he commenced so to direct attention to them, between his wares, services or business, and the wares, services or business of another;

   (b)   pass off other wares or services as and for those ordered or requested.

Chapter 6: Protecting Product Shape and Appearance

1. INTRODUCTION

Product shape and appearance are tangible elements of a brand. Both elements can affect the image and values associated with the brand, as well as serving to differentiate the brand from other brands.

A familiar example of a brand being expressed through product shape is the COCA-COLA® bottle, which is one of the world's most widely recognized product shapes. The effectiveness of the bottle is evident in its use as a brand identifier on cans and in advertising. In addition, it has been protected in many countries through trade mark registrations.

In a number of markets product shape is a key element of the brand. The sale of spirits and pharmaceuticals are good examples. However, the importance of product shape is not limited to these sectors as is evident from the distinctive shape of PERRIER® and EVIAN® brand water containers or FERRERO® brand chocolates.

Product shape and appearance can be positively coordinated with the brand image in a number of ways. First, product shape and appearance should be consistent with the brand's positioning. For example, if the positioning of a fabric softener emphasizes, softness the container will not project this attribute if it is a cold, hard metal can. To avoid such a problem the container for COLGATE® PALMOLIVE® SOFT AND GENTLE brand fabric treatment was modified in some markets through the use of textured inks, varnishing and the tooling to give it a finish which was softer to the touch. Second, an innovative product shape may result in a product which is easier to dispense or which delivers improved product freshness. For example, fresh soups and pasta sauces have been successfully delivered in tetrapak containers and bottled water has been delivered in crushable plastic containers. Finally, in markets characterized by container homogeneity, differentiation may provide a competitive advantage.

The primary methods of protecting product shape and appearance are registration under the *Trade-marks Act* as a distinguishing guise, registration under the *Industrial Design Act* and common law actions for passing off. Registration under the *Industrial Design Act* is time sensitive and must occur within one year of publication of the design in Canada or elsewhere.

2. DISTINGUISHING GUISE

The *Trade-marks Act* contains provisions which allow for the registration of product "get-up" as a trade mark. A distinguishing guise is defined to mean a shaping of the wares or their containers or a mode of wrapping or packaging wares, the appearance of which is used by a person for the purpose of distinguishing wares manufactured, sold, leased, or hired by it from those manufactured, sold, leased, hired or performed by others.[624] A distinguishing guise is registrable only if:

(a)   it has been used in Canada by the applicant[625] to such an extent as to have become distinctive at the date of filing of an application for its registration; and

(b)   the exclusive use by the applicant of the distinguishing guise in association with the wares or services with which it has been used is not likely unreasonably to limit the development of an art or an industry.

The registration of a distinguishing guise will not interfere with the use of any utilitarian feature embodied in the distinguishing guise.[626]

The definition of "trade-mark" includes a "distinguishing guise". Presumably, this was done in order to ensure that the owner of a distinguishing guise has the same rights as those available to a trade mark owner.

An applicant seeking to register a distinguishing guise must provide evidence similar to that required to establish acquired distinctiveness or

---

[624] Section 2 of the *Trade-marks Act.*
[625] Use by a predecessor in title accrues to the benefit of the applicant.
[626] Section 13 of the *Trade-marks Act.*

secondary meaning concerning a regular trade mark.[627] The registration of the distinguishing guise may be limited to a defined area of Canada.[628] The standard of proof is similar to that required to show acquired distinctiveness or secondary meaning.[629]

A distinguishing guise incorporating functional features of a product that relate primarily or essentially to the product itself should not be registrable. In a case relating to registered trade marks for two-dimensional representations of a triple-headed rotary shaver assembly and registrations for distinguishing guises of the same assembly, all of the registrations were expunged on appeal to the Federal Court of Appeal.[630] With respect to the trade mark design registrations, the Court considered whether these registrations were invalid on the basis of functionality. After reviewing the case law, the Court concluded that if functionality relates either to the trade mark itself (for example, a transparent moisture proof wrapper for cigarettes[631] or differently coloured bands encircling capsules containing pharmaceuticals[632] or to the wares, such as a design which accentuated the darker colouring of the grain of the wood of tool handles)[633] then it is essentially or primarily inconsistent with registration. However, if the functionality is

---

[627] Subsection 32(1) of the *Trade-marks Act*. The colour, shape and size of a medicinal tablet may not be sufficiently recognized by consumers to allow applicants to obtain distinguishing guise registrations. *Glaxo Wellcome Inc. v. Novopharm Ltd.* (2000), 8 C.P.R. (4th) 448 (Fed. T.D.). See also the practice notice in the *Trade-marks Journal*, Volume 47, No. 2408, December 20, 2000 dealing with Trade Mark Office practice.

[628] Subsection 32(2) of the *Trade-marks Act*.

[629] *Glaxo Wellcome Inc. v. Novopharm Ltd.* (2000), 8 C.P.R. (4th) 448 (Fed. T.D.); *Molson Breweries, A Partnership v. John Labatt Ltd.* (2000), 5 C.P.R. (4th) 180 (Fed. C.A.), leave to appeal refused (2000), 7 C.P.R. (4th) vi (S.C.C.). Third party use of similar designs is relevant *Gillette Canada Inc. v. Mennen Canada Inc.* (1992), 40 C.P.R. (3d) 76 (Fed. T.D.).

[630] *Remington Rand Corp. v. Philips Electronics N.V.* (1995), 64 C.P.R. (3d) 467 (Fed. C.A.), leave to appeal to the S.C.C. refused (1996), 67 C.P.R. (3d) vi (note) (S.C.C.); *Thomas & Betts Ltd. v. Panduit Corp.* (2000), 4 C.P.R. (4th) 498 (Fed. C.A.), leave to appeal refused (2000), 264 N.R. 191 (note) (S.C.C.); and see Donald A. Cameron and Patricia Corneil, *Functional Trade-marks in Canada* 20 C.I.P.R. 167.

[631] *Imperial Tobacco Co. v. Canada (Registrar of Trade Marks)*, [1939] 2 D.L.R. 65 (Can. Ex. Ct.).

[632] *Parke, Davis & Co. v. Empire Laboratories Ltd.* (1964), 43 C.P.R. 1 (S.C.C.).

[633] *Elgin Handles Ltd. v. Welland Vale Manufacturing Co.* (1964), 43 C.P.R. 20 (Can. Ex. Ct.).

merely secondary or peripheral, like a telephone number with no essential connection to the wares,[634] then it does not act as a bar to registration.

With respect to distinguishing guise registrations, the Court observed that every form of trade mark, including a distinguishing guise, is characterized by its distinctiveness. Since a distinguishing guise is not different in essence from a design mark, it must be governed by the same considerations relating to functionality and public policy. It is permissible to allow a trade mark owner to distinguish their wares from their competitors by monopolizing the mark used in relation to them but not by monopolizing the wares. The Court concluded that to the extent that functionality relates primarily or essentially to the wares themselves, it will invalidate a trade mark registration of a distinguishing guise.

In the case of *Kirkbi AG v. Ritvik Holdings Inc. / Gestions Ritvik Inc.*, a similar result was arrived at with respect to an unregistered distinguishing guise, which was found to be primarily functional. The plaintiff had been seeking to protect the distinguishing guise in an action for passing off but failed at trial.[635] On appeal, the Court observed that a trade mark that is purely functional cannot be a valid trade mark. The purpose of the doctrine of functionality is to ensure that no one indirectly achieves the status of a patent holder through the guise of a trade mark. It would be abusive and unfair to the public to allow a person to gain the benefits of a patent by merely holding a trade mark, especially when a person otherwise could not obtain a patent or when the patent in issue has expired. The functionality doctrine applies to both registered and unregistered trade marks.[636]

The fact that a distinguishing guise may be registrable as an industrial design does not prevent its registration as a trade mark.[637]

The registration of a distinguishing guise may be expunged by the Federal Court of Canada on the application of any interested person if the Court decides that the registration is likely to unreasonably limit the development of any art or industry.[638]

---

[634] *Pizza Pizza Ltd. v. Canada (Registrar of Trade Marks)* (1989), 26 C.P.R. (3d) 355 (Fed. C.A.).

[635] (2002), (sub nom. *Kirkbi AG v. Ritvik Holdings Inc.*) 20 C.P.R. (4th) 224 (Fed. T.D.), affirmed (2003), 26 C.P.R. (4th) 1 (Fed. C.A.), leave to appeal allowed (2004), 2004 CarswellNat 1211, 2004 CarswellNat 1212 (S.C.C.).

[636] *Kirkbi AG v. Ritvik Holdings Inc. / Gestions Ritvik Inc.* (2003), 26 C.P.R. (4th) 1 (Fed. C.A.), leave to appeal allowed (2004), 2004 CarswellNat 1211, 2004 CarswellNat 1212 (S.C.C.).

[637] *W.J. Hughes & Sons "Corn Flower" Ltd. v. Morawiec* (1970), 62 C.P.R. 21 (Can. Ex. Ct.).

[638] Subsection 13(3) of the *Trade-marks Act* and see *WCC Containers Sales Ltd. v. Haul-All Equipment Ltd.* (2003), 28 C.P.R. (4th) 175 (F.C.).

Since the definition of a trade mark includes a distinguishing guise, an action may be brought for the infringement of a distinguishing guise pursuant to sections 19 and 20. In the case of infringement of a trade mark consisting of a distinguishing guise, the appeal to the eye will be particularly important in determining whether infringement has occurred.

3. INDUSTRIAL DESIGNS

a) The Basic Elements of a Design

Product shape or appearance may be protected under the *Industrial Design Act*.[639] The Act provides that "design" means features of shape, configuration, pattern or ornament and any combination of those features that, in a finished article, appeal to and are judged solely by the eye.[640] The definition is limited by section 5.1, which provides that no protection afforded by the Act extends to:

(a)   features applied to a useful article that are dictated solely by a utilitarian function of the article; or

(b)   any method or principle of manufacture or construction.

The Act contains two additional definitions relevant to section 5.1. First, "useful article" means an article that has a utilitarian function and includes a model of any such article.[641] Second, "utilitarian function" in respect of an article means a function other than merely serving as a substrate or carrier for artistic or literary matter.[642]

The reference in the definition to "any combination of those features" makes it clear that a design may be made up of one or more of the features of shape, configuration, pattern or ornament.

Shape and configuration are important components of a "design". Each term signifies something in three dimensions. "Shape" relates to the external form of the product, while "configuration" relates to the arrangement or the physical relationship of the components of the design to each other by which

---

[639] R.S.C. 1985, c. I-9 as amended.

[640] *Industrial Design Act* R.S.C. 1985 c. I-9 as amended section 2.

[641] Section 2. See *U & R Tax Services Ltd. v. H & R Block Canada Inc.* (1995), 62 C.P.R. (3d) 257 (Fed. T.D.).

[642] Section 2.

the shape of the composite product is arrived at.[643] For example, in a design for a hot water bottle, a series of diagonal ribs both on the front and on the back of the bottle extending up to a narrow strip at the union of the back and front were found to constitute configuration.[644]

Shape is the dominant feature of registered industrial designs. Even if the feature of the design which is original is one of configuration, pattern, or ornament, it is often the shape of the configured item, the shape of the elements of the pattern and the shape of the ornamental features which is protected.

Pattern and ornament may also be protected. In the majority of cases, they can be treated as practically synonymous.[645] Typically, they consist of something that is placed on a product for its decoration. The term "pattern" denotes a design made up of repetitive elements which are all the same.[646] Ornamentation must only distinguish the appearance of the product; there is no requirement that it beautify it.[647]

Colour is not referred to as a design feature in the Act or the *Industrial Design Rules*[648] and normally does not form an element of a design. In most cases, it is a trade variant which does not alter the identity of a design. In determining whether a design has been infringed, a difference in colour is not relevant.[649]

The *Industrial Design Procedure Manual*[650] makes it clear that photographs and drawings must be black and white. However, it is observed that it is possible to register contrasting tones which create a "pattern".

---

[643] *Gramophone Co. Ltd. v. Magazine Holder Co.* (1910), 27 R.P.C. 152 at 159, (1911), 28 R.P.C. 221 and see Canadian Intellectual Property Office (Industrial Design Office), *Canadian Industrial Design Procedures Manual* (Ottawa: Industry Canada, 1998).

[644] *P.B. Cow & Co. v. Cannon Rubber Manufacturers Ltd.*, [1959] R.P.C. 347 (U.K. C.A.); *N.C. Sommer Allibert (U.K.) Ltd. v. Flair Plastics Ltd.*, [1987] R.P.C. 599 (U.K. C.A.).

[645] *Cimon Ltd. v. Bench Made Furniture Corp.* (1964), [1965] 1 Ex. C.R. 811 (Can. Ex. Ct.) at 833.

[646] Canadian Intellectual Property Office (Industrial Design Office), *Canadian Industrial Design Procedures Manual* (Ottawa: Industry Canada, 1998).

[647] *DRG Inc. v. Datafile Ltd.* (1991), 35 C.P.R. (3d) 243 (Fed. C.A.).

[648] *Industrial Design Regulation*, SOR/99-460.

[649] *Calder Vale Mfg. Co. Ltd.'s Registered Design, Re* (1935), 52 R.P.C. 117; *Associated Colour Printers Ltd.'s Application* (1937), 54 R.P.C. 203.

[650] Canadian Intellectual Property Office (Industrial Design Office), *Canadian Industrial Design Procedures Manual* (Ottawa: Industry Canada, 1998) and see *Industrial Design Rules*, C.R.C. 1978, c. 964, repealed SOR/99-459 and now see section 13 of the *Industrial Design Regulations* SOR/99-460.

The Act provides that "article" means any thing that is made by hand, tool or machine[651] and includes manufactured products. The words "in a finished article" mean in a physical embodiment divorcing the design from a mere scheme or preliminary conception of an idea.[652]

b) Appeal to and be Judged Solely by the Eye

To be protected under the Act, the design must appeal to and be judged solely by the eye. These words limit the generality of the definition of design. The eye which makes the determination is the eye of a customer. A design must appeal to the eye of some customers and the limitation excludes cases where a customer might choose an article of that shape, not because of its appearance, but because they thought the shape made it more useful.[653] Artistic merit or aesthetic value is not required.[654]

A design must be capable of being applied to an article in such a way that the article to which it has been applied shows to the eye of potential customers the particular shape, configuration, pattern or ornament, which constitutes the design. If an article to which a design is applied is so small that the features of the design cannot be appreciated by the naked eye it is doubtful that the design can be protected.[655] Unmagnified vision is the appropriate reference.[656]

c) Features Applied to a Useful Article Dictated Solely by Utilitarian Function

As previously set out, section 5.1 provides that no protection afforded by the Act extends to features applied to a useful article that are dictated solely by a utilitarian function of the article.[657] "Useful article" means an article that has a utilitarian function and includes a model of any such

---

[651] Section 2.

[652] *Milliken & Co. v. Interface Flooring Systems (Canada) Inc.*, [1998] 3 F.C. 103 (Fed. T.D.), additional reasons at (1998), 149 F.T.R. 125 (Fed. T.D.), affirmed (2000), 5 C.P.R. (4th) 209 (Fed. C.A.).

[653] *Amp Inc. v. Utilux Pty. Ltd.*, [1972] R.P.C. 103 (U.K. H.L.).

[654] *Walker, Hunter & Co. v. Falkirk Iron Co.* (1887), 4 R.P.C. 390; *Clarke's Design* (1896), 13 R.P.C. 351.

[655] *Stenor Ltd. v. Whitesides (Clitheroe) Ltd.* (1946), 63 R.P.C. 81 (U.K. H.L.), affirmed (1947), 64 R.P.C. 1 (U.K. H.L.).

[656] *Amp Inc. v. Utilux Pty. Ltd.*, [1970] R.P.C. 397 (Eng. C.A.), reversed [1972] R.P.C. 103 (U.K. H.L.).

[657] A similar exception to protection is contained in subsection 64.1(1) of the *Copyright Act*.

article[658] and "utilitarian function" in respect of an article, means a function other than merely serving as a substrate or carrier for artistic or literary matter.[659]

In substance, protection cannot be obtained for a feature applied to an article that is dictated by a utilitarian function of the article. This restriction does not apply to ornamental non-functional features. In order for the exclusion to apply, every feature must be dictated solely by functional considerations. If there are features of the design which are not dictated solely by function, the design as a whole may still be protectable.[660]

Section 5.1 also provides that no protection afforded by the Act shall extend to any method or principle of manufacture or construction. Presumably this limitation should not apply if the method is incidentally disclosed by an otherwise valid design.

It is unclear whether designs for soft articles, whose shape is not completely definite, are registrable.[661] In the case of a design for an article subject to being manipulated by flexion, the validity of the design and whether it may be infringed should be determined on the basis that the application of the design to the article disclosed in the application is not capable of being modified by flexion. As a result this issue should be considered in relation to the representations set out in the description of the design.[662]

d) Sets and Kits

The Act deals specifically with the rights associated with kits and sets. The following definitions apply:

"Kit" means a complete or substantially complete number of parts that can be assembled to construct a finished article;

"Set" means a number of articles of the same general character ordinarily on sale together or intended to be used together, to each of which the same design or variants thereof are applied;

---

[658] Section 2.
[659] Section 2.
[660] *Amp Inc. v. Utilux Pty. Ltd.*, [1972] R.P.C. 103 (U.K. H.L.); *Interlego A.G. v. Tyco Industries Inc.*, [1988] R.P.C. 343 (Hong Kong P.C.); *Industrial Design Application No. 1998-2446, Re* (2003), (sub nom. *LTI Corp. Industrial Design Application 1998-2446, Re*) 25 C.P.R. (4th) 256 (Can. Pat. App. Bd. & Pat. Commr.).
[661] *Travers Ltd.'s Application* (1951), 68 R.P.C. 255.
[662] *Schmittzehe v. Roberts* (1955), 72 R.P.C. 122.

"Variants" means designs applied to the same article or set and not differing substantially from one another.

A design which is applied to a finished article assembled from a kit may be protected if the following conditions are met:

(a)   all, or substantially all of the parts required to construct the article are sold together as a unit;
(b)   the parts must assemble to create a finished article;
(c)   the description must refer to features in the completely assembled view; and
(d)   the completely assembled view must be illustrated in the drawings or photographs.[663]

Frequently, articles are sold as a set, such as cutlery or glassware. All of the individual pieces of the set can be protected in a single design application, so long as:

(a)   all of the pieces are of the same general character;
(b)   the same design or variant thereof is applied to each piece of the set; and
(c)   all of the articles in the set must normally be on sale together or intended to be used together.[664]

4. INDUSTRIAL DESIGNS AND OTHER INTELLECTUAL PROPERTY RIGHTS

a) Trade Marks

Registration as an industrial design does not preclude the subsequent registration of a distinguishing guise relating to the product to which the design is applied.[665]

---

[663] Canadian Intellectual Property Office (Industrial Design Office), *Canadian Industrial Design Procedures Manual* (Ottawa: Industry Canada, 1998) at p 6-4.

[664] Canadian Intellectual Property Office (Industrial Design Office), *Canadian Industrial Design Procedures Manual* (Ottawa: Industry Canada, 1998) at p 6-1.

[665] *United States Playing Card Company's Application, Re* (1907), [1908] 1 Ch. 197, 77 L.J. Ch. 204 (Eng. Ch. Div.); *Sobrefina S.A.'s Trademark Application, Re*, [1974] R.P.C. 672 (Eng. Ch. Div.).

b) Copyright

Protection under the *Copyright Act* does not affect protection under the *Industrial Design Act*, but sections 64 and 64.1 of the *Copyright Act* limit protection available under that Act for useful article features.

Subsection 64(1) of the *Copyright Act* contains definitions of the terms "article", "design", "useful article" and "utilitarian function" which apply to section 64 and 64.1 and are similar to the definitions contained in the *Industrial Design Act*.

Under section 64, the concept of a "design" is applicable only to finished articles which are useful; the section does not apply to works such as sculptures. The words "in a finished article" in the definition of design contained in section 64 mean in a physical embodiment, as opposed to a mere scheme or preliminary conception of an idea.[666]

Sections 64 and 64.1 only apply to useful articles which are defined to mean articles, including models, which have a utilitarian function, that is a function other than merely serving as a substrate or carrier for artistic or literary matter.

Subsection 64(2) provides that where copyright subsists in a design applied to a useful article, or in an artistic work from which the design is derived and, by or under the authority of the person who owns the copyright in Canada or elsewhere:

(a)   the article is reproduced in a quantity of more than fifty; or

(b)   where the article is a plate,[667] engraving or cast, the article is used for producing more than fifty useful articles,

it is not an infringement of the copyright or the moral rights for anyone

(c)   to reproduce the design of the article or a design not differing substantially from the design of the article by:

(i)   making the article; or

(ii)   making a drawing or other reproduction in any material form of the article; or

---

[666] *Milliken & Co. v. Interface Flooring Systems (Canada) Inc.*, 83 C.P.R. (3d) 470, [1998] 3 F.C. 103 (Fed. T.D.), additional reasons at (1998), 149 F.T.R. 125 (Fed. T.D.), affirmed (2000), 5 C.P.R. (4th) 209 (Fed. C.A.).

[667] The term "plate" is defined in section 2 of the *Copyright Act* and includes any stereotype or other plate, stone, block, mould, matrix, transfer or negative used or intended to be used for printing or reproducing copies of any work.

(d)   to do with an article, drawing or reproduction that is made as described in paragraph (c) anything that the owner of the copyright has the sole right to do with the design or artistic work in which the copyright subsists.[668]

The subsection restricts copyright protection for eye-appealing features of useful articles since it provides the actions which would otherwise constitute infringement are not actionable. The subsection only applies to useful articles which have a utilitarian function, that is a function other than merely serving as a substrate or carrier for artistic or literary matter. The section does not preclude protection under the *Industrial Design Act.*

The subsection also applies to an artistic work from which the design is derived. For example, if a drawing or plan portrays the design, the section will be applicable to a design derived from the artistic work. Similar considerations apply to a model of a useful article which is included in the definition of "useful article".

If the conditions of paragraphs 64(2)(a) and (b) are not satisfied, the copyright in the work is unaffected. The burden of proof in an action involving the applicability of these subsections will be on the party attempting to take advantage of them. The intent of the owner of the copyright is not relevant.

If the conditions of paragraphs 64(2)(a) and (b) are satisfied, paragraphs 64(2)(c) and (d) are applicable. As a result, anyone may reproduce the design of the article or a design not differing substantially from the design of the article by making the article or a drawing, or other reproduction in any material form of the article or otherwise doing anything that the owner of the copyright has the sole right to do without infringing copyright.

The following artistic works are exempted from subsection 64(2) and fully protected by copyright, if it is otherwise available and even if the works have been reproduced in quantities in excess of 50:

(a)   a graphic or photographic representation that is applied to the face of an article;

(b)   a trade mark or a representation thereof, or a label;[669]

(c)   material that has a woven or knitted pattern or that is suitable for piece goods or surface coverings or for making wearing apparel;

---

[668] Subsection 64(2) and see *Milliken & Co. v. Interface Flooring Systems (Canada) Inc.*, 83 C.P.R. (3d) 470, [1998] 3 F.C. 103 (Fed. T.D.), additional reasons at (1998), 149 F.T.R. 125 (Fed. T.D.), affirmed (2000), 5 C.P.R. (4th) 209 (Fed. C.A.).

[669] See *Specialty Sports Ltd. v. Kimpex International Inc.* (1997), 72 C.P.R. (3d) 538 (Fed. T.D.).

   (d)   a representation of a real or fictitious being, event or place that is applied to an article as a feature of shape, configuration, pattern or ornament;

   (e)   articles that are sold as a set, unless more than fifty sets are made; or

   (f)   such other work or article as may be prescribed by regulation.[670]

Subsections 64(2) and (3) apply only in respect of designs created after June 8, 1988. The *Copyright Act*[671] and the *Industrial Design Act*,[672] as they read immediately before June 8, 1988, as well as the rules made under them, continue to apply in respect of designs created before that date.[673]

The *Copyright Act* contains further provisions to clarify the protection available concerning useful article features. Section 64.1 provides that the following acts do not constitute infringement of the copyright or moral rights in a work:

   (a)   applying to a useful article features that are dictated solely by a utilitarian function of the article;

   (b)   by reference solely to a useful article, making a drawing or other reproduction in any material form of any features that are dictated solely by a utilitarian function of the article;

   (c)   doing with a useful article having features described in paragraph (a), or with a drawing or reproduction made as described in paragraph (b), anything that the owner of the copyright has the sole right to do with the work; and

   (d)   using any method or principle of manufacture or construction.[674]

Section 64.1 deals with the application to a useful article of features which are dictated solely by a utilitarian function of the article, unlike subsection 64(2) which deals with the application of designs, which appeal to and are judged solely by the eye, to useful articles.

Under paragraph 64.1(1)(a), the application to a useful article of features which are dictated solely by a utilitarian function of the article does not constitute infringement of the copyright or moral rights in the work from which they are copied. Paragraph 64.1(1)(b) makes it clear that the process

---

[670] Subsection 64(3).

[671] R.S.C. 1985, c. C-42.

[672] R.S.C. 1985, c. I-9.

[673] Subsection 64(4). See John S. McKeown, *Fox on Copyright and Industrial Designs*, 4th ed.

[674] Subsection 64.1(1). See John S. McKeown, *Fox on Copyright and Industrial Designs*, 4th ed., looseleaf, p. 10-10 to 10-20.

of reverse engineering to create a drawing or other reproduction, in any material form, of any features that are dictated solely by a utilitarian function of the article, does not constitute infringement. However, this does not justify the copying of drawings of such features which may still be an infringement.

Subsections 64(2) and (3) apply only in respect of designs created after June 8, 1988.[675]

c) Patents

A patent grants an absolute monopoly during its term and gives to the patentee, for the term of the patent, the exclusive right, privilege and liberty of making, constructing and using the invention and selling it to others to be used.[676] Whether a product or component of the product is protected by a patent and the enforcement of such rights is not directly related to the brand and is not dealt with in this text.

5. ORIGINALITY

To register a design, the applicant (proprietor) must deposit a declaration that the design was not, to the proprietor's knowledge, in use by any person other than the first proprietor at the time the design was adopted by the first proprietor.[677] Originality is not limited to Canada and is universal. An individual cannot copy a design which has been published outside Canada and then attempt to register it on the basis that it is original in Canada. The Act also provides that the Minister shall register the design if the Minister finds that it is not identical with, or does not so closely resemble any other design already registered so as to be confounded therewith.[678]

The use of the word "original" suggests the exercise of intellectual activity to originate, for the first time, something by applying a pattern,

---

[675] Subsection 64(4) and see *Milliken & Co. v. Interface Flooring Systems (Canada) Inc.*, 83 C.P.R. (3d) 470, [1998] 3 F.C. 103 (Fed. T.D.), additional reasons at (1998), 149 F.T.R. 125 (Fed. T.D.), affirmed (2000), 5 C.P.R. (4th) 209 (Fed. C.A.).

[676] *Patent Act*, R.S.C. 1985, c. P-4, s. 42.

[677] Subsection 4(1) (b).

[678] Subsection 6(1). Subsection 7(3) of the Act also contains an implied requirement that a design must be original in order to be registerable. Subsection 6(2) provides for the refusal of a registration of a design which does not comply with the provisions of Part 1 of the *Act* (subsection 3-18). See *Industrial Design Application No. 1998-2666, Re* (2003), 25 C.P.R. (4th) 373 (Can. Pat. App. Bd. & Pat. Commr.).

shape or ornament to subject-matter to which it had not been applied before.[679] The design is the focus of consideration, not the article to which it is applied.

To be original there must be a substantial difference between the design in issue and pre-existing designs. A minor change or other insubstantial variation from pre-existing designs will not be sufficiently original to allow a registration to be obtained.[680] Originality requires at least a spark of inspiration on the part of the designer to create a new design or a new application of an old design.[681]

The primary consideration in determining whether a design is original is appeal to the eye.[682] However, the eye should be that of a knowledgeable individual who is aware of what was common to the trade for the class of articles to which the design is applied.[683] Expert evidence is frequently of assistance.[684] The determination is a question of fact.[685]

The application of an old shape or pattern to a new subject matter may be original. For example, a representation of Westminster Abbey was registered as a design for a handle for a spoon. It was alleged, in defence to an action for infringement, that the picture of Westminster Abbey was not original and registration was invalid. It was held that the originality of the design did not depend upon the originality of the picture.[686]

---

[679] *Clatworthy & Son Ltd. v. Dale Display Fixtures Ltd.*, [1928] Ex. C.R. 159 (S.C.C.); *Cimon Ltd. v. Bench Made Furniture Corp.* (1964), [1965] 1 Ex. C.R. 811 (Can. Ex. Ct.) at 843; *Carr-Harris Products Ltd. v. Reliance Products Ltd.* (1969), 58 C.P.R. 62 (Can. Ex. Ct.), affirmed (1970), 65 C.P.R. 158n.

[680] *Clatworthy & Son Ltd. v. Dale Display Fixtures Ltd.*, [1929] S.C.R. 429 (S.C.C.) at 433; *Industrial Design Application No. 1996-0991, Re* (2000), 5 C.P.R. (4th) 317 (Can. Pat. App. Bd. & Pat. Commr.); *Industrial Design Application No. 1997-2244, Re* (2001), 14 C.P.R. (4th) 59 (Can. Pat. App. Bd. & Pat. Commr.).

[681] *Bata Industries Ltd. v. Warrington Inc.* (1985), 5 C.P.R. (3d) 339 (Fed. T.D.).

[682] Section 2 definition of "design". *Industrial Design Application No. 1998-2446, Re* (2003), (sub nom. *LTI Corp. Industrial Design Application 1998-2446, Re*) 25 C.P.R. (4th) 256 (Can. Pat. App. Bd. & Pat. Commr.); *Industrial Design Application No. 1998-2666, Re* (2003), 25 C.P.R. (4th) 373 (Can. Pat. App. Bd. & Pat. Commr.).

[683] *Phillips v. Harbro Rubber Co.* (1920), 37 R.P.C. 233 at 239.

[684] *Birkin & Co. v. Pratt Hurst & Co. Ltd.* (1895), 12 R.P.C. 371; *Werner Motors Ltd. v. Gamage Ltd.* (1904), 21 R.P.C. 141.

[685] *Clatworthy & Son Ltd. v. Dale Display Fixtures Ltd.*, [1929] S.C.R. 429, [1929] 3 D.L.R. 11 (S.C.C.).

[686] *Saunders v. Wiel* (1892), 9 R.P.C. 459 at 467, (1893), 10 R.P.C. 29.

If the design is old, its application for a purpose analogous to its original application will not likely be original for the purpose of the Act.[687] However, the application of the design to a different material for a different purpose may be sufficiently original.[688]

It is possible to take old designs and combine them to form a new design for which a valid registration may be obtained, so long as the combination results in an original design which is substantially different from any of the old designs or any known combination of them.[689] For example, a design applied to a tent peg which combined a number of old elements or designs resulting in a new combination which was original.[690] If a design comprises old elements, it is the design as a whole that is protected. It is not necessary to distinguish the part of it that is new from the part that is old.[691]

The introduction of ordinary trade variations into a design, or a change in the mode of construction, is not sufficient to make a design original.[692] Potential purchasers are entitled to a choice of ordinary trade variations for their use.[693] Changes to a design which result in differences in size or scale will, in general, not be original.[694]

In order to determine what are ordinary trade variants, evidence specific to the trades or industries involved must be presented to the Court.[695]

---

[687] *Dover Ltd. v. Núrnberger Celluloidwaren Fabrik Gebrader Wolff* (1910), 27 R.P.C. 175 at 498.

[688] *Clatworthy & Son Ltd. v. Dale Display Fixtures Ltd.*, [1929] S.C.R. 429, [1929] 3 D.L.R. 11 (S.C.C.).

[689] *Clatworthy & Son Ltd. v. Dale Display Fixtures Ltd.*, [1928] Ex. C.R. 159 (Can. Ex. Ct.), affirmed [1929] S.C.R. 429, [1929] 3 D.L.R. 11 (S.C.C.) at 162 [Ex. C.R.]; *Bata Industries Ltd. v. Warrington Inc.* (1985), 5 C.P.R. (3d) 339 (Fed. T.D.).

[690] *Carr-Harris Products Ltd. v. Reliance Products Ltd.* (1969), 58 C.P.R. 62 (Can. Ex. Ct.), affirmed (1970), 65 C.P.R. 158n.

[691] *Carr-Harris Products Ltd. v. Reliance Products Ltd.* (1969), 58 C.P.R. 62 (Can. Ex. Ct.), affirmed (1970), 65 C.P.R. 158n.

[692] *Renwal Manufacturing Co. v. Reliable Toy Co.*, [1949] Ex. C.R. 188, 9 C.P.R. 67 (Can. Ex. Ct.); *Angelstone Ltd. v. Artistic Stone Ltd.*, [1960] Ex. C.R. 286, 33 C.P.R. 155 (Can. Ex. Ct.).

[693] *Kaufman Rubber Co. v. Miner Rubber Co.*, [1926] Ex. C.R. 26 (Can. Ex. Ct.) at 30; *Clatworthy & Son Ltd. v. Dale Display Fixtures Ltd.*, [1928] Ex. C.R. 159 (Can. Ex. Ct.), affirmed [1929] S.C.R. 429, [1929] 3 D.L.R. 11 (S.C.C.) at 164 [Ex. C.R.].

[694] *Canadian William A. Rogers Ltd. v. International Silver Co.*, [1932] Ex. C.R. 63 (Can. Ex. Ct.); *Angelstone Ltd. v. Artistic Stone Ltd.*, [1960] Ex. C.R. 286, 33 C.P.R. 155 (Can. Ex. Ct.).

[695] *Phillips v. Harbro Rubber Co.* (1918-20), 35 R.P.C. 276, 36 R.P.C. 79, 37 R.P.C. 233.

Originality is assessed as of the date of the creation of the design, not the date of its registration.[696] Prior publications, including patent specifications, may be referred to. However, such prior documents must contain clear and unmistakable directions to make the article in the shape of the industrial design in order to invalidate it.[697]

6. PUBLICATION

Subsection 6(3) of the Act provides that the Minister shall refuse to register a design if the application for registration is filed in Canada more than one year after the publication of the design in Canada or elsewhere.

In specified circumstances, section 29 extends a six month grace period for an application which has been filed in a specified foreign country.[698] If the proprietor files an application for the same design in Canada within the grace period, the Canadian application will obtain the benefit of the foreign priority filing date. However, for the purposes of subsection 6(3), section 29 does not apply in determining when an application for registration is filed.

Publication, for this purpose, must generally be of a commercial type. The sale[699] or exhibition[700] of the article to which the design is applied will be sufficient. Communicating a design to engravers and other similar individuals in a confidential capacity in order to have them work on the design does not constitute publication.[701]

In one case, prior to committing itself to the production of a breakfast nook product, a manufacturer had shown a plastic prototype to buyers for most of the large retail stores and chains in Canada. In addition, the product was displayed at housewares expositions and shows in Canada and the U.S. It was found that the appellant's registered design was "published" in Can-

---

[696] *Bata Industries Ltd. v. Warrington Inc.* (1985), 5 C.P.R. (3d) 339 (Fed. T.D.).

[697] *Rosedale Associated Manufacturers Ltd. v. Airfix Ltd.*, [1957] R.P.C. 239.

[698] The term foreign country is defined in section 29.

[699] *Durable Electric Appliance Co. v. Renfrew Electric Products Ltd.*, [1926] 4 D.L.R. 1004, 59 O.L.R. 527 (Ont. C.A.), affirmed (1927), [1928] S.C.R. 8 (S.C.C.); *Epstein v. O-Pee-Chee Co.*, [1927] Ex. C.R. 156, [1927] 3 D.L.R. 160 (Can. Ex. Ct.).

[700] *Algonquin Mercantile Corp. v. Dart Industries Canada Ltd.* (1984), 1 C.P.R. (3d) 75 (Fed. C.A.), leave to appeal refused (1984), 5 C.I.P.R. xlviii (S.C.C.).

[701] *Ribbons (Montreal) Ltd. v. Belding Corticelli Ltd.*, [1961] Ex. C.R. 388, 36 C.P.R. 65 (Can. Ex. Ct.).

ada more than one year before its registration and that the registration was invalid.[702]

Prior publication may occur in a printed document if it gives to the public, in substance, the information necessary to make the design.[703] The decisions in patent cases may be of some assistance but must be carefully considered due to differences in statutory language and the underlying concepts.[704]

7. APPLICATION AND REGISTRATION

a) Applications

The proprietor of a design may apply to register it by paying the prescribed fees and filing an application in prescribed form with the industrial design section of the Office of Commissioner of Patents. The application must include:

(a)   a drawing or photograph of the design and a written description of the design;[705]

(b)   a declaration that the design was not, to the proprietor's knowledge, in use by any other person than the first proprietor at the time the design was adopted by the first proprietor; and

(c)   any prescribed information.[706]

The application must include a title identifying the article. The title is intended to identify the specific type of finished article to which the design is applied by its common or generic name.[707]

An application must relate to one design applied to a single article or set, or to variants.[708] Where the Office of Commissioner of Patents ascertains

---

[702] *Algonquin Mercantile Corp. v. Dart Industries Canada Ltd.* (1984), 1 C.P.R. (3d) 75 (Fed. C.A.), leave to appeal refused (1984), 5 C.I.P.R. xlviii (S.C.C.).

[703] *Plimpton v. Malcomson* (1875), 44 L.J. Ch. 257.

[704] *Rosedale Associated Manufacturers Ltd. v. Airfix Products Ltd.*, [1956] R.P.C. 360, [1957] R.P.C. 239.

[705] See *Industrial Design Application No. 1997-1768, Re* (1999), 3 C.P.R. (4th) 254 (Can. Pat. App. Bd. & Pat. Commr.), where a description defining the features of the design in the alternative was in contravention of the Rules.

[706] Subsection 4(1) and see *Industrial Design Regulations*, SOR/99, as amended SOR/2003-210 subsections 9&10.

[707] *Industrial Design Regulations*.

[708] *Industrial Design Regulations*, section 10. See *Industrial Design Application No. 1998-0950, Re* (2001), 14 C.P.R. (4th) 213 (Can. Pat. App. Bd. & Pat.

that the application relates to more than one design, the applicant must, on being so advised, limit the application to one design only. Any other design disclosed may be made the subject of a separate application if it is filed before the registration of a design based on the original application.[709]

On receipt of an application, the application is classified, searched and examined by an examiner. The examination is carried out to ascertain whether the design meets the requirements of the Act for registration. If a design does not meet the requirements a report is sent to the applicant setting out the objections and specifying a period for reply. [710] Included among the requirements of the Act are that:

(a)   the design was not in use by any other person at the time the design was first adopted by the applicant;[711]

(b)   the design is not identical with or does not so closely resemble any other design already registered so as to be confounded therewith;[712] and

(c)   the application was not filed more than one year after the publication of the design in Canada or elsewhere.[713]

The applicable sections of the Act and the *Industrial Design Regulations* must be complied with, otherwise the registration will be invalid.[714]

The procedural steps to be taken with respect to reports are set out in the *Canadian Industrial Design Procedures Manual*.[715]

Although not referred to in the Act, the Patent Appeal Board deals with replies received in response to final reports. The Patent Appeal Board will arrange a hearing, after which recommendations are made to the Commis-

---

Commr.) for a discussion of whether different embodiments of a design shown in the drawings required separate applications or were variants which did not.

[709] *Industrial Design Regulations*, section 10.

[710] Section 5.

[711] Subsection 4(1)(a).

[712] Subsection 6(1).

[713] Subsection 6(3).

[714] *Kaufman Rubber Co. v. Miner Rubber Co.*, [1926] Ex. C.R. 26, [1926] 1 D.L.R. 505 (Can. Ex. Ct.).

[715] See Canadian Intellectual Property Office (Industrial Design Office), *Canadian Industrial Design Procedures Manual* (Ottawa: Industry Canada, 1998) section 2.8. Also see *Industrial Design Practice Notices* dealing with Electronic Icons, Descriptions, Drawings and Photographs at *http:/strategis.ic.gc.ca*.

sioner of Patents as to whether the decision should be allowed to stand or be reversed.[716]

If it is decided that a design is not registrable, the applicant may apply to the Federal Court to review the Commissioner's decision.[717] Presumably, such proceedings will be dealt with by way of application.[718]

b) Protection of Separate Features

The description must indicate whether the design relates to the appearance of the entirety of the article or to the appearance of a portion of the article.[719] Where the design is limited to the appearance of a portion of the article, the description must indicate what the relevant portion is. The description must make clear which of the visual features shown in the drawings comprise the design. It is acceptable to include in a description a statement that a particular feature is considered to be an important feature of the design. However, it must still be clear from the description what constitutes the design.

The description will have a material impact in an action for infringement. In conjunction with the drawing or photograph of the design, the description sets out the scope of the monopoly claimed in the design. In the absence of any limitation, the design will be taken to be the shape or pattern as a whole. This will be the context in which the validity and infringement of the design is considered. It is not appropriate to treat design registrations in the same fashion as the patent claims.[720]

---

[716] Canadian Intellectual Property Office (Industrial Design Office), *Canadian Industrial Design Procedures Manual* (Ottawa: Industry Canada, 1998) at section 2.9.

[717] Section 22(1).

[718] See Rule 300, *Federal Court Rules*, 1998 SOR/98- 106.

[719] Canadian Intellectual Property Office (Industrial Design Office), *Canadian Industrial Design Procedures Manual* (Ottawa: Industry Canada, 1998) at p 9-1. See.*Industrial Design Application No. 1997-1768, Re* (1999), 3 C.P.R. (4th) 254 (Can. Pat. App. Bd. & Pat. Commr.), where a description defining the features of the design in the alternative was in contravention of s. 12(2) of the Rules.

[720] *Alkot Industries Inc. v. Consumers Distributing Co./Cie distribution aux consommateurs* (1986), 11 C.P.R. (3d) 276 (Fed. T.D.).

c) Registration

An exclusive right for an industrial design is acquired by registration of the design under the Act.[721] During the existence of an exclusive right, no person shall, without the licence of the proprietor of the design,

(a)   make, import for the purpose of trade or business, sell, rent, or offer or expose for sale or rent, any article in respect of which the design is registered and to which the design or a design not differing substantially therefrom has been applied; or

(b)   do, in relation to a kit, anything specified in paragraph (a) that would constitute an infringement if done in relation to an article assembled from the kit.[722]

Once an application has been allowed, a certificate is signed by the Minister, the Commissioner of Patents or an officer, clerk or employee of the Commissioner's office stating that the design has been registered in accordance with this Act.[723] The certificate shows the date of registration, the name and address of the proprietor and the registration number.
In the absence of proof to the contrary, the certificate is sufficient evidence of

(a)   the design,
(b)   the originality of the design,
(c)   the name of the proprietor,
(d)   the person named as proprietor being proprietor,
(e)   the commencement and term of registration, and
(f)   compliance with the Act.[724]

Clear and convincing proof is required to displace these presumptions.[725]

A certificate issued under the Act is admissible in evidence in all courts without proof of the signature or official character of the person appearing to have signed it.[726]

---

[721] Section 9.

[722] Subsection 11(1).

[723] Subsection 7(4).

[724] Subsection 7(2).

[725] *Ribbons (Montreal) Ltd. v. Belding Corticelli Ltd.*, [1961] Ex. C.R. 388, 36 C.P.R. 65 (Can. Ex. Ct.); *Alkot Industries Inc. v. Consumers Distributing Ltd.* (1985), 6 C.P.R. (3d) 168 (Fed. T.D.); *Uniformes Town & Country Inc. v. Labrie* (1992), 44 C.P.R. (3d) 514 (Fed. C.A.).

[726] Subsection 7(4).

8. MARKING

The Act does not require that articles be marked with an indication that they are protected by an industrial design registration. However, for designs registered after June 9, 1993, they may be marked with the capital letter "D" in a circle and the name, or the usual abbreviation of the name of the proprietor of the design.

Section 17[727] of the Act provides for a defence relating to the defendant's lack of knowledge that a design was registered. Under the section, the plaintiff's remedies are limited to an injunction, if the defendant establishes that, at the time of the act that is the subject of the proceedings, the defendant was not aware and had no reasonable grounds to suspect that the design was registered. The defence does not apply if the plaintiff establishes that the capital letter "D" in a circle and the name or the usual abbreviation of the name of the proprietor of the design was marked on all, or substantially all, of the articles to which the registration pertains and that were distributed in Canada by or with the consent of the proprietor before the act complained of or the labels or packaging associated with those articles.

For designs registered before June 9, 1993, the Act provided that after registration, the name of the proprietor must appear on the article to which the design applies by being marked, if the manufacture is a woven fabric, on one end thereof, together with the letters "Rd" and, if the manufacture is of any other substance, with the letters "Rd" and the year of registration at the edge or on any convenient part thereof.[728] Under this provision substantial compliance with the marking requirements was sufficient but the effect of non-compliance was uncertain.[729]

9. THE PROPRIETOR

a) The First Proprietor

The Act provides that the author of a design is the first proprietor of the design, unless the author executed the design for another person for consideration, in which case the other person is the first proprietor.[730] The

---

[727] Subsection 17(1) does not apply to a design registered on the basis of an application filed before June 9, 1993, if after the registration the name of the proprietor of the design appears on the article to which the design applies by being marked with the letters "–Rd" or "–ENR" or both "–Rd" and "–ENR" and, the year of registration. See section 29.1(2).

[728] *Industrial Design Act*, R.S.C. 1985, c.I-8, section 14.

[729] *L.M. Lipski Ltd. v. Dorel Industries Inc.*, [1988] 3 F.C. 594 (Fed. T.D.).

[730] Subsection 12(1).

right of another person to the property in a design shall only be co-extensive with the right acquired.[731]

The Act does not contain a definition of the word "author" and there is little authority on point. Presumably the author of a design is the person who gives visual expression to the design by personally making the drawing or model. The determination is a question of fact[732] and the personal involvement of the "author" in the development of the design must be considered.[733]

While cases which have considered who is the author of a work subject to copyright may be considered,[734] under the Act the emphasis must be given to determining who has developed the elements which make up the design.

b) Designs Executed for Consideration

If the author of a design executed it for another person for consideration, the other person is the first proprietor of the design.[735] This provision will apply when an independent contractor is specifically paid to develop a design.

The provision also applies to designs produced by individuals in the course of their employment.[736] The receipt of a salary by an employee constitutes consideration and, as a result, the employer will be the proprietor of designs made in the course of employment.[737]

An employee who has made designs in the ordinary course of employment is not entitled after the termination of employment to use them. If such an employee personally registers a design, the registration may be invalidated.[738] The invalidity cannot be cured by an assignment to the employer.[739]

---

[731] Subsection 12(2).

[732] *Ribbons (Montreal) Ltd. v. Belding Corticelli Ltd.*, [1961] Ex. C.R. 388, 36 C.P.R. 65 (Can. Ex. Ct.).

[733] *Renwal Manufacturing Co. v. Reliable Toy Co.*, [1949] Ex. C.R. 188 (Can. Ex. Ct.); *Comstock Canada v. Electec Ltd.* (1991), 38 C.P.R. (3d) 29.

[734] See John S. McKeown, *Fox on Canadian Law of Copyright and Industrial Designs,* 4th ed.

[735] Subsection 12(1).

[736] *Renwal Manufacturing Co. v. Reliable Toy Co.*, [1949] Ex. C.R. 188, 9 C.P.R. 67 (Can. Ex. Ct.).

[737] *Angelstone Ltd. v. Artistic Stone Ltd.*, [1960] Ex. C.R. 286, 33 C.P.R. 155 (Can. Ex. Ct.); *Ribbons (Montreal) Ltd. v. Belding Corticelli Ltd.*, [1961] Ex. C.R. 388, 36 C.P.R. 65 (Can. Ex. Ct.).

[738] *Angelstone Ltd. v. Artistic Stone Ltd.*, [1960] Ex. C.R. 286, 33 C.P.R. 155 (Can.

10. ASSIGNMENT AND LICENCE

a) Requirements

The Act provides that every design, whether registered or unregistered, is assignable in law, either as to the whole interest or any undivided part, by an instrument in writing, which shall be recorded in the office of the Commissioner of Patents on payment of the prescribed fees.[740] After an assignment is made, the name of proprietor at the time the article, labels or packaging were marked, should be shown for the purposes of the Act.[741]

If the proprietor assigns their rights prior to filing an application, the assignee is entitled to apply to register the design.[742]

Every proprietor of a design may grant and convey an exclusive right to make, use and vend and to grant to others the right to make, use and vend the design, within and throughout Canada or any part thereof, for the unexpired term of its duration or any part thereof.[743] Such a grant and conveyance shall be called a licence and must be recorded in the same manner as an assignment.[744]

The reference to "an exclusive right" follows from the nature of the rights granted to the proprietor and does not restrict the proprietor to granting exclusive licences only. Non-exclusive licences may be granted.

A design is assignable only by an instrument in writing, but it is not clear whether a licence may be made orally.[745]

b) Registration

Under the Act, it is not clear whether it is necessary to register an assignment or exclusive licence in order to institute an action for infringement. Section 13, dealing with assignments, requires recordal in the office

---

Ex. Ct.); *Hassenfeld Brothers Inc. v. Parkdale Novelty Co.*, [1967] 1 Ex. C.R. 277 (Can. Ex. Ct.).

[739] *Renwal Manufacturing Co. v. Reliable Toy Co.*, [1949] Ex. C.R. 188 (Can. Ex. Ct.).

[740] Subsection 13(1).

[741] Subsection 17(2) and (3).

[742] Canadian Intellectual Property Office (Industrial Design Office), *Canadian Industrial Design Procedures Manual* (Ottawa: Industry Canada, 1998) at p 3-1 and see subsection 13(1); *Milliken & Co. v. Interface Flooring Systems (Canada) Inc.* (1994), 55 C.P.R. (3d) 30 (Fed. T.D.).

[743] Subsection 13(2).

[744] Subsection 13(3).

[745] See *Griffiths v. Hughes*, [1892] 3 Ch. 105.

of the Commissioner of Patents. Section 15, relating to the right to bring an action, contains no direction.[746]

11. TERM

So long as the prescribed fee is paid, the term of protection is ten years beginning on the date of registration of the design. In order to maintain the exclusive right, the proprietor must pay to the Commissioner of Patents an additional fee before the fifth anniversary of the registration. If the fee is not received in a timely fashion, there is a grace period of six months and a further fee must be paid. If the design is not renewed within five years and six months the term expires the next day.[747]

12. AMENDMENT OF THE REGISTER

a) Statutory Provisions

Sections 22 to 24 of the Act provide for rectification and alteration of the register of Industrial Designs. The Federal Court has exclusive jurisdiction, on the information of the Attorney General or at the suit of any person aggrieved, to make orders making, expunging or varying any entry in the register.[748]

Section 23 sets out the procedure for adding to or altering a registered industrial design in other than an essential particular by order of the Federal Court. Notice of any intended application to the Federal Court under the section must be given to the Minister and the Minister is entitled to be heard on the application.

b) Expungement

The Federal Court has exclusive jurisdiction to hear and determine proceedings for rectification and alteration of registrations of designs.[749] The Court may make such order for making, expunging or varying any

---

[746] Subsection 15(2) requires that the proprietor of the design shall be or be made a party to any action for infringement.

[747] *North American Free Trade Agreement Implementation Act*, S.C. 1993, c. 44, section 163 and see section 30(4) of the Act for the transitional provisions.

[748] Subsection 22(1).

[749] Subsection. 22(4); *Epstein v. O-Pee-Chee Co.*, [1927] Ex. C.R. 156, [1927] 3 D.L.R. 160 (Can. Ex. Ct.) at 158 [Ex. C.R.]; *Gamache v. Cie des industries de Sherbrooke Ltée* (1945), [1946] Que. P.R. 277 (Que. S.C.).

entry in the register as the Court thinks fit, or the Court may refuse the application.

The section also gives the Federal Court jurisdiction to make such order with respect to the costs of the proceedings as the Court thinks fit and to decide any question that may be necessary or expedient to decide for the rectification of the register.[750]

A person aggrieved by an omission without sufficient cause to make an entry in the Register of Industrial Designs, or by any entry made without sufficient cause in the register may institute proceedings. A design is registered without sufficient cause if its registration should have been refused.[751]

The term "person aggrieved" has been broadly interpreted[752] and includes any one who may possibly be injured by the continuance of the design on the register.[753] A person is a "person aggrieved" if, as one of the public, an impugned design registration prevents them from using it.[754] The term has also been held to be synonymous with the expression "persons interested". which is the expression used in a similar section of the *Trademarks Act*.[755]

13. INFRINGEMENT

Section 9 of the Act provides that: "[a]n exclusive right for an industrial design may be acquired by registration of the design under this Part". The nature of the exclusive right is defined by reference to what others are precluded from doing. Subsection 11(1)[756] provides that;

During the existence of an exclusive right, no person shall, without the licence of the proprietor of the design,

---

[750] Subsection 22(2) and (3).

[751] *Lamont, Corliss & Co. v. Star Confectionery Co.*, [1924] Ex. C.R. 147 (Can. Ex. Ct.).

[752] *John De Kuyper & Son v. Van Dulken, Weiland & Co.* (1895), 24 S.C.R. 114 (S.C.C.).

[753] *Bergeron, Whissell & Co. v. Jonkopings & Vulcans Tandsticksfabriksaktiebolag* (1915), 51 S.C.R. 411, 24 D.L.R. 621 (S.C.C.) at 413 [S.C.R.].

[754] *Epstein v. O-Pee-Chee Co.*, [1927] Ex. C.R. 156, [1927] 3 D.L.R. 160 (Can. Ex. Ct.) at 158 [Ex. C.R.].

[755] R.S.C. 1985, c. T-13, as amended, section 57 and see **Chapter 4, part 9(c)**.

[756] Section 11 was amended pursuant to the *North American Free Trade Agreement Implementation Act*, was S.C. 1993, c. 44 and was brought into force January 1, 1994. It is quite different from the section which preceded it.

    (a)   make, import for the purpose of trade or business, or sell, rent or offer, or expose for sale or rent, any article in respect of which the design is registered and to which the design or a design not differing substantially therefrom has been applied; or

    (b)   do, in relation to a kit, anything specified in paragraph (a) that would constitute an infringement if done in relation to an article assembled from the kit.

An action for infringement of the exclusive right may be brought in any court of competent jurisdiction by the proprietor of the design or by an exclusive licensee of any right therein, subject to any agreement between the proprietor and the licensee.[757]

Subsection 11(1)(a) of the Act relates to any article in respect of which the design is registered and to which the design or a design not differing substantially therefrom has been applied. The making, importation for commercial purposes, selling, renting, or offering or exposing for sale or rent of such articles is an infringement of the exclusive right.

As previously set out, designs are registered in association with a specifically identified article. Infringement will occur when the design or a design not differing substantially therefrom has been applied to the article for which the design was registered.

Subsection 11(1)(b) relates to kits consisting of a complete or substantially complete number of parts that can be assembled to construct a finished article.[758] Carrying out any of the actions described in subsection 11(1)(a) that would constitute an infringement if done in relation to an article assembled from the kit is an infringement.

For the purposes of subsection 11(1), when considering whether differences are substantial, the extent to which the registered design differs from any previously published design may be taken into account.[759]

In order to determine whether infringement has occurred, three matters must be considered:

    (a)   whether the defendant has engaged in one of the activities prescribed in section 11;

    (b)   whether the allegedly infringing article is an article in respect of which the design has been registered; and

    (c)   whether the design or a design not differing substantially from the design has been applied to the allegedly infringing article.

---

[757] Section 15.
[758] Section 2.
[759] Subection 11(2).

The exclusive right which may be acquired under the Act is limited to Canada. As a result, the activities must occur within Canada to be actionable. If, however, goods bearing the design are manufactured in a foreign country and then imported into Canada for sale, this will amount to actionable infringement.[760]

The activities must also take place during the term of the exclusive right in order to be actionable. The term begins on the date of registration of the design[761] and expires at the conclusion of the term.[762]

In order to show that infringement has occurred, the plaintiff must show that the defendant has engaged in at least one of the activities described in the section in relation to the article in respect of which the plaintiff's design has been registered. Unless the defendant's article corresponds there can be no infringement.

If the design itself has been applied to an article in respect of which the plaintiff's design has been registered, there will be no difficulty in finding infringement has occurred. However, in many cases there will be differences which must be considered to ascertain whether the designs differ substantially. The design as a whole must be considered, not specific elements which may make up the design.[763]

In light of the reference in the definition of "design" to "features.... that, in a finished article, appeal to and are judged solely by the eye" infringement must be determined on an ocular basis from the point of view of a customer.[764] The primary concern is what the article looks like not what it does. The emphasis is on the visual image conveyed by the article.[765]

The appearance of the allegedly infringing article must be compared to the appearance of the registered design. Reference must be made to the drawings or photographs of the design and the description of it which accompanied the application. It is appropriate to view articles which embody the registered design but care must be taken to avoid giving consideration to any features not disclosed in the design.[766]

The Act provides that in considering whether differences are substantial, the extent to which the registered design differs from any previously

---

[760] *Dunlop Rubber Co. v. A.A. Booth & Co.* (1926), 43 R.P.C. 139.

[761] Section 10(1).

[762] Section 10(3).

[763] *Benchairs Ltd. v. Chair Centre Ltd.*, [1974] R.P.C. 429 (U.K. C.A.); *UPL Group Ltd. v. DUX Engineers Ltd.*, [1989] 3 N.Z.L.R. 135 (New Zealand C.A.).

[764] See **part 3 of this chapter**.

[765] *Interlego (Attorney General) v. Tyco Industries Inc.* (1988), [1988] 3 W.L.R. 678 (England P.C.).

[766] *Benchairs Ltd. v. Chair Centre Ltd.*, [1974] R.P.C. 429 (U.K. C.A.); *Sommer Allibert (U.K.) Ltd. v. Flair Plastics Ltd.*, [1987] R.P.C. 599 (U.K. C.A.).

published design may be taken into account. A design which has substantial originality may have a broader scope of protection than a design which is close to designs which had been published before it.[767] Where the design is limited to the shape or configuration of the article, the plaintiff must show similarity approaching identity.[768]

Infringement is a question of fact.[769] Expert evidence is admissible to point out similarities and dissimilarities, what is common to the trade[770] and what has been disclosed in previously published designs.

It is not necessary to show any intention to infringe. If there is infringement, an intention in good faith not to infringe will not be a defence.[771]

The absence of knowledge and the absence of reasonable grounds for suspecting that the design was registered may preclude the plaintiff from claiming damages.[772] In addition, the absence of intention may be relevant in assessing the amount of damages for infringement.

14. TRADE DRESS OR GET-UP OF GOODS

a) General

Even though not registered as a distinguishing guise under the *Trade-marks Act*,[773] the dress or get-up of goods, if distinctive, has always been regarded by the common law as something that ought to be protected against unfair competition.[774] For example, plaintiffs have successfully asserted

---

[767] *UPL Group Ltd. v. DUX Engineers Ltd.*, [1989] 3 N.Z.L.R. 135 (New Zealand C.A.).

[768] *Sommer Allibert (U.K.) Ltd. v. Flair Plastics Ltd.*, [1987] R.P.C. 599 (U.K. C.A.).

[769] *Chudzikowski v. Sowak*, [1957] R.P.C. 111 at 117.

[770] *Holdsworth v. McCrea* (1867), L.R. 2 H.L. 380 (U.K. H.L.).

[771] *Mitchell v. Henry* (1880), 15 Ch. D. 181 (U.K.); *Walker v. Hecla Foundry Co.* (1888), 5 R.P.C. 365 at 367.

[772] Section 17 and **see part 7 of this chapter**.

[773] See sections 2 and 13 of the *Trade-marks Act* and **part 2 of this chapter**.

[774] *Ayerst, McKenna & Harrison Inc. v. Apotex Inc.* (1982), 134 D.L.R. (3d) 668 (Ont. H.C.), reversed (1983), 41 O.R. (2d) 366 (Ont. C.A.); *Ciba-Geigy Canada Ltd. v. Apotex Inc.* (1992), 44 C.P.R. (3d) 289 (S.C.C.); *Kirkbi AG v. Ritvik Holdings Inc. / Gestions Ritvik Inc.* (2002), (sub nom. *Kirkbi AG v. Ritvik Holdings Inc.*) 20 C.P.R. (4th) 224 (Fed. T.D.), affirmed 2003 FCA 297 (Fed. C.A.), leave to appeal allowed (2004), 2004 CarswellNat 1211, 2004 CarswellNat 1212 (S.C.C.).

rights relating to a lemon shaped lemon juice dispenser[775] and the shape and colour of a snow brush and ice scraper.[776]

Claims relating to the dress or get-up of goods are typically asserted by bringing an action for passing off or the statutory codification of it contained in subsections 7(b) and 7(c) of the *Trade-marks Act*. In order to assert such claims, a plaintiff must prove the three elements previously described[777] or in summary the existence of goodwill, deception of the public due to a misrepresentation and damage.[778]

Get-up can include the shape, appearance, packaging,[779] the lettering and arrangement of the label[780] or the adornment[781] of a product. It is the external appearance of the goods in the form in which they are likely to be seen prior to purchase.[782] In the context of prescription drugs the final consumer of the product includes physicians, pharmacists, dentists and patients.[783]

---

[775] *Reckitt & Colman Products Ltd. v. Borden Inc.*, [1990] 1 All E.R. 873 (U.K. H.L.).

[776] *Ray Plastics Ltd. v. Dustbane Products Ltd.* (1990), 33 C.P.R. (3d) 219 (Ont. H.C.).

[777] See **part 5 of Chapter 5**.

[778] *Ciba-Geigy Canada Ltd. v. Apotex Inc.* (1992), 44 C.P.R. (3d) 289 (S.C.C.).

[779] *Atkinson & Yates Boatbuilders Ltd. v. Hanlon* (2003), 27 C.P.R. (4th) 195 (N.L. T.D.).

[780] *Anheuser-Busch Inc. v. Canada Bud Breweries Ltd.*, [1933] O.R. 75 (Ont. S.C.); *General Mills Canada Ltd. v. Maple Leaf Mills Ltd.* (1980), 52 C.P.R. (2d) 218 (Ont. H.C.).

[781] *Tommy Hilfiger Licensing Inc. v. International Clothiers Inc.* (2003), 29 C.P.R. (4th) 39 (F.C.).

[782] *Mr. Submarine Ltd. v. Bikas* (1975), 24 C.P.R. (2d) 135 (Ont. H.C.); *Syntex Inc. v. Novopharm Ltd.* (1983), 74 C.P.R. (2d) 110 (Ont. H.C.); *Ciba-Geigy Canada Ltd. v. Apotex Inc.* (1992), 44 C.P.R. (3d) 289 (S.C.C.) at 301; *Searle Canada Inc. v. Novopharm Ltd.* (1994), 56 C.P.R. (3d) 213 (Fed. C.A.); *Eli Lilly & Co. v. Novopharm Ltd.* (1997), 73 C.P.R. (3d) 371 (Fed. T.D.), affirmed (2000), 10 C.P.R. (4th) 10 (Fed. C.A.), leave to appeal to the S.C.C. refused (2001), 275 N.R. 200 (note) (S.C.C.); *Kraft Jacobs Suchard (Schweiz) AG v. Hagemeyer Canada Inc.* (1998), 78 C.P.R. (3d) 464 (Ont. Gen. Div.); *Greystone Energy Systems Inc. v. International Conduits Ltd.* (2003), 27 C.P.R. (4th) 421 (N.B. Q.B.).

[783] *Ciba-Geigy Canada Ltd. v. Apotex Inc.* (1992), 44 C.P.R. (3d) 289 (S.C.C.) at 315; *Hanlon v. Atkinson & Yates Boatbuilders Ltd.* (2003), 35 C.P.C. (5th) 195 (N.L. T.D.).

b) Similarity of Get-up

It is not necessary for every part of the get-up to be imitated. It is sufficient if enough of the plaintiff's get-up is imitated such that there is a probability that the defendant's wares would be passed off as those of the plaintiff.[784] This is a question of fact.

Colour alone, even when combined with size, is not generally sufficient to form the basis of an action for passing off.[785]

The addition of distinctive matter may eliminate the probability of deception.[786] However, marking the goods with the name of the manufacturer is not necessarily sufficient,[787] although it may be important in showing the defendant's good faith.[788]

An Australian case illustrates the application of these principles in a brand context. Red Bull GmbH, through Red Bull Australia Pty. Ltd., sold a product in Australia known as RED BULL brand energy drink. Substantial amounts of money were spent in promoting the product in Australia. The marketing campaign focused on a slimline 250 ml can which was smaller in diameter than cans widely used for other kinds of soft drinks.

Much of the product was supplied to the market through distributors. Sydneywide Distributors Pty. Ltd. commenced to distribute the product in February 2000, and was fully briefed concerning the RED BULL brand product. Shortly after Sydneywide placed its last order for the product, Red Bull became aware that Sydneywide had commenced to sell its own energy drink in a 250ml can in association with the trade mark LIVEWIRE.

---

[784] *Renwal Manufacturing Co. v. Reliable Toy Co.* (1949), 9 C.P.R. 67 (Can. Ex. Ct.); *Canadian Converters' Co. v. Eastport Trading Co.* (1968), 56 C.P.R. 204 (Can. Ex. Ct.); *Oxford Pendaflex Canada Ltd. v. Korr Marketing Ltd.* (1982), 134 D.L.R. (3d) 271 (S.C.C.); *Green v. Schwarz* (1986), 9 C.I.P.R. 290 (Ont. H.C.).

[785] *Prairie Maid Cereals Ltd. v. Christie, Brown & Co.* (1966), 48 C.P.R. 289 (B.C. C.A.); *Sheres Co. v. Texpol Trading Co.* (1969), 58 C.P.R. 136 (Ex. Ct.); *Ciba-Geigy Canada Ltd. v. Novopharm Ltd.* (1986), 12 C.P.R. (3d) 76 (Ont. H.C.); *Irwin Toy Ltd. v. Marie-Anne Novelties Inc.* (1986), 12 C.P.R. (3d) 145 (Ont. H.C.); *Smith, Kline & French Canada Ltd. v. Apotex Inc.* (1985), 12 C.P.R. (3d) 479 (Ont. H.C.).

[786] *Renwal Manufacturing Co. v. Reliable Toy Co.* (1949), 9 C.P.R. 67 (Can. Ex. Ct.); *Parke, Davis & Co. v. Empire Laboratories Ltd.* (1963), [1964] Ex. C.R. 399 (Can. Ex. Ct.), affirmed [1964] S.C.R. 351 (S.C.C.).

[787] *Canadian Converters' Co. v. Eastport Trading Co.* (1968), 56 C.P.R. 204 (Can. Ex. Ct.).

[788] *Renwal Manufacturing Co. v. Reliable Toy Co.* (1949), 9 C.P.R. 67 (Can. Ex. Ct.).

Red Bull brought proceedings and alleged that Sydneywide had passed off its product for the RED BULL brand product. The plaintiff relied on the evidence of an expert who focused on what he described as the "gestalt" of the brand. He described the gestalt as the overall identity of a brand as it relates to consumers including not only the name, colour, physical properties and packaging, but also associations with the brand and brand name devices used to create associations including its advertising and the channels through which it is sold. He said that many buyers of packaged goods recognize and differentiate between brands on the basis of the overall look and feel of the product and its total image, particularly where no single brand identity element is dominant. Where the gestalts of the two products are almost identical, without more information about the products he concluded that some consumers were likely to perceive them as comprising the same brand and/or as derived from the same source.

The trial judge inferred that Sydneywide identified distinct advantages of its LIVEWIRE product and the appropriate approach to be adopted for its packaging and get up by reason of its substantial involvement with the RED BULL brand product. The trial judge also concluded that recognition of the colour of a particular brand on products and product displays may be central to the promotion of the brand and the likelihood of purchase by consumers. Apart from colour, physical properties such as shape and size, together with graphic elements such as symbols and label design, can be important to visually identify a brand and to create brand associations.

As a result the trial judge found that Sydneywide had passed off its LIVEWIRE product for the plaintiff's RED BULL brand product. The trial judge's conclusion was based on the fact that there was substantial similarity in the appearance of the two cans particularly in colouring and the diagonal thrust of the design elements and that Sydneywide had deliberately adopted a get-up which included elements of the Red Bull get-up in an effort to benefit from the latter's market position and marketing efforts.

On appeal, the Federal Court of Australia upheld the trial judge's conclusions and in particular the concept of looking at the "gestalt" of each product as presented by the expert witnesses.[789]

c) Functionality

Generally speaking, any combination of elements which are primarily designed to perform a function are not protectable under the *Trade-marks*

---

[789] *Sydneywide Distributors Pty. Ltd. v. Red Bull Australia Pty. Ltd.*, [2002] FCAFC 157 (F.C.A.).

Act or at common law.[790] The fact that the party seeking protection obtained a patent relating to the article in question is evidence of functionality.[791]

d) Common to the Trade

A brand owner may make use of the characteristic features of the get-up used in the trade in which it is engaged.[792] However, if a brand owner develops a distinctive get-up for its goods, even though each individual item of the get-up may, in itself, be common to the trade, they may succeed with an action for passing off if the get-up is sufficiently well known and associated with its wares.[793]

e) Substitution of Goods

Passing off a competitor's wares or services as and for those ordered or requested is actionable.[794] In order to succeed the plaintiff must show that a misrepresentation occurs relating to the fact that its wares or services are known and ordered or requested by a brand name.

---

[790] *Canadian Shredded Wheat Co. v. Kellogg Co.*, [1938] 1 All E.R. 618, [1938] 2 D.L.R. 145 (Ontario P.C.); *Parke, Davis & Co. v. Empire Laboratories Ltd.* (1963), 41 C.P.R. 121 (Can. Ex. Ct.), affirmed [1964] S.C.R. 351 (S.C.C.); *Elgin Handles Ltd. v. Welland Vale Manufacturing Co.* (1964), 43 C.P.R. 20 (Can. Ex. Ct.); *Remington Rand Corp. v. Philips Electronics N.V.* (1995), 64 C.P.R. (3d) 467 (Fed. C.A.), leave to appeal refused (1996), 67 C.P.R. (3d) vi (note) (S.C.C.); *Thomas & Betts Ltd. v. Panduit Corp.* (2000), 4 C.P.R. (4th) 498 (Fed. C.A.), leave to appeal refused (2000), 264 N.R. 191 (note) (S.C.C.); *Kirkbi AG v. Ritvik Holdings Inc. / Gestions Ritvik Inc.* (2002), (sub nom. *Kirkbi AG v. Ritvik Holdings Inc.*) 20 C.P.R. (4th) 224 (Fed. T.D.), affirmed (2003), 26 C.P.R. (4th) 1 (Fed. C.A.), leave to appeal allowed (2004), 2004 CarswellNat 1211, 2004 CarswellNat 1212 (S.C.C.).

[791] *Parke, Davis & Co. v. Empire Laboratories Ltd.* (1963), 41 C.P.R. 121 (Can. Ex. Ct.), affirmed [1964] S.C.R. 351 (S.C.C.).

[792] *Hodgkinson & Corby Ltd. v. Wards Mobility Services Ltd.*, [1995] F.S.R. 169 (Eng. Ch. Div.); *Abbott Laboratories Ltd. v. Apotex Inc.* (1998), 81 C.P.R. (3d) 85 (Ont. Gen. Div.); *Kun Shoulder Rest Inc. v. Joseph Kun Violin & Bow Maker Inc.* (1998), 83 C.P.R. (3d) 331 (Fed. T.D.), reconsideration refused (1999), 172 F.T.R. 149 (Fed. T.D.).

[793] *Oxford Pendaflex Canada Ltd. v. Korr Marketing Ltd.* (1982), 134 D.L.R. (3d) 271 (S.C.C.).

[794] Subsection 7(c) of the *Trade Marks Act*.

15. SUMMARY AND CHECKLIST

To ensure that product shape and appearance are protected the following matters should be considered.

1. The primary methods of protecting product shape and appearance are registration under the *Trade-marks Act* as a distinguishing guise, registration under the *Industrial Design Act* and common law actions for passing off.
2. The *Trade-marks Act* contains provisions which allow for the registration of a distinguishing guise. Such a guise means a shaping of the wares or their containers or a mode of wrapping or packaging wares, the appearance of which is used by a person for the purpose of distinguishing wares or services manufactured, sold, leased or hired by it from those manufactured, sold, leased or hired by others.
3. An applicant seeking to register a distinguishing guise must provide evidence similar to that required to establish acquired distinctiveness or secondary meaning concerning a regular trade mark. A guise incorporating functional features of a product which relate primarily or essentially to the product itself is not likely registrable.
4. Features of shape, configuration, pattern or ornament or any combination of those features which, in a product, appeal to and are judged solely by the eye may be protected under *Industrial Design Act.* Protection cannot be obtained for a feature applied to an article that is dictated by a utilitarian function of the article. However, if there are features of the design which are not dictated solely by function, the design as a whole may still be protectable.
5. The *Industrial Design Act* requires that a design be original and there must be some substantial difference between the new design and pre-existing designs. A slight change of outline or configuration or an insubstantial variation will not be sufficient to obtain a registration.
6. An application for registration of an industrial design must be filed in Canada within one year of the publication of the design in Canada or elsewhere in the world. Publication means offering or making a design available to the public.
7. The author of a design is the first proprietor of the design, unless the author executed the design for another person for consideration, in which case the other person is the first proprietor. This applies to designs produced by individuals in the course of their employment.
8. The duration of the right granted is ten years, beginning on the date of registration of the design. However, in order to maintain the exclusive right, the proprietor must pay to the Commissioner of Patents an additional fee before the fifth anniversary of the registration.

9. An exclusive right for an industrial design will be acquired on registration. During the existence of an exclusive right, no person shall, without the licence of the proprietor of the design,

    (a) make, import for the purpose of trade or business, or sell, rent, or offer or expose for sale or rent, any article in respect of which the design is registered and to which the design or a design not differing substantially therefrom has been applied; or

    (b) do, in relation to a kit, anything specified in paragraph (a) that would constitute an infringement if done in relation to an article assembled from the kit.

10. It is prudent that articles be marked with the capital letter "D" in a circle and the name or the usual abbreviation of the name of the proprietor of the design in order to preclude defences alleging lack of knowledge of the design.

11. Even though not registered as a distinguishing guise under the *Trade-marks Act,* the dress or get-up of goods, if distinctive, has always been regarded by the common law as something that ought to be protected against unfair competition. Claims relating to the dress or get-up of goods can be asserted by bringing an action for passing off or the statutory codification of it contained in subsections 7(b) and 7(c) of the *Trade-marks Act.*

Chapter 7: **Protecting Product Packaging**

1. INTRODUCTION

Product packaging is one of the tangible elements of a brand. The packaging of a product, in addition to its functional purpose, must visually express the brand image and the values the image symbolizes. The package design is a manifestation of the brand and must work harmoniously with other aspects of the brand communication and all of the elements of the packaging, such as colours, graphics, typography and structure, must also be consistent with the brand image and its values.

Packaging plays a key role in influencing the choices that consumers make. The packaging is the spokesperson for the brand which helps communicate the brand's uniqueness and importance. Retail shelves are flooded with thousands of products and many purchasing decisions are made in-store. Successful packaging can help a product break out from the clutter.

Packaging may also be used to make it more difficult to counterfeit a product. For example, in a recent situation involving an exporter of premium synthetic motor oil, counterfeiters were opening the containers, pouring out the premium oil, refilling it with used oil and then seaming on a new package end for re-sale. The exporter, with the assistance of its supplier, developed an aluminum closure for its containers which was laborious to replicate and difficult to re-seam, making it easy for consumers to spot the counterfeit product.[795]

---

[795] See article contained in *Canadian Packaging Magazine* dated October 1, 2002, published by MacLean Hunter Canadian Publishing Inc.

Product packaging may be protected under the *Copyright Act* as a literary or artistic work or as a compilation. Registration under the *Trade-marks Act* is also possible but there may be practical problems.

2. TRADE MARKS

While it is possible to register the label or package design as a trade mark and thereby protect it,[796] there may be practical problems with this approach. First, it may be difficult to determine exactly what constitutes the trade mark.[797] For example, if there are a number of different models or signs of a product with different designations or descriptors, each separate presentation may have to be independently registered. If an application is filed relating only to the common elements of the label presentation, the registration obtained may be open to attack on the basis that only unregistered variations of the registered trade mark are being used.[798]

Second, while the actual brand name may not change, the label presentation may be changed from time to time with the result that new trade mark application(s) should be filed. Depending on the frequency of the changes or the length of the life of the product, maintaining trade mark registrations may be uneconomic in light of the cost of obtaining new registration(s).

Third, disclaimers may be required for descriptive elements of the label presentation such as text relating to the product, number of units, etcetera. The existence of the disclaimers may result in a trade mark registration which gives the trade mark owner little more protection than a registration of the brand name itself or the design presentation of the brand name.[799]

On the other hand, if the product packaging is sufficiently durable and distinct, it may be independently protected by a trade mark registration. For example, Seiko[800] sought to protect its watch boxes in addition to its watches, by extending the existing Seiko trade mark registration to include watch

---

[796] See for example *Tavener Rutledge Ltd. v. Specters Ltd.*, [1959] R.P.C. 83.

[797] See for example *Domtar Inc. v. Ottawa Perma-Coating Ltd.* (1985), 3 C.P.R. (3d) 302 (T.M. Opp. Bd.); *Molson Breweries, A Partnership v. Great Western Brewing Co.* (1996), 67 C.P.R. (3d) 394 (T.M. Opp. Bd.); *Molson Breweries, A Partnership v. Oland Breweries Ltd./Brasseries Oland Ltée* (1999), (sub nom. *Molson Breweries, A Partnership v. Oland Breweries Ltd.*) 1 C.P.R. (4th) 239 (T.M. Opp. Bd.).

[798] See **Chapter 4, part 3** concerning trade mark use.

[799] See *Molson Cos. v. Scottish & Newcastle Breweries Ltd.* (1985), 4 C.P.R. (3d) 124 (T.M. Opp. Bd.).

[800] *Impenco Ltd. v. Kabushiki Kaisha Hattori Seiko* (1999), (sub nom. *Kabushiki Kaisha Hattori Seiko v. Impenco Ltd.*) 4 C.P.R. (4th) 374 (Fed. T.D.), reversing (1998), 86 C.P.R. (3d) 398 (T.M. Opp. Bd.).

boxes. The application was opposed and the Trade-marks Opposition Board found that the existence of the trade mark on the watch box did not constitute trade mark use in association with the watch box, but the product contained in the box, namely the watch. On appeal to the Federal Court, the decision was reversed as it was found that there were in fact two distinct wares in respect of which the Seiko trade mark was being used and that a registration for use in association with watch boxes was appropriate.[801]

3. COPYRIGHT

a) Acquisition

The expression of brand image and other information on product packaging may be protected under the *Copyright Act*.[802] Copyright protection in Canada does not depend on registration or other formal steps.[803] Copyright subsists automatically without any act beyond the creation of an original literary or artistic work or compilation in the circumstances set out in the Act.[804] Registration is permissive[805] but prudent if it is likely an action will be brought for infringement.

Copyright protection extends to authors of works who are Canadian nationals as well as to the nationals of other countries. As a signatory to the Berne Convention (Paris Revisions, 1971), the agreement establishing the World Trade Organization (WTO) and the agreement on Trade-Related Aspects of Intellectual Property Rights, including trade in Counterfeit Goods (TRIPs), which was annexed to the Agreement establishing the WTO, Canada is bound to give protection to the nationals of other countries.

After September 1, 1997,[806] copyright subsists in Canada, in every original literary and artistic work if any one of the following conditions is met:

(a)   in the case of any work, whether published or unpublished, the

---

[801] For a discussion of the case, see Ruth M. Corbin and David Aylen, *Product Containers Take Flight from Packaging* (2000), 14 I.P.J. 361.

[802] R.S.C. 1985, c. C-42 as amended.

[803] *Zamacoïs v. Douville* (1943), 2 C.P.R. 270, [1943] 2 D.L.R. 257 (Can. Ex. Ct.); *King Features Syndicate Inc. v. O. & M. Kleemann Ltd.*, [1941] 2 All E.R. 403 (U.K. H.L.).

[804] See section 5.

[805] *Circle Film Enterprises Inc. v. Canadian Broadcasting Corp.*, [1959] S.C.R. 602 (S.C.C.).

[806] Different rules apply to works created before this date. See John S. McKeown, *Fox on Canadian Law of Copyright and Industrial Designs*, 4th ed., Chapter 6.

author was, at the date of the making of the work, a citizen or subject of, or a person ordinarily resident in, a treaty country;[807] or

(b)   in the case of a published work, the first publication in such a quantity as to satisfy the reasonable demands of the public, having regard to the nature of the work, occurred in a treaty country.

The first publication described above is deemed to have occurred in a treaty country notwithstanding that it occurred previously elsewhere, if the interval between those two publications did not exceed thirty days.[808] Under the Act, "publication" is defined to mean in relation to works, the making of copies of a work available to the public.

b) Originality

Copyright subsists only in *original* works. The originality required by the Act relates to the expression of thought in which the work is presented. For a work to be "original" it must be more than a mere copy of another work. At the same time, it need not be creative in the sense of being novel or unique. What is required to attract copyright protection in the expression of an idea is an exercise of skill and judgment. Skill in this context means the use of an individual's knowledge, developed aptitude or practiced ability in producing the work. Judgment means the use of one's capacity for discernment or ability to form an opinion or an evaluation by comparing different possible options in producing the work. The exercise of skill and judgment will necessarily involve intellectual effort. Such an exercise must not be so trivial that it could be characterized as a purely mechanical exercise. For example, any skill and judgment that might be involved in simply changing the font of a work to produce another work would be too trivial to merit copyright protection as "original" work.[809]

The amount of skill and judgment required cannot be defined in precise terms and each case must be decided on its own facts.[810] In addition, the

---

[807] The definition of "treaty country" in section 2 of the Act includes countries which are a party to the Berne Convention or a WTO Member.

[808] Subsection 5(1.1).

[809] *CCH Canadian Ltd. v. Law Society of Upper Canada*, 2004 SCC 13 (S.C.C.). This case has changed the requirements for originality and previously decided cases must be read subject to it.

[810] *Interlego A.G. v. Tyco Industries Inc.* (1988), [1989] A.C. 217 (Hong Kong P.C.).

type of work in issue may influence the determination; for example, a photograph is considered in different terms than other works.[811]

Copyright has nothing to do with the literary merit of the author's work.[812] It may exist in a list of advertisements,[813] or the advertisements themselves.[814]

Generally speaking, a work which is a slavish copy of an earlier work will not be entitled to copyright as it is not original.[815] Skill and judgment relating solely to the process of copying cannot confer originality.[816] However, a work which is substantially derived from pre-existing material may still be the proper subject matter of copyright if sufficient skill and judgment have been bestowed on it.[817]

The owner of copyright is not entitled to a monopoly in the protected work. Other individuals may produce the same work so long as they do so independently and their work is original in the sense in which that word is used in the Act.[818]

Copyright does not extend to schemes, systems, or methods,[819] even if they are original, but is confined to their expression.[820]

---

[811] *Viceroy Homes Ltd. v. Ventury Homes Inc.* (1991), 34 C.P.R. (3d) 385 (Ont. Gen. Div.), affirmed (1996), 69 C.P.R. (3d) 459 (Ont. C.A.).

[812] *Walter v. Lane*, [1900] A.C. 539 (U.K. H.L.).

[813] *Lamb v. Evans*, [1893] 1 Ch. 218 (Eng. C.A.).

[814] *Maple & Co. v. Junior Army and Navy Stores* (1882), 21 Ch. D. 369 (Eng. C.A.); *Promotions Atlantiques Inc. v. Hardcraft Industries Ltd.* (1987), 17 C.P.R. (3d) 552 (Fed. T.D.).

[815] *University of London Press v. University Tutorial Press Ltd.*, [1916] 2 Ch. 601 (Eng. Ch. Div.); *Ladbroke (Football) Ltd. v. William Hill (Football) Ltd.*, [1964] 1 All E.R. 465 (U.K. H.L.).

[816] *Interlego A.G. v. Tyco Industries Inc.* (1988), [1989] A.C. 217 (Hong Kong P.C.).

[817] *Interlego A.G. v. Tyco Industries Inc.* (1988), [1989] A.C. 217 (Hong Kong P.C.); and see W.J. Braithwaite, "Derivative Works in Canadian Copyright Law" (1982), 20 Osgoode Hall L. J. 191.

[818] *Ladbroke (Football) Ltd. v. William Hill (Football) Ltd.*, [1964] 1 All E.R. 465 (U.K. H.L.).

[819] *Ladbroke (Football) Ltd. v. William Hill (Football) Ltd.*, [1964] 1 All E.R. 465 (U.K. H.L.).

[820] *Commercial Signs v. General Motors Products of Canada Ltd.*, [1937] O.W.N. 58, [1937] 2 D.L.R. 310 (Ont. H.C.), affirmed [1937] 2 D.L.R. 800 (Ont. C.A.); *Moreau v. St. Vincent*, [1950] Ex. C.R. 198, 12 C.P.R. 32, [1950] 3 D.L.R. 713 (Can. Ex. Ct.); *Stevens v. Robert Simpson Co.* (1964), 41 C.P.R. 204 (Ont. S.C.).

c) Fixation

In order for a work to be entitled to copyright, it must be expressed in material form, capable of identification and having a character of reasonable substance or permanence.[821] For example, where the plaintiff developed an idea for certain types of window display features and the defendant used display features embodying the idea of the plaintiff, but did not copy any substantial portion of the plaintiff's work, the plaintiff could not recover.[822] It is not an infringement of copyright to adopt the ideas of another or to publish information derived from another, so long as there is no copying of the language or expression in which the ideas or the information have previously been presented.[823]

d) Compiliations

The Act provides that a "compilation" means

a)   a work resulting from the selection or arrangement of literary, dramatic, musical or artistic works or parts thereof; or

b)   a work resulting from the selection or arrangement of data.[824]

A compilation containing two or more of the categories of literary, dramatic, musical or artistic works is deemed to be a compilation of the category making up the most substantial part of the compilation.[825] The mere fact that a work is included in a compilation does not increase, decrease or otherwise affect the protection conferred by the Act in respect of the copyright in the work or the moral rights in respect of the work.[826] The information contained in a product label or leaflet may be protected as a compilation under the Act.[827]

---

[821] *Canadian Admiral Corp. v. Rediffusion Inc.*, [1954] Ex. C.R. 382, 20 C.P.R. 75 (Can. Ex. Ct.).

[822] *Stevens v. Robert Simpson Co.* (1964), 41 C.P.R. 204 (Ont. S.C.) and see *Moreau v. St. Vincent*, [1950] Ex. C.R. 198, 12 C.P.R. 32, [1950] 3 D.L.R. 713 (Can. Ex. Ct.).

[823] *Deeks v. Wells* (1930), [1931] O.R. 818 (Ont. H.C.), affirmed [1931] 4 D.L.R. 533 (Ont. C.A.), affirmed (1932), [1933] 1 D.L.R. 353 (Ontario P.C.).

[824] Section 2.

[825] Subsection 2.1(1).

[826] Subsection 2.1(2).

[827] *Slumber-Magic Adjustable Bed Co. v. Sleep-King Adjustable Bed Co.* (1984), 3 C.P.R. (3d) 81 (B.C. S.C.); *Elanco Products Ltd. v. Mandops (Agrochemical Specialists) Ltd.*, [1979] F.S.R. 46 (U.K. C.A.).

A part of a work by itself may be entitled to copyright, while other parts of the work are not (for example, a work consisting of parts from the public domain and original material).[828] However, the entire work may be entitled to protection as a compilation[829] independently from any copyright which may subsist in the parts.[830]

e) Derivative Works

A work which is derived from pre-existing material will be protected by copyright if sufficient skill and judgment has been directed to its creation.[831] For works such as photographs, the requirement for originality will be satisfied by the "expression" of the images contained in the photograph.

Since the exclusive rights, which include the rights to make derivative works, are vested in the author, another individual who wishes to make a "derivative" work will require the consent of the author, unless the work is in the public domain. In the absence of consent, the "derivative" work may infringe the author's rights.

4. LITERARY WORKS

a) What is Protected

The category of "literary works" covers a wide field, including all works that are expressed in print or writing irrespective of their literary quality or merit.[832] The sole requirements for protection of a literary work is that it be expressed in print or writing[833] and be original. Literary quality or merit, in the sense of aesthetic quality or virtue, is not required.[834]

---

[828] *Canadian Admiral Corp. v. Rediffusion Inc.*, [1954] Ex. C.R. 382, 20 C.P.R. 75 (Can. Ex. Ct.); *Leslie v. Young & Sons*, [1894] A.C. 335 (U.K. H.L.).

[829] Section 2.

[830] *Chappell & Co. v. Redwood Music Ltd.*, [1980] 2 All E.R. 817 (U.K. H.L.) and *Slumber-Magic Adjustable Bed Co. v. Sleep-King Adjustable Bed Co.* (1984), 3 C.P.R. (3d) 81 (B.C. S.C.).

[831] *Interlego A.G. v. Tyco Industries Inc.* (1988), [1989] A.C. 217 (Hong Kong P.C.) and see W.J. Braithwaite, "Derivative Works in Canadian Copyright Law" (1982), 20 Osgoode Hall L. J. 191.

[832] *University of London Press v. University Tutorial Press Ltd.*, [1916] 2 Ch. 601 (Eng. Ch. Div.).

[833] *Apple Computer Inc. v. Mackintosh Computers Ltd.* (1987), [1988] 1 F.C. 673 (Fed. C.A.), affirmed (1990), 30 C.P.R. (3d) 257 (S.C.C.).

[834] *Ladbroke (Football) Ltd. v. William Hill (Football) Ltd.*, [1964] 1 All E.R. 465 (U.K. H.L.).

In the case of *Édutile Inc. v. Automobile Protection Assn. (APA)*,[835] Édutile Inc. published a used car price guide intended for consumers. The guide presented trade-in values, private sale information and retail sales information in three vertical columns, with the private sale column being in the middle flanked by the trade-in value on the left and the retail value on the right. The Court found that copyright subsisted in the selection and layout of two juxtaposed columns, one dealing with the private sale market and the other dealing with the retail or commercial market.

Copyright has been denied with respect to the words of a slogan,[836] but protection under the *Trade-marks Act* is possible.[837]

b) The Rights Associated with a Literary Work

Copyright in a literary work includes the sole right:

(a)   to produce or reproduce the work or any substantial part in any material form whatever;

(b)   to perform the work or any substantial part of it in public, (the public performance right);

(c)   if unpublished, to publish the work or any substantial part of it;

(d)   to produce, reproduce, perform or publish any translation of the work;

(e)   in the case of a novel or other non-dramatic work, to convert it into a dramatic work, by way of performance in public or otherwise;

(f)   to make any sound recording, cinematograph film or other contrivance by means of which the work may be mechanically reproduced or performed;

(g)   to reproduce, adapt and publicly present the work as a cinematographic work;

(h)   to communicate the work by telecommunication;

---

[835] (2000), 188 D.L.R. (4th) 132 (S.C.C.).

[836] See for example *Sinanide v. La Maison Kosmeo* (1928), 139 L.T. 365, 44 T.L.R. 371, 574, where the plaintiff, an electrotherapist, used in his advertisements of face treatments a phrase that he claimed to have invented—namely, that beauty was a "social necessity, not a luxury". The defendant, who carried on the same type of business, used in his advertisements the words "a youthful appearance is a social necessity". It was held by the English Court of Appeal that the plaintiff's phrase was not an "original literary work" within the meaning of the *Copyright Act*.

[837] See **Chapter 8, part 2**.

and to authorize such acts.[838]

5. ARTISTIC WORKS

a) What is Protected

The Act provides that copyright subsists in "every original . . . artistic work".[839] The term "artistic work" is defined to include paintings,[840] drawings, maps, charts, plans, photographs, engravings, sculptures and works of artistic craftsmanship,[841] and compilations of artistic works. Product labels have been protected as artistic works.[842]

"Photograph"[843] is defined to include a "photo-lithograph and any work expressed by any process analogous to photography".[844]

An artistic work may be derived from another—for example, an engraving may be made from a work of sculpture or a painting. Such a work may be the proper subject matter of copyright if sufficient skill and judgment have been bestowed upon it, even though it is a reproduction in a different medium of an already existing artistic work. For example, a photograph of an engraving[845] has been protected by copyright.

b) The Rights Associated with an Artistic Work

Copyright in an artistic work includes the sole right:

(a)   to produce or reproduce the work or any substantial part of it in any material form whatever;

(b)   to perform the work or any substantial part of it in public;

(c)   if unpublished, to publish the work or any substantial part of it;

---

[838] Section 3.

[839] Section 5.

[840] *Mansell v. Star Printing & Publishing Co. of Toronto*, [1937] 3 All E.R. 912, [1937] A.C. 872, [1937] 4 D.L.R. 1 (Ontario P.C.).

[841] In *Eldon Industries Inc. v. Reliable Toy Co.* (1965), [1966] 1 O.R. 409, 54 D.L.R. (2d) 97 (Ont. C.A.) it was held that a toy truck is not a work of artistic craftsmanship.

[842] *Charles Walker & Co. Ltd. v. The British Picker Co. Ltd.*, [1961] R.P.C. 57 (Ch. Div.); *Tavener Rutledge Ltd. v. Specters Ltd.*, [1959] R.P.C. 83.

[843] Section 2.

[844] *Canadian Admiral Corp. v. Rediffusion Inc.*, [1954] Ex. C.R. 382, 20 C.P.R. 75 (Can. Ex. Ct.).

[845] *Walker, Re, Ex parte Graves* (1869), 4 Q.B. 715, 10 B. & S. 680, 39 L.J. Q.B. 31 (U.K.).

(d) to produce, reproduce, perform or publish any translation of the work;

(e) to convert the work into a dramatic work, by way of performance in public or otherwise;

(f) to reproduce, adapt and publicly present the work as a cinematographic work;

(g) to communicate the work to the public by telecommunication;

and to authorize such acts.[846]

The ability to exercise the rights associated with an artistic work may be restricted in the case of a design applied to a useful article or the application to a useful article of features dictated solely by utilitarian function as defined in subsections 64 and 64.1 of the Act, but not for a work consisting of a trade mark or representation of it or a label.[847]

Copyright in artistic works does not extend to ideas, conceptions, schemes, systems or methods, but is confined to their expression in material form.[848] Just as there is no copyright in ideas expressed in a literary work, the subject of an artistic work is generally not protected by copyright.

In the case of *Kenrick & Co. v. Lawrence & Co.,*[849] copyright in an election card bearing a representation of a hand holding a pencil in the act of completing a cross within a square on a ballot was considered. The cards were being used to assist illiterate voters in the marking of ballots. The defendants published similar cards with a hand holding a pencil completing a cross in a square on a ballot. The hand on the defendant's card was in a slightly different position, but it was alleged that the idea had been copied from the plaintiff's card. The action was dismissed. There was no copyright in the subject or idea expressed in the card. Copyright was limited to the specific drawing shown and only an exact literal reproduction of such a drawing would constitute infringement.[850]

Under the Act, "artistic work" is a defined term which includes certain types of works. The use of the word "artistic" refers only to the nature of the works referred to in the statutory definition as "literary" does in the definition of literary work. It also provides a general description of works

---

[846] Section 3.
[847] See **Chapter 6, part 4(b)**.
[848] *Canadian Admiral Corp. v. Rediffusion Inc.*, [1954] Ex. C.R. 382, 20 C.P.R. 75 (Can. Ex. Ct.).
[849] (1890), 25 Q.B. 99 (Q.B.).
[850] *Kenrick & Co. v. Lawrence & Co.* (1890), 5 Q.B. 99 (Q.B.); see also *Nottage v. Jackson* (1883), 11 Q.B. 627 (Q.B.).

which are expressed in a visual medium as opposed to works of literary, musical or dramatic expression.[851]

A work may be protected as an artistic work without considering its artistic merit or aesthetic value.[852] In the context of protecting product packaging, as long as the other requirements for obtaining copyright are satisfied, the fact that the work is used for business or advertising purposes is irrelevant.[853]

6. REGISTRATION AND MARKING

As discussed, copyright protection in Canada does not depend on registration or other steps such as marking. Protection is automatic.[854] Registration is permissive and is unnecessary for the subsistence of copyright.[855]

a) The Effect of Registration

The registration of copyright or an assignment of copyright or a licence granting an interest in a copyright will have a number of generally advantageous consequences for the owner and which are discussed below.

Copies of entries on the Register of Copyrights certified by the Commissioner of Patents are admissible in all courts in Canada without further proof or production of originals.[856]

A certificate of registration of copyright in a work is evidence that copyright subsists in the work, and that the person registered is the owner

---

[851] *DRG Inc. v. Datafile Ltd.* (1987), 18 C.P.R. (3d) 538 (Fed. T.D.), affirmed (1991), 35 C.P.R. (3d) 243 (Fed. C.A.).

[852] *King Features Syndicate Inc. v. O. & M. Kleemann Ltd.*, [1941] 2 All E.R. 403 (U.K. H.L.).

[853] *Church v. Linton* (1894), 25 O.R. 131 (Ont. H.C.); *Toronto Carton Co. v. Manchester McGregor Ltd.*, [1935] O.R. 144, [1935] O.W.N. 105, [1935] 2 D.L.R. 94 (Ont. H.C.); *Van Dusen v. Kritz*, [1936] 2 K.B. 176, 105 K.B. 498 (Eng. K.B.); *Tavener Rutledge Ltd. v. Specters Ltd.*, [1959] R.P.C. 83; *Klarmann (H.) Ltd. v. Henshaw Linen Supplies*, [1960] R.P.C. 150; *Charles Walker & Co. Ltd. v. The British Picker Co. Ltd.*, [1961] R.P.C. 57 (Ch. Div.).

[854] *Zamacoïs v. Douville* (1943), 2 C.P.R. 270, [1943] 2 D.L.R. 257 (Can. Ex. Ct.).

[855] *Circle Film Enterprises Inc. v. Canadian Broadcasting Corp.*, [1959] S.C.R. 602 (S.C.C.).

[856] Subsection 53(1) and (3) and see *Blue Crest Music Inc. v. Canusa Records Inc.* (1974), 17 C.P.R. (2d) 149 (Fed. T.D.), affirmed (1976), 30 C.P.R. (2d) 11 (Fed. C.A.), reversed on other grounds (1976), 30 C.P.R. (2d) 14 (Fed. C.A.), affirmed *Compo Co. v. Blue Crest Music Inc.* (1979), [1980] 1 S.C.R. 357 (S.C.C.).

of the copyright.[857] A certificate of registration of an assignment of copyright is evidence that the right recorded on the certificate has been assigned and that the assignee registered is the owner of that right.[858] A certificate of registration of a licence granting an interest in a copyright is evidence that the interest recorded on the certificate has been granted and that the licensee registered is the holder of that interest.[859]

The certificate of registration of copyright is *prima facie* evidence that copyright exists, but is not conclusive.[860] However, the matters set out above will be presumed to be as described in the certificate and the party seeking to dispute them will bear the onus of leading credible evidence to the contrary.[861]

It is not clear what effect will be given to a registration which was obtained after an alleged infringement. In one case, a trial judge refused to give retroactive effect to a late registration.[862]

In response to a statement of claim based on and pleading a certificate of registration, a defendant is not entitled to rely upon a simple denial but must allege material facts which could, if proven, bring into question the matters set out in the registration.[863]

Under section 39 of the Act, a defendant who alleges that they were not aware and had no reasonable ground for suspecting that copyright existed in a work is not liable to any other remedy against them other than an injunction. However, the section provides that, if at the date of the infringement, the copyright in the work was duly registered under the Act, the

---

[857] Subsection 53(2) and see *King Features Syndicate Inc. v. O. & M. Kleemann Ltd.*, [1941] 2 All E.R. 403 (U.K. H.L.).

[858] Subsection 53(2.1).

[859] Subsection 53(2.2).

[860] *Underwriters' Survey Bureau Ltd. v. Massie & Renwick Ltd.*, [1940] S.C.R. 218 (S.C.C.), special leave to appeal refused [1940] S.C.R. 219 (note) (S.C.C.); *Bishop v. Stevens* (1985), 4 C.P.R. (3d) 349 (Fed. T.D.), reversed (1987), (sub nom. *Bishop v. Télé-Métropole Inc.*) 80 N.R. 302 (Fed. C.A.), affirmed [1990] 2 S.C.R. 467 (S.C.C.).

[861] *Circle Film Enterprises Inc. v. Canadian Broadcasting Corp.*, [1959] S.C.R. 602 (S.C.C.); *Blue Crest Music Inc. v. Canusa Records Inc.* (1974), 17 C.P.R. (2d) 149 (Fed. T.D.), affirmed (1976), 30 C.P.R. (2d) 11 (Fed. C.A.), reversed on other grounds *Compo Co. v. Blue Crest Music Inc.* (1976), 30 C.P.R. (2d) 14 (Fed. C.A.), affirmed *Compo Co. v. Blue Crest Music Inc.* (1979), [1980] 1 S.C.R. 357 (S.C.C.).

[862] *Grignon v. Roussel* (1991), 38 C.P.R. (3d) 4 (Fed. T.D.).

[863] *Samsonite Canada Inc. v. Costco Wholesale Corp.* (1993), 48 C.P.R. (3d) 5 (Fed. T.D.); *Samsonite Canada Inc. v. Costco Wholesale Corp.* (1995), 61 C.P.R. (3d) 293 (Fed. T.D.); *Glaxo Canada Inc. v. Apotex Inc.* (1994), 58 C.P.R. (3d) 1 (Fed. T.D.), reversed on appeal (1995), 64 C.P.R. (3d) 191 (Fed. C.A.).

defendant shall be deemed to have had reasonable grounds for suspecting that copyright subsisted in the work.[864] Copyright must be registered at the time of the alleged infringement.[865]

Any grant of an interest in copyright either by assignment or licence will be void against a subsequent assignee or licensee for valuable consideration, unless the prior assignment or licence is registered.[866]

In the absence of a registration the presumptions set in the Act relating to ownership of copyright will apply.[867] A certificate of registration will prevail over the presumption that the author is the owner of copyright unless there is evidence to contradict the certificate.[868]

b) Marking

Using a copyright notice is permissive. However, if copies of the work published with the authority of the author or copyright owner bear the copyright symbol © accompanied by the name of the copyright owner and the year of first publication placed in such manner and location as to give reasonable notice of claim of copyright, there will be two advantageous results. First, such a notice will likely be sufficient to avoid a defence under section 39 of the Act. Second, if in any proceedings for infringement of copyright, the defendant puts in issue the existence of copyright or the plaintiff's title thereto and no assignment or licence granting an interest in the copyright has been registered, the person whose name is printed or indicated on the work in the usual manner shall, unless the contrary is proved, be presumed to be the owner of the copyright in question.[869]

7. TERM OF PROTECTION

Section 6 of the Act provides that the term for which copyright shall subsist, except as otherwise expressly provided in the Act, is the life of the

---

[864] Section 39; *Gribble v. Manitoba Free Press Co.*, [1931] 3 W.W.R. 570 (Man. C.A.); *Canadian Performing Right Society Ltd. v. Ford Hotel*, [1935] 2 D.L.R. 391 (Que. S.C.).

[865] *MCA Canada Ltd. (Ltée) v. Gillberry & Hawke Advertising Agency Ltd.* (1976), 28 C.P.R. (2d) 52 (Fed. T.D.).

[866] Subsection 57(3) and see *Kelley Estate v. Roy* (2002), (sub nom. *Winkler v. Roy*) 21 C.P.R. (4th) 539 (Fed. T.D.).

[867] Subsection 34(4).

[868] *Circle Film Enterprises Inc. v. Canadian Broadcasting Corp.* (1959), 31 C.P.R. 57 (S.C.C.); *Glaxo Canada Inc. v. Apotex Inc.* (1994), 58 C.P.R. (3d) 1 (Fed. T.D.), reversed on appeal (1995), 64 C.P.R. (3d) 191 (Fed. C.A.).

[869] Subsection 34.1 (2)(b).

author, the remainder of the calendar year in which the author dies, and a period of fifty years following the end of that calendar year. The Act contains exceptions from the general term of protection for works of joint authorship and photographs.

The Act provides that a "work of joint authorship" means a work produced by the collaboration of two or more authors in which the contribution of one author is not distinct from the contribution of the other author or authors.[870] Except as provided in section 6.2,[871] copyright shall subsist during the life of the author who dies last, for the remainder of the calendar year of that author's death, and for a period of fifty years following the end of that calendar year. References in the Act to the period after the expiration of any specified number of years from the end of the calendar year of the death of the author are construed as references to the period after the expiration of the like number of years from the end of the calendar year of the death of the author who dies last.[872]

The Act provides that "photograph" includes photo-lithograph and any work expressed by any process analogous to photography.[873] Where the owner of the copyright in the photograph is a corporation, the term for which copyright subsists is the remainder of the year of the making of the initial negative or plate from which the photograph was derived or, if there is no negative or plate, of the initial photograph, plus a period of fifty years.[874] Where the owner is an individual, the term for which copyright subsists is that set out in section 6: the life of the author, the remainder of the calendar year in which the author dies, and a period of fifty years following the end of that calendar year. Where the owner is a corporation, the majority of the voting shares of which are owned by a natural person who would have qualified as the author of the photograph, except for the deeming provisions of subsection 10(2) of the Act the term of copyright is the term set out in section 6.

8. OWNERSHIP

a) The General Principle

Subsection 13(1) provides that, subject to the Act, the author of a work shall be the first owner of the copyright in the work. The owner of the

---

[870] Section 2.
[871] Section 6.2 applies where the identity of all the authors of a work of joint authorship is unknown.
[872] Section 9.
[873] Section 2.
[874] Subsection 10(1).

copyright of a work is entitled to exercise the rights set out in section 3 of the Act, including the right to authorize others to exercise such rights.[875] In addition, the author is entitled to exercise the moral rights associated with the work. There are exceptions to this general principle of ownership for engravings, photographs or portraits[876] and works made in the course of employment.[877]

b) The Author

The Act does not define the term "author", but generally the author of a work is the person who actually creates it. In most cases it will be readily apparent who the author of a work is, but there are some situations which are unclear. In these situations it must be determined who has exercised the skill and judgment resulting in the expression of the work in material form.[878]

In the case of *Commercial Signs v. General Motors Products of Canada Ltd.*,[879] the defendants wished to use designs consisting of four stars in advertisements. One of its employees had made five pencil sketches of the designs. He gave them to the co-defendant, Adams, and requested that he submit sketches drawn to scale, following the pencil drawings, using specified lettering and colours together with a quotation of prices for a supply of the advertisements. It was held that Adams was not the author of the sketches as no artistic skill was displayed in the preparation of the sketches, but merely the mechanical task of putting them in a specific form.

Apart from the provisions of section 10 relating to photographs, a corporation will not likely be an author, although it may be the owner of copyright.

c) Computer Generated Works

Ascertaining who the author is may be difficult in cases concerning works that have been generated by a programmed computer. There are

---

[875] Section 3; and see *Underwriters' Survey Bureau Ltd. v. Massie & Renwick Ltd.*, [1938] Ex. C.R. 103, [1938] 2 D.L.R. 31 (Can. Ex. Ct.), varied (1940), [1940] 1 D.L.R. 625 (S.C.C.), special leave to appeal refused [1940] S.C.R. 219 (note) (S.C.C.).

[876] Subsection 13(2).

[877] Subsection 13(3).

[878] *New Brunswick Telephone Co. v. John Maryon International Ltd.* (1982), 141 D.L.R. (3d) 193 (N.B. C.A.), leave to appeal refused (1982), 46 N.R. 262 (S.C.C.).

[879] [1937] O.W.N. 58, [1937] 2 D.L.R. 310 (Ont. H.C.), affirmed [1937] 2 D.L.R. 800 (Ont. C.A.).

many situations where such technology is used to generate works which would otherwise be protected by copyright. To date no Canadian case has considered this problem.

In the case of *Express Newspapers PLC v. Liverpool Daily Post & Echo PLC*,[880] ownership of copyright in grids and letter sequences generated by a computer program were considered. The grids were used in connection with a promotional contest which allowed customers to attempt to match cards distributed to them with grids published in the plaintiff's newspaper. On a motion for an interlocutory injunction, it was found that the computer was no more than a tool by which the varying grids were produced. The computer program was similar to a pen used by an author to write a work.

d) Compilations

The individual who selects and arranges the material which makes up a compilation is its author.[881] As with literary or artistic works, it must be determined who exercised the skill and judgment resulting in the expression of the work in material form.

In the case of contributions to compilations, the contributions by themselves may also be protected by copyright. The requirements of the Act relating to authorship, originality and fixation, among others, must be satisfied for each contribution. Each case will turn on its own facts.

e) Photographs

Subsection 10(2) of the Act provides that the person who was the owner of the initial negative or other plate[882] at the time when that negative or other plate was made, or was the owner of the initial photograph at the time when that photograph was made, where there was no negative or other plate, is deemed to be the author of the photograph. The individual who takes the photograph is not necessarily the author and the owner of copyright in the photograph.

Where the owner of the initial negative or plate is a corporation, the corporation is deemed, for the purposes of the Act, to be ordinarily resident in a treaty country[883] if it has established a place of business therein.

---

[880] [1985] 3 All E.R. 680 (Ch. Div.).

[881] See *Waterlow Publishers Ltd. v. Rose*, [1995] F.S.R. 207 (U.K. C.A.).

[882] "Plate" is defined in section 2 to include any stereotype or other plate, stone, block, mould, matrix, transfer or negative used or intended to be used for printing or reproducing copies of any work.

[883] Section 2 and see **part 3(a) of this chapter**.

Subsection 13(2) provides that in the case of an engraving, photograph or portrait, if the plate or other original was ordered by a person other than the creator of the work and was made for valuable consideration, and the consideration was paid, in pursuance of that order, in the absence of any agreement to the contrary, the person placing the order is the first owner of the copyright.

While subsection 10(2) is applied to determine who the author is of the photograph, subsection 13(2), when applicable, overrides the provisions of subsection 13(1) and determines who is the first owner of copyright. It is an exception to the general rule that the author is the first owner of copyright.[884]

In order for subsection 13(2) to apply it must be shown that:

(a)   the plate, which is defined to include a negative, or other original was ordered by some other person;

(b)   the order was made for valuable consideration;

(c)   the consideration was paid;

(d)   the plate or other original was made in pursuance of the order;[885] and

(e)   there is no agreement to the contrary.

The application of this subsection can be less than clear. The requirement to show that the photograph was made pursuant to an order can be a problem, as there is no requirement that the order be in writing. There are uncertainties concerning the requirement that the order was made for valuable consideration; for example, the courts have implied an obligation to pay for services rendered or accepted nominal consideration depending on the facts of the case. Finally, the custom or practice in a specific industry may be sufficient to constitute an agreement to the contrary.

A photographer may use a standard form of contract to avoid the application of the subsection. In the case of *Christopher Bede Studios Ltd. v. United Portraits Ltd.*,[886] the plaintiff was in the business of selling photographs taken at customers' homes. Each customer signed a contract which provided that copyright in all photographs taken or supplied would be owned by the plaintiff. When the proofs were sent to customers, an endorsement

---

[884] *Christopher Bede Studios Ltd. v. United Portraits Ltd.*, [1958] N.Z.L.R. 250 (New Zealand S.C.).

[885] *Toronto Carton Co. v. Manchester McGregor Ltd.*, [1935] O.R. 144, [1935] O.W.N. 105, [1935] 2 D.L.R. 94 (Ont. H.C.).

[886] [1958] N.Z.L.R. 250 (New Zealand S.C.) and see *Pro Arts Inc. v. Campus Crafts Holdings Ltd.* (1980), 50 C.P.R. (2d) 230 (Ont. H.C.).

on the back of each proof stated that, although the proof was the customer's property, only the studio had the right to reproduce the proof in any form.

In an action brought against another photographer who was reproducing proofs of pictures taken by the plaintiff and left with customers, an injunction was granted restraining the defendant's activities. The Court concluded that the contract between the plaintiff and the customer was an agreement to the contrary sufficient to overcome the subsection.

In the case of *Allen v. Toronto Star Newspapers Ltd.*,[887] the Court found an agreement to the contrary as a result of the practice or custom in the trade. A freelance photographer was commissioned by a magazine to take a photograph of a politician. The photograph was used for the front cover of an issue of the magazine and the photographer was paid for his work. Later, the defendant newspaper reproduced the cover of the magazine, without obtaining the photographer's consent. The photographer testified that he had been requested to take the photograph and had received a negotiated fee plus disbursements. According to the practice or custom in the trade, after completing his work the photographs and negatives were returned to him. There was no written agreement with the magazine and no specific discussion took place as to who owned the photograph. The evidence of both the plaintiff and the defendant confirmed the custom or practice in the industry was that if the photograph was to be used again, an additional fee would be paid to the photographer. Based on this evidence, it was concluded that the photographer was the owner of the copyright in the photograph.

As with other works, where a photograph was taken and the author was in the employment of some person under a contract of service or apprenticeship and the work was made in the course of such employment by that person, the person who employed the author is, in the absence of an agreement to the contrary, the first owner of the copyright.[888]

In the case of *Global Upholstery Co. v. Galaxy Office Furniture Ltd.*,[889] the plaintiff had contracted with a photographer, but it was unclear which individuals had actually taken the photographs. At the trial, the defendant submitted that the plaintiff had to prove that the agreement relating to the photographs was made with the individuals who had actually taken them. The Court disagreed, as it would be contrary to the normal course of business if the person ordering the photograph, in order to obtain the ownership in the copyright, had to make an agreement concerning it with someone in the

---

[887] (1995), 63 C.P.R. (3d) 517 (Ont. Gen. Div.), reversed on appeal on other grounds (1997), 36 O.R. (3d) 201 (Ont. Div. Ct.).
[888] Subsection 13(3).
[889] (1976), 29 C.P.R. (2d) 145 (Fed. T.D.).

service of the firm the order had been placed with. It was sufficient to contract with the owner of the copyright.

f) Engravings

"Engravings" are defined by the Act[890] as including "etchings, lithographs, woodcuts, prints and other similar works, not being photographs". The provisions of subsection 13(2) apply to such works, and principles set out above will apply to engravings in the same manner as they apply to photographs.

In the case of *Con Planck Ltd. v. Kolynos Inc.*,[891] the plaintiffs claimed to be the owner of the copyright in two sketches. The sketches were shown to the defendants, who suggested that the colours be changed and then ordered a quantity of them to be reproduced lithographically for advertisements at a price that gave the plaintiffs a considerable profit. When the defendants ordered further quantities from another source, an action for infringement of copyright was brought but successfully defended. An engraving had been ordered by the defendants and was made for valuable consideration pursuant to the order without any agreement to the contrary. The defendants who ordered the original engraving were the first owners of the copyright relating to it.[892]

In order to fall within the subsection, the plate or other original of the engraving, photograph or portrait must have been made for valuable consideration, which consideration was paid in pursuance of the order of some other person. If the plate or other original of such works was made in the hope that the maker could sell them, the works do not fall within the terms of the subsection.[893]

g) Sketches and Drawings

The application of subsection 13(2) is limited to "an engraving, photograph or portrait". It does not extend to other artistic works such as sketches and drawings from which no engraving has been made, even

---

[890] Section 2.

[891] [1925] 2 K.B. 804 (Eng. K.B.).

[892] See also *Nicol v. Barranger*, [1921] Macg. Cop. Cas. 219; *Banco de Portugal v. Waterlow & Sons Ltd.*, [1932] A.C. 452 (U.K. H.L.), in which it was held that a bank note was an engraving, the copyright therein belonging to the bank at whose order the design was executed.

[893] *Toronto Carton Co. v. Manchester McGregor Ltd.*, [1935] O.R. 144, [1935] O.W.N. 105, [1935] 2 D.L.R. 94 (Ont. H.C.).

though the sketch may have been intended to be used as the original for an engraving but was not used for this purpose.[894]

In the case of *Cselko Associates Inc. v. Zellers Inc.*,[895] a judge relied on the custom of the trade relating to drawings to avoid an unexpected result from the point of view of Zellers. In this case, Zellers contracted with a third party to obtain drawings for advertising purposes. The plaintiff knew that the illustrations which had been commissioned were going to be used by Zellers for advertising purposes and no limitation on their use was ever discussed. The plaintiff was paid for the services which had been provided. When the plaintiff discovered that reproductions of the drawings were being sold separately in frames, an action was brought for copyright infringement. On a motion for summary judgment, it was shown that the practice in the trade was that a commercial artist assigns all rights in the work to the customer and that this was so widely known that a written assignment was rarely executed. The plaintiff's claim was dismissed on the basis of an implied licence to use the work arising from the conduct of the parties which did not need to be in writing.

h) Contracts of Service

Subsection 13(3) provides that where the author of a work was in the employment of some other person under a contract of service or apprenticeship and the work was made in the course of employment by that person, the person by whom the author was employed shall, in the absence of any agreement to the contrary, be the first owner of the copyright.

The author's employment will have a definite effect on the first ownership of copyright. While subsection 13(1) is presumably still applicable to determine who the author of a work is, subsection 13(3), when applicable, overrides the provisions of subsection 13(1) and determines who the first owner is of copyright. It is an exception to the general rule that the author is the first owner of copyright.

In order for the subsection to apply:

(a) the author of the work must be in the employment of some other person under a contract of service or apprenticeship;

(b) the work must be made in the course of employment by that person; and

(c) there must be the "absence of any agreement to the contrary."

---

[894] *Toronto Carton Co. v. Manchester McGregor Ltd.*, [1935] O.R. 144, [1935] O.W.N. 105, [1935] 2 D.L.R. 94 (Ont. H.C.).

[895] (1992), 44 C.P.R. (3d) 56 (Ont. Gen. Div.).

If these conditions are satisfied, the author's employer will be the first owner of copyright in the work without any assignment being necessary.

The contract must be a "contract of service or apprenticeship" and not a "contract for services".[896] In many cases, it will not be difficult to make this determination.[897] Each case will depend upon its own facts[898] and there is no universal test which applies in all cases. However, there are a number of tests which can be of assistance including tests applied in labour or tax cases.[899]

i) The Control Test

A number of older cases emphasized the degree of control exercised by the employer over the individual involved as the determining factor. A contract of service is not the same thing as a contract for service, and the existence of direct control by the employer, the degree of independence on the part of the person providing the services and the place where the service is rendered are all matters to be considered in determining whether there is a contract of service.[900] A contract of service involves the existence of a servant and an obligation to obey the orders of the employer. A servant is a person who is subject to the commands of a master as to the manner in which the servant does the work that is required.[901]

In *Massie & Renwick v. Underwriters' Survey Bureau Ltd. et al.*,[902] the ownership of insurance plans and revisions made by salaried employees, under a prescribed work method, was in issue. It was concluded the persons

---

[896] *Harold Drabble Ltd. v. Hycolite Manufacturing Co.* (1928), 44 T.L.R. 264 (Eng. Ch. Div.).

[897] For example, an agreement to write a work is a contract "for services" and not a contract "of service", see *Ward, Lock & Co. Ltd. v. Long*, [1906] 2 Ch. 550.

[898] *Simmons v. Heath Laundry Co.*, [1910] 1 K.B. 543 (Eng. C.A.).

[899] *Marotta v. R.*, [1986] 2 F.C. 221 (Fed. T.D.); *Amusements Wiltron Inc. c. Mainville* (1991), 40 C.P.R. (3d) 521 (Que. S.C.).

[900] *Simmons v. Heath Laundry Co.*, [1910] 1 K.B. 543 (Eng. C.A.); see also *Leicestershire County Council v. Michael Faraday & Partners Ltd.*, [1941] 2 All E.R. 483 (Eng. C.A.); *Cassidy v. Ministry of Health*, [1951] 2 K.B. 343 (Eng. K.B.); *Stephenson, Jordan & Harrison Ltd. v. MacDonald & Evans*, [1952] 1 T.L.R. 101, 69 R.P.C. 10 (Eng. C.A.).

[901] See also *Evans v. Liverpool*, [1906] 1 K.B. 160 (Eng. K.B.); *Beeton & Co., Re*, [1913] 2 Ch. 279 (U.K.); *Park v. Wilsons & Clyde Coal Co. Ltd.*, [1928] Sess. Cas. 121; *National Federation of Sub-Postmasters v. Minister of Health* (1939), 161 L.T. 337; *Short v. Henderson Ltd.* (1946), 39 B.W.C.C. 62 (Scotland H.L.).

[902] *Underwriters' Survey Bureau Ltd. v. Massie & Renwick Ltd.*, [1940] S.C.R. 218, [1940] 1 D.L.R. 625 (S.C.C.), special leave to appeal refused [1940] S.C.R. 219 (note) (S.C.C.).

involved in the actual production of a plan could not in the ordinary course be fairly described as independent contractors and this was sufficient evidence to support the inference that they were performing services under contracts of service.[903]

The control test is helpful in situations where the activities in issue are closely prescribed. The more control, the more likely a contract of service;[904] however, where professional or other highly skilled individuals are involved, the control test may be less appropriate.

ii) The Organization or Integration Test

The integration test is predicated on the fact that, under a contract of service, an individual is employed as part of a business and their work is done as an integral part of the business. Under a contract for services, the work, although done for the business, is not integrated into it, but is only an accessory to it.[905]

This integration test has also been described somewhat differently as follows:[906]

> Is the person who has engaged himself to perform these services performing as a person in business on his own account? If the answer to that question is "yes" the contract is a contract for services. If the answer is "no" then the contract is a contract of service.[907]

iii) The Economic Reality Test

Under the "economic reality" test, the focus of the inquiry is a determination of whether the individual involved is carrying on the business alone or on his or her own behalf and not merely for a superior. In this regard a fourfold test consisting of a complex made up of (a) control; (b) ownership of tools; (c) chance of profit; and (d) risk of loss is applied.

---

[903] See also *Ware v. Anglo-Italian Commercial Agency*, [1922] Macg. Cop. Cas. 346; *Harold Drabble Ltd. v. Hycolite Manufacturing Co.* (1928), 44 T.L.R. 264 (Eng. Ch. Div.); *Massine v. De Basil* (1938), 82 Sol. Jo. 173.

[904] *Simmons v. Heath Laundry Co.*, [1910] 1 K.B. 543 (Eng. C.A.).

[905] *Stephenson, Jordan & Harrison Ltd. v. MacDonald & Evans* (1952), 69 R.P.C. 10; *Gould v. Minister of National Insurance*, [1951] 1 All E.R. 368 (Eng. K.B.).

[906] *Market Investigations v. Minister of Social Security* (1968), [1969] 2 Q.B. 173 (Eng. Q.B.).

[907] *Market Investigations v. Minister of Social Security* (1968), [1969] 2 Q.B. 173 (Eng. Q.B.); *Belof v. Pressdome*, [1973] 1 All. E.R. 241 (U.K.).

Control in itself is not always conclusive. The whole of the various elements which make up the relationship must be considered.[908]

iv) The Work Must be Made in the Course of Employment

In order for subsection 13(3) to apply, the work must have been made by the author in the course of the employment. For example, a person permanently employed on the editorial staff of a newspaper was directed to translate and summarize a speech. He did the work in his own time and separately from his ordinary duties, and it was held that in doing so he did not act under a contract of service.[909]

A director of a company, in the absence of a specific contract of service, may not come within the subsection. For example, in one case, an action was brought alleging infringement of drawings relating to furniture. The defendants successfully objected to the claims relating to drawings which had been made by the plaintiff's managing director, since it was not shown that such drawings were made under a contract of service and there had been no assignment.[910]

v) Absence of Agreement to the Contrary

In order for the subsection to apply there must be an "absence of any agreement to the contrary". There is nothing in the Act to prevent parties from contracting out of some its provisions.[911] Such an agreement need not be in writing to be enforceable[912] and an implied term of a contract may be sufficient.[913]

---

[908] *Montreal (City) v. Montreal Locomotive Works Ltd.* (1946), [1947] 1 D.L.R. 161 (Canada P.C.).

[909] *Bryne v. Statist Co.*, [1914] 1 K.B. 622 (Eng. K.B.); *Stephenson, Jordan & Harrison Ltd. v. MacDonald & Evans* (1952), 69 R.P.C. 10 (Eng. C.A.); *Noah v. Shuba*, [1991] F.S.R. 14 (Ch. Div.); *Noah v. Shuba*, [1991] F.S.R. 14 (Ch. Div.).

[910] *Antocks Lairn Ltd. v. I. Bloohn Ltd.*, [1972] R.P.C. 219 (Ch. Div.).

[911] *Harold Drabble Ltd. v. Hycolite Manufacturing Co.* (1928), 44 T.L.R. 264 (Eng. Ch. Div.).

[912] *Canavest House Ltd. v. Lett* (1984), 2 C.P.R. (3d) 386 (Ont. H.C.).

[913] *Noah v. Shuba*, [1991] F.S.R. 14 (Ch. Div.).

9. MORAL RIGHTS

Subsection 14.1(1) of the Act provides that the author of a work has, subject to section 28.2, the right to the integrity of the work and, in connection with an act mentioned in section 3, the right where reasonable in the circumstances, to be associated with the work, as its author by name or under a pseudonym, and the right to remain anonymous.

The right of integrity is made available to the author of a work subject to section 28.2. Section 28.2 provides the author's right to the integrity of a work is infringed only if the work is, to the prejudice of the honour or reputation of the author:

(a)   distorted, mutilated or otherwise modified; or

(b)   used in association with a product, service, cause or institution.

The scope of the right of integrity is controlled by the requirement that an author alleging infringement of the right must show prejudice to his or her honour or reputation. The assessment of whether a distortion, mutilation or other modification is prejudicial to an author's honour or reputation requires an objective evaluation of the prejudice based on public or expert opinion.[914]

Under the Act, moral rights may not be assigned, but may be waived in whole or in part.[915] An assignment of copyright in a work does not by that act alone constitute a waiver of any moral rights.[916]

The right to the integrity of the work and the right to be associated with the work or to remain anonymous can be waived either separately or simultaneously. In addition, different rights may be waived in favour of different persons and in association with different uses of the work.

The Act does not prescribe the form of a waiver and presumably, a waiver need not be in writing, but may be verbal and could presumably be implied. However, it is prudent to obtain a written waiver.

---

[914] *Prise de parole Inc. v. Guérin, éditeur Ltée* (1995), 66 C.P.R. (3d) 257 (Fed. T.D.), affirmed (1996), 73 C.P.R. (3d) 557 (Fed. C.A.).

[915] Subsection 14.1(2).

[916] Subsection 14.1(3).

10. ASSIGNMENT

a) The Statutory Provisions

Subsection 13(4) provides that:

> The owner of the copyright in any work may assign the right, either wholly or partially, and either generally or subject to limitations relating to territory, medium or sector of the market or other limitations relating to the scope of the assignment, and either for the whole term of the copyright or for any other part thereof, and may grant any interest in the right by licence, but no assignment or grant is valid unless it is in writing signed by the owner of the right in respect of which the assignment or grant is made, or by the owner's duly authorized agent.

The Act also makes it clear that a right of action for infringement of copyright may be assigned and that a grant of an exclusive licence constitutes the grant of an interest in the copyright by licence. Subsections 13(6) and (7) of the Act are as follows:

> (6) For greater certainty, it is deemed always to have been the law that a right of action for infringement of copyright may be assigned in association with the assignment of the copyright or the grant of an interest in the copyright by licence.
> (7) For greater certainty, it is deemed always to have been the law that a grant of an exclusive licence in a copyright constitutes the grant of an interest in the copyright by licence.

b) Must Be In Writing

An assignment or grant of an interest in a copyright must be in writing, signed by the owner of the right in respect of which the assignment or grant is made or by the owner's duly authorized agent. An assignment of copyright in a work does not by that act alone constitute a waiver of moral rights.[917]

The requirement that an assignment be in writing and signed by the owner or by the owner's duly authorized agent has been generally interpreted by the courts in Canada as a substantive rule of law, not just a rule of evidence.[918] An assignment which does not comply will not be enforce-

---

[917] Subsection 14.1(3).
[918] *Motel 6 Inc. v. No. 6 Motel Ltd.* (1981), 56 C.P.R. (2d) 44 (Fed. T.D.); *Guillemette c. Centre coopératif de Loisirs & de Sports du Mont Orignal* (1986), 15 C.P.R. (3d) 409 (Fed. T.D.); *Jeffrey Rogers Knitwear Productions Ltd. v. R.D. International Style Collections Ltd.* (1986), 19 C.P.R. (3d) 217 (Fed. T.D.).

able. However, evidence of the existence of a written assignment may be made by way of oral testimony and without producing the actual written assignment.[919]

A mark or a facsimile of a signature is acceptable if there is evidence to prove that it is the customary method of identification of the person involved. This element gives the facsimile the authenticity needed.[920]

While English cases have given effect to equitable assignments which were not in writing, it is unlikely that a Canadian court would give effect under the Act to an equitable assignment in light of the statutory limitations.[921] Subsection 13(4) provides that an assignment of copyright must be in writing; section 89 provides that no person is entitled to copyright or any similar right in any work otherwise than under and in accordance with the Act.[922]

Even if an assignment is not in writing as required by the Act, the "owner" of a work made pursuant to either an oral contract or one that can be implied from the conduct of the parties may be precluded from exercising their statutory rights as against the other party to the contract.[923]

c) Subject Matter

Copyright consists of the sole right to exercise, and to restrain others from exercising, specific statutory rights relating to protected works. The owner of the copyright in the work may assign these rights, either wholly or partially, and either generally or subject to limitations relating to territory, medium or sector of the market or other limitations relating to the scope of the assignment, and either for the whole term of the copyright or for any other part thereof.

The ownership of copyright is independent from the ownership or the physical possession of the physical object protected by copyright. Copyright is an intangible set of statutory rights separate from any material object such as a manuscript or plate used for printing. The copyright owner has the

---

[919] *Motel 6 Inc. v. No. 6 Motel Ltd.* (1981), 56 C.P.R. (2d) 44 (Fed. T.D.).

[920] *Milliken & Co. v. Interface Flooring Systems (Canada) Inc.*, [1998] 3 F.C. 103, 83 C.P.R. (3d) 470 (Fed. T.D.), affirmed (2000), 5 C.P.R. (4th) 209 (Fed. C.A.).

[921] A claim could be made for breach of trust in appropriate circumstances and see *Downing v. General Synod of Church of England in Canada*, [1943] O.R. 652 (Ont. C.A.).

[922] *Downing v. General Synod of Church of England in Canada*, [1943] O.R. 652 (Ont. C.A.).

[923] *Cselko Associates Inc. v. Zellers Inc.* (1992), 44 C.P.R. (3d) 56 (Ont. Gen. Div.); *Robert D. Sutherland Architects Ltd. v. Montykola Investments Inc.* (1996), 150 N.S.R. (2d) 281 (N.S. C.A.).

exclusive right to deal with these rights. The person in possession of the object has no interest in the copyright unless obtained by written assignment. For example, the delivery of a letter to the addressee may transfer ownership in the paper the letter is written on, but does not affect the ownership of copyright in the letter.

Subsection 14(1) contains a limitation on the right of the author if the author is the first owner of the copyright to make an assignment or grant an interest in copyright. Such an assignment, except in relation to collective works, otherwise than by will, does not operate to vest in the assignee any rights in the copyright for more than twenty-five years after the author's death and the reversionary interest, notwithstanding any agreement to the contrary, devolves on the author's legal representatives as part of the author's estate.

An author of a work is not the first owner of the copyright where

(a)   the author was in the employment of some other person under a contract of service or apprenticeship, and the work was made in the course of employment by that person, in the absence of any agreement to the contrary;[924]

(b)   in the case of an engraving, photograph or portrait, the plate or other original was ordered by some other person and was made for valuable consideration and the consideration was paid in pursuance of that order, in the absence of any agreement to the contrary.[925]

11. INFRINGEMENT

a) Direct Infringement

The Act deals with two types of infringement. First, the direct infringement of the rights of the copyright owner or author which are defined by reference to the rights conferred on the owner of the copyright[926] or the author in the case of moral rights.[927] The second type of infringement is secondary in nature and is typically directed toward the unauthorized dealing with infringing articles.

---

[924] Subsection 13(3) and see **part 8(h)** of this chapter.

[925] Subsection 13(2) and see **part 8(e)** of this chapter.

[926] *Ash v. Hutchinson & Co. (Publishers)*, [1936] 2 All E.R. 1496 (Eng. C.A.); *Jennings v. Stephens*, [1936] 1 All E.R. 409 (Eng. C.A.).

[927] Section 28.2 specifies what constitutes infringement of the author's right to the integrity of the work.

Subsection 27(1) provides that it is an infringement of copyright for any person to do, without the consent of the owner of the copyright, anything that, according to the Act, only the owner of the copyright has the right to do.

The rights available consist of the sole right to engage in the activities set out in the Act. Copyright is, in essence, a negative right to prevent others from exercising the rights available under the Act.[928] As a result, the question of infringement should be approached by inquiring whether or not the act alleged to be an infringement would, if done by the owner of the copyright, have been an exercise of the rights conferred solely on the owner by the Act.[929]

Each infringement is a separate cause of action.[930] For example, in the case of a literary work the copyright owner is entitled to the sole right to produce or reproduce the work and, if unpublished, to publish the work. If an infringing work is printed and published by different persons, the printer will be liable for infringing the right to reproduce, while the publisher may be liable for infringing the right to publish and also for authorizing the reproduction.[931]

Moral rights are dealt with in a different fashion. Under section 28.1, any act or omission that is contrary to any of the moral rights of the author of a work is, in the absence of consent by the author, an infringement of the moral rights. However, section 28.2 specifies the acts which constitute infringement of the author's right to the integrity of a work.

The Act contains a number of provisions referred to as exceptions which describe activities that do not constitute infringement of copyright.[932]

b) Secondary Infringement

It is an infringement of copyright for any person to

---

[928] *Canadian Admiral Corp. v. Rediffusion Inc.*, [1954] Ex. C.R. 382, 20 C.P.R. 75 (Can. Ex. Ct.); *Corelli v. Gray* (1913), 29 T.L.R. 570 (Eng. Ch. Div.), affirmed (1913), 30 T.L.R. 116 (Eng. C.A.).

[929] *Jennings v. Stephens*, [1936] 1 All E.R. 409 (Eng. C.A.).

[930] *Ash v. Hutchinson & Co. (Publishers)*, [1936] 2 All E.R. 1496 (Eng. C.A.) and see *Compo Co. v. Blue Crest Music Inc.* (1979), [1980] 1 S.C.R. 357 (S.C.C.) and *Bishop v. Stevens*, [1990] 2 S.C.R. 467 (S.C.C.).

[931] See for example *Compo Co. v. Blue Crest Music Inc.* (1979), [1980] 1 S.C.R. 357 (S.C.C.).

[932] Sections 29, 29.1, 29.2, 29.4, 29.5, 29.6, 29.7, 30.1, 30.2, 30.3, 30.6, 30.7, 30.8 and 30.9.

(a)   sell or rent out,[933]
(b)   distribute to such an extent as to affect prejudicially the owner of the copyright,[934]
(c)   by way of trade distribute, expose or offer for sale or rental or exhibit in public,[935] or
(d)   possess for the purpose of doing an activity proscribed in paragraphs (a) through (c) (a "Proscribed Activity"),
(e)   import into Canada for the purpose of doing a Proscribed Activity,

a copy of a work that the person knows or should have known infringes copyright or would infringe copyright if it had been made in Canada by the person who made it.

In determining whether there is an infringement in the case of a Proscribed Activity or possession for the purpose of a Proscribed Activity, in relation to a copy that was imported for the purpose of a Proscribed Activity, it is irrelevant whether the importer knew or should have known that the importation of the copy infringed copyright.[936]

The subsection is unlike subsection 27(1) in that it must be shown that the alleged infringer has engaged in a Proscribed Activity or possession for the purpose of carrying out a Proscribed Activity, which the person knows or should have known infringes copyright or would infringe copyright if it had been made in Canada by the person who made it. This is an essential element of the cause of action for infringement under subsection 27(2).

It is possible that imported copies of a work may have been lawfully made outside of Canada, but they may be infringing if imported into Canada under the subsection.

12. SUMMARY AND CHECKLIST

To ensure that product packaging is protected, the following matters should be considered.

1.   While it is possible to register the label or package design as a trade mark, there may be practical problems with this approach. However, if the product packaging will be in place without change for a reasonable period of time it may be protected by a trade mark registration.

---

[933] Subsection 27(2)(a).
[934] Subsection 27(2)(b).
[935] Subsection 27(2)(c).
[936] Subsection 27(2).

2. The expression of brand image and other information on product packaging may be protected under the *Copyright Act*. Copyright protection in Canada does not depend on registration or other formal steps and subsists automatically without any act beyond the creation of an original literary or artistic work or a compilation in the circumstances set out in the Act. Product packaging may frequently be protected within these categories.

3. Under the Act, in order to acquire copyright, "connecting factors" or "points of attachment" must be present in relation to the subject matter of the work, either as regards to the nationality of the author or the place of first publication.

4. Copyright subsists only in *original* works. The originality required by the Act relates to the expression of thought in which the work is presented. The requirement for originality means that the work must originate from the author in the sense that it is the result of a substantial degree of skill and judgment.

5. A part of a work by itself may be entitled to copyright while other parts of the work are not. However, the entire work may be entitled to protection as a compilation independently from any copyright which may subsist in the parts.

6. A work which is derived from pre-existing material will be protected by copyright if sufficient skill and judgment have been bestowed on it.

7. Literary works cover a wide field, including all works that are expressed in print or writing irrespective of their literary quality or merit. The sole distinguishing characteristic of a literary work is not its quality as literature or art but simply that it is in print or writing and original.

8. A "compilation" is a work resulting from the selection or arrangement of literary, dramatic, musical or artistic works or parts thereof.

9. Artistic works include paintings, drawings, maps, charts, plans, photographs, engravings, sculptures and works of artistic craftsmanship and compilations of artistic works. A work may be protected as an artistic work without considering its artistic merit or aesthetic value.

10. Copyright in a work includes, among other rights, the sole right:

    (a)   to produce or reproduce the work or any substantial part of it in any material form whatever,

    (b)   if unpublished, to publish the work or any substantial part of it,

    (c)   to produce, reproduce, perform or publish any translation of it,

    and to authorize such acts.

11. Registration is permissive and is unnecessary for the subsistence of copyright. However, the registration of copyright, an assignment of

copyright or a licence granting an interest in a copyright will generally be advantageous to the copyright owner.

12. Using a copyright notice is permissive. However, it is prudent to use the copyright symbol © accompanied by the name of the copyright owner and the year of first publication on product packaging in order to give reasonable notice of claim of copyright to third parties.

13. Generally, the author of a work is the first owner of the copyright in the work, but there are exceptions relating to engravings, photographs, portraits and works made in the course of employment. The owner of the copyright in a work is entitled to exercise the rights relating to the work, including the right to authorize others to exercise such rights. The author is also entitled to exercise the moral rights associated with the work.

14. In the case of an engraving, photograph or portrait, if the work was ordered by a person other than the creator of the work and was made for valuable consideration, and the consideration was paid as required by the order, in the absence of any agreement to the contrary, the person placing the order is the first owner of the copyright. It is open to the creator of the work, such as a photographer, to use a standard form of contract to overcome this result.

15. Where the author of a work was in the employment of some other person under a contract of service or apprenticeship and the work was made in the course of employment by that person, the person by whom the author was employed shall, in the absence of any agreement to the contrary, be the first owner of the copyright. The contract must be a "contract of service or apprenticeship" and not a "contract for services". A written assignment of copyright should be obtained from an independent service provider.

16. Subject to section 28.2, the author of a work has moral rights consisting of the right to the integrity of the work and the right, where reasonable in the circumstances, to be associated with the work, as its author by name or under a pseudonym, and the right to remain anonymous. Section 28.2 provides the author's right to the integrity of a work is infringed only if the work is, to the prejudice of the honour or reputation of the author:

  (a) distorted, mutilated or otherwise modified; or
  (b) used in association with a product, service, cause or institution.

17. Moral rights may not be assigned, but may be waived in whole or in part. An assignment of copyright in a work does not by that act alone constitute a waiver of any moral rights. It is prudent to obtain a written waiver.

18. An assignment or grant of an interest in a copyright must be in writing, signed by the owner of the right assigned or granted or by the owner's duly authorized agent. An assignment which does not comply with these requirements will not be enforceable.

19. The ownership of copyright is independent from the ownership or the physical possession of the physical object protected by copyright. Copyright is an intangible set of statutory rights separate from any material object, such as a manuscript or plate used for printing. The copyright owner has the exclusive right to deal with these rights. The person in possession of the object has no interest in the copyright unless obtained by written assignment.

20. The *Copyright Act* deals with two types of infringement. First, the direct infringement of the rights of the copyright owner or author, which are defined by reference to the rights conferred on the owner of the copyright or the author in the case of moral rights. The second type of infringement is secondary in nature and is typically directed toward the unauthorized dealing with infringing articles.

Chapter 8: Protecting Brand Advertising

1. INTRODUCTION

The term "brand execution" is used to refer to the communication of brand image to customers. As previously discussed, brand image is made up of the consumer perception of brand attributes and associations from which consumers derive symbolic value.[937] Once established, the brand image defines the meaning customers associate with the brand or what the brand stands for.

Brand execution is the total experience created by the brand owner. It begins with the way the telephone is answered and includes how products and services are delivered, quality and service philosophies, sales procedures, communications and value.

A brand association is anything that is linked in a consumer's memory with a brand, for example, McDonald's is linked to the cartoon character Ronald McDonald. A link to a brand is stronger when it is based on many experiences or exposures rather than a few. A brand image is a set of associations organized in a meaningful way. A brand is positioned by emphasizing strong associations.[938]

From the consumer's point of view the brand must deliver the image and the values it symbolizes. The brand is the brand owner's promise to consistently deliver the components which make it up. The promise operates at different levels which vary from product to product. For items which are commodities, tangible attributes and price may be more important but for products driven by image the emphasis is on the intangible.

The terms "brand position" or "brand positioning" are used to mean the message that a brand owner wishes to imprint in the minds of customers

---

[937] M. Patterson, "Re-appraising the Concept of Brand Image", (1999) Volume 6, No. 6 *The Journal of Brand Management* at 409 –26.

[938] David Aaker, *Managing Brand Equity, Capitalizing on the Value of Brand Name*, (New York: The Free Press, 1991) at 109.

about its brand and how it differs from and offers something better than its competitors. Frequently, this is accomplished through advertising consisting of a motivating, persuasively communicated message that provides targeted prospects with a reason why they should consider and remember the advertised product as being able to deliver the brand owner's promise.

Advertising is an integral part of brand execution. It is important to understand how advertising can be protected and the legal rules applicable to it.

2. TRADE MARK PROTECTION

a) Slogans and Taglines

While advertising as a whole will not be protected under the *Trademarks Act,* slogans, sometimes referred to as taglines, may be. A slogan is a group of words or a phrase used to encourage consumers to purchase goods or services. A slogan may be used for the purpose of distinguishing the wares or services of the brand owner from those of others and function as a trade mark. In other cases the slogan will simply be part of the advertising used by the brand owner. Examples of well known slogans are Nike's "Just Do It" and General Electric's "GE Brings Good Things To Life".

If a slogan functions as a trade mark, consideration should be given to obtaining a trade mark registration.[939] In this regard, the slogan must be registrable,[940] distinguish the brand owner's wares or services from the wares and services of others and be "used" within the meaning of the *Trademarks Act.*[941] The filing of a trade mark application and obtaining a registration will serve to protect the slogan. However, to the extent that a slogan is made up of common words or is descriptive, the scope of its protection may be somewhat limited.[942]

---

[939] See **Chapter 2, part 9**, and see *General Mills Canada Ltd. v. Procter & Gamble Inc.* (1985), 6 C.P.R. (3d) 551 (T. M. Opp. Bd.); *Thomas J. Lipton v. HVR Co.* (1995), 64 C.P.R. (3d) 552 (T.M. Opp. Bd.); *Hudson's Bay Co. v. Sears Canada Inc.* (2002), (sub nom. *Governor & Co. v. Sears Canada Inc.*) 26 C.P.R. (4th) 457 (T.M. Opp. Bd.).

[940] *Quaker Oats Co. of Canada/Cie Quaker Oats du Canada v. Ralston Purina Canada Inc.* (1987), 18 C.P.R. (3d) 108 (T.M. Opp. Bd.); *Westfair Foods Ltd. v. Jim Pattison Industries Ltd.* (1989), 26 C.P.R. (3d) 28 (B.C. S.C.), affirmed (1990), 30 C.P.R. (3d) 174 (B.C. C.A.); *Wal-Mart Stores Inc. v. Tough Stuff Distributors Inc.* (1999), 1 C.P.R. (4th) 271 (T.M. Opp. Bd.).

[941] *Sports & Entertainment Inc. v. SkyDome Corp.* (2002), 28 C.P.R. (4th) 240 (T.M. Opp. Bd.).

[942] See **Chapter 5, part 2(b)**.

Interested third parties may use parodies of slogans to direct criticism at brand owners.[943] The courts have been reluctant to find that a parody of a trade mark constitutes trade mark infringement, since typically there is no trade mark "use" as required by the Act.[944]

3. COPYRIGHT PROTECTION

a) Ownership

The principles relating to the ownership of copyright have been previously discussed.[945] In order to ensure that brand advertising can be protected, the brand owner should own the copyright in the advertising material that is prepared at its request. Where the author of the work was in the employment of the brand owner under a contract of service or apprenticeship and the work was made in the course of employment by that person, the brand owner will be the copyright owner in the absence of the agreement to the contrary.[946] In addition, since the author of the work will be entitled to moral rights, notwithstanding their status as an employee, a waiver of moral rights should be obtained by the brand owner.

Individuals who are the authors of advertising copy but who are not employed by the brand owner will be the author and first owner of the copyright unless they were acting in the course of their employment with an advertising agency or the like, in which case their employer will own the copyright in the work. In light of this a written assignment of copyright in the relevant work should be obtained from any advertising agencies, photographers or other individuals involved in the preparation of advertising materials.[947] In addition, waivers of moral rights should be obtained from the individual authors.

---

[943] See **part 3(b) of this chapter and Chapter 3, part 4(b)**.

[944] *Cie générale des établissements Michelin - Michelin & Cie v. CAW-Canada* (1996), (sub nom. *Cie Générale des Établissements Michelin-Michelin & Cie v. C.A.W. -Canada*) 71 C.P.R. (3d) 348 (Fed. T.D.) and see *Pro-C Ltd. v. Computer City In*c. (2001), 55 O.R. (3d) 577 (Eng.) (Ont. C.A.) concerning use in general.

[945] See **Chapter 7, part 8**.

[946] *Copyright Act*, R.S.C. 1985, c. C-42, subsection 13(3).

[947] See **Chapter 7, Part 10** which summarizes the legal requirements relating to assignments of copyright.

b) Parodies

Traditionally, parody in a literary context consists of a composition in which the characteristic style of an author is mimicked and made to appear ridiculous, especially by applying such a style to inappropriate subjects.[948] More recently there have been a number of cases where parody web sites or sites for critical commentary have been directed at a specific business. Frequently a domain name is obtained which consists of the subject of the site's trade mark combined with the word "sucks", but other methods are used.[949]

In the case of *Schweppes Ltd. v. Wellingtons Ltd.*,[950] the plaintiff brought proceedings to enforce the copyright in its label for Indian tonic water. The defendant's label was substantially similar to the plaintiff's, but instead of using the plaintiff's trade mark "Schweppes" the defendant's labels used in the same place the word "Schlurpps". The defendant argued that its labels were a parody of the plaintiff's labels. The trial judge stated that the sole issue to be determined was whether the defendant's work reproduced a substantial part of the plaintiff's copyright work.

A number of Canadian cases have also held that parody or burlesque is not a defence to a claim for copyright infringement.[951] In each case, an assessment must be made as to whether the parody or burlesque reproduces the work in issue or a substantial part of it. A parody or burlesque may also constitute an infringement of the author's moral rights.[952]

4. COMMON LAW RIGHTS — PASSING OFF

The nature of these rights has previously been discussed.[953] A number of cases have found that where a defendant has promoted its product or

---

[948] Leon R. Yankwich, "Parody and Burlesque in the Law of Copyright", (1955) 33 Can. Bar Rev. 1130 at 1130-1.

[949] See **Chapter 3, part 4(b)**.

[950] [1984] 10 S.C.R. 210 (Eng. Ch.) and see *Williamson Music Ltd. v. Pearson Partnership Ltd.,* [1987] F.S.R. 97 (Eng. Ch.).

[951] *Cie générale des établissements Michelin - Michelin & Cie v. CAW-Canada* (1996), (sub nom. *Cie Générale des Établissements Michelin-Michelin & Cie v. C.A.W. -Canada)* 71 C.P.R. (3d) 348 (Fed. T.D.); *Productions Avanti Ciné-Vidéo Inc v. Favreau* (1997), 79 C.P.R. (3d) 385 (Que. S.C.), reversed (1999), 1999 CarswellQue 2742 (Que. C.A.), leave to appeal refused (2000), 2000 CarswellQue 946 (S.C.C.); *British Columbia Automobile Assn. v. O.P.E.I.U., Local 378* (2001), 10 C.P.R. (4th) 423 (B.C. S.C.).

[952] See **Chapter 7, part 9**.

[953] See **Chapter 5, part 5**.

business in such a way as to create the false impression that its product or business is in some way approved, authorized or endorsed by the plaintiff, or that there is some business connection between the defendant and plaintiff will constitute passing off.[954]

5. MISLEADING ADVERTISING

a) Introduction

From the consumer's point of view, the brand must deliver the image and the values it symbolizes. The brand is the brand owner's promise to consistently deliver its wares or services. A brand owner should not make promises that it cannot keep. If advertising appropriately communicates information relating to the brand, misleading advertising should not be a concern. However, for those cases where mistakes occur, it is helpful to understand the rules concerning misleading advertising. In addition, the rules are useful in assessing the activities of competitors.

b) The Legislative Framework

Generally, advertising law in Canada is governed by the Federal *Competition Act.*[955] The purpose of the Act is to maintain and encourage competition in Canada so as to promote the efficiency and adaptability of the Canadian economy. The provisions of the Act directed at misleading representations aim to improve the quality and accuracy of marketplace information and discourage deceptive marketing practices.

Provisions relating to misleading advertising can also be found in other federal acts, such as those dealing with packaging and labeling[956] and food and drugs.[957] In addition, each of the provinces typically has its own consumer protection and business practices laws.

The misleading advertising provisions of the Act are administered and enforced by the Commissioner of Competition (the "Commissioner")

---

[954] *British Columbia Automobile Assn. v. O.P.E.I.U., Local 378* (2001), 10 C.P.R. (4th) 423 (B.C. S.C.); *National Hockey League v. Pepsi-Cola Canada Ltd.* (1992), 42 C.P.R. (3d) 390 (B.C. S.C.), affirmed (1995), (sub nom. *National Hockey League v. Pepsi-Cola Canada Ltd. (No. 2)*) 59 C.P.R. (3d) 216 (B.C. C.A.), where such a claim was dismissed on the basis the defendant had a legitimate connection.

[955] R.S.C. 1985, c. C-34 as amended.

[956] *Consumer Packaging and Labelling Act*, R.S.C. 1985, c. C-36.

[957] *Food and Drugs Act*, R.S.C. 1985, c. F-27.

through the Competition Bureau ("the Bureau"). The Fair Business Branch is the branch of the Bureau responsible for administering the provisions of the Act directed to false or misleading advertising.

Most inquiries under the Act are initiated by the Bureau on the basis of complaints made by individuals, government employees, businesses or competitors. Complaints by competitors are given more weight. The Bureau publishes guidelines which outline the relevant policies which apply to violations of the Act.

Persons and corporations may also commence a civil action against a wrongdoer pursuant to the statutory civil right of action contained in the *Competition Act*, where that person or corporation has suffered damage as a result of the wrongdoer's breach of the provisions of Part VI of the Act[958] which sets out criminal offences in relation to competition or the failure to comply with an order of the Competition Tribunal (the "Tribunal") or another court under the Act.[959] In any civil action under this provision, the record of proceedings in the court in which that person was convicted of an offence under Part VI or convicted of or punished for failure to comply with an order of the Tribunal or another court under the Act is, in the absence of any evidence to the contrary, proof that the person against whom the action is brought engaged in such conduct and any evidence given in those proceedings as to the effect of those acts or omissions on the person bringing the action is evidence thereof in the action.[960]

The burden of proof in a civil action where criminal conduct forms the basis of the action remains on the balance of probabilities, but a trial judge is justified in scrutinizing the evidence with greater care if there are serious allegations to be established by the proof offered. [961]

There has been a trend towards implementing class action legislation and to date specific acts have been brought into force in the provinces of Quebec, Ontario and British Columbia. While plaintiffs have argued that the breach of the Act could be the appropriate subject matter of a class action, the courts have not agreed, at least in the context of indirect purchasers alleging damages from a price fixing conspiracy in violation of the Act. In this context, the term "indirect purchaser" has been used to refer to

---

[958] Part VI includes conspiracy to unduly limit competition under section 45 and knowingly or recklessly making a representation to the public that is false or misleading in a material respect. However, all of the offences in this section are criminal and require proof of intent.

[959] *Competition Act*, section 36.

[960] *Competition Act*, section 36(2).

[961] *Continental Insurance Co. v. Dalton Cartage Co.*, [1982] 1 S.C.R. 164 (S.C.C.); *Janelle Pharmacy Ltd. v. Blue Cross of Atlantic Canada* (2003), 217 N.S.R. (2d) 50 (N.S. S.C.).

a person or entity who had purchased the relevant product indirectly from a member of the alleged conspiracy, such as someone further down the chain of distribution.[962]

The Commissioner has the option under the Act to enforce the misleading advertising provisions of the Act as civil matters reviewable by the Competition Tribunal or the civil courts, or as offences prosecuted in the criminal justice system. The choice to proceed under either regime is entirely within the discretion of the Commissioner. The choice of one route precludes proceeding with the other.

The Bureau has published an Information Bulletin[963] dealing with the criteria to be applied. In order to proceed on the criminal track the Bureau has stated that both of the following criteria must be satisfied:

(a) there must be clear and compelling evidence suggesting that the accused knowingly or recklessly made a false or misleading representation to the public. An example of such evidence is the continuation of a practice by the accused after complaints have been made by consumers directly to the accused; and

(b) if there is clear and compelling evidence that the accused knowingly or recklessly made a false or misleading representation to the public, and this evidence is available, the Bureau must also be satisfied that the criminal prosecution would be in the public interest.

c) Criminal Offences

Under the Act, it is a criminal offence to

(a) knowingly or recklessly make a representation to the public that is false or misleading in a material respect,[964] or

(b) to send or cause to be sent by electronic or regular mail a deceptive notice of winning a prize, if the notice gives the general impression that the recipient has won, will win or will on doing a particular act win, a prize or other benefit and if the recipient is asked

---

[962] *Chadha v. Bayer Inc.* (2001), 54 O.R. (3d) 520 (Ont. Div. Ct.), affirmed (2003), 63 O.R. (3d) 22 (Ont. C.A.), additonal reasons at (2003), 2003 CarswellOnt 1205 (Ont. C.A.), leave to appeal refused (2003), 2003 CarswellOnt 2810 (S.C.C.).

[963] *Misleading Representations and Deceptive Marketing Practices: Choice of Criminal or Civil Track under the Competition Act*, available at the Bureau's website at *www.strategis.ic.gc.ca*.

[964] *Competition Act*, section 52.

or given the option to pay money, incur a cost or do anything that will incur a cost,[965] or

(c) to engage in deceptive telemarketing, including failing to make required disclosure or making a representation to the public that is false or misleading in a material respect.[966]

The Crown must show all of the elements of the particular offence exist beyond a reasonable doubt. If the accused can show a reasonable doubt with respect to any of the elements this may be a defence. For example, if an impugned representation is capable of multiple interpretations not all of which are false and misleading the accused should be acquitted.[967]

The Crown may proceed by way of indictment or by way of summary conviction. Indictments are reserved for the most serious cases and the amount of the fine is in the discretion of the Court. A term of imprisonment, not exceeding five years, may also be imposed.[968] In summary conviction proceedings the maximum fine which can be awarded for each offence is $200,000.00. A term of imprisonment of one year may also be imposed.

d) Reviewable Matters

The activities which may be reviewed by the Tribunal or a court rather than prosecuted criminally include:

(a) the making of false or misleading representations to the public;[969]

(b) the making of claims relating to performance, efficacy or length of life of a product that are not based on adequate and proper tests;[970]

(c) the making of false or misleading warranty or guarantee claims;[971]

(d) the making of misleading claims relating to a "regular" price;[972]

(e) the making of false or misleading representations relating to performance tests or product testimonials;[973]

---

[965] *Competition Act*, section 53.

[966] *Competition Act*, section 52.1.

[967] *R. v. Lowe Real Estate Ltd.* (1978), (sub nom. *R. v. R.M. Lowe Real Estate Ltd.*) 39 C.P.R. (2d) 266 (Ont. C.A.).

[968] *Competition Act*, section 52(5) and 52.1(9).

[969] *Competition Act*, section 74.01(1)(a).

[970] *Competition Act*, section 74.01(1)(b).

[971] *Competition Act*, section 74.01(1)(c).

[972] *Competition Act*, subsection 74.01(2) and 74.01(3).

[973] *Competition Act*, section 74.02.

(f)   bait and switch selling;[974]

(g)   sale above advertised price;[975] and

(h)   carrying on a promotional contest in a prohibited manner.[976]

Only the Commissioner can bring an application to have particular reviewable conduct prohibited. Such proceedings are subject to the civil burden of proof. Unlike criminal proceedings, the respondent will have an obligation to advance a defence and adverse inferences may be drawn against the respondent who fails to do so.

e) Responsibility for Representations

For the purposes of both the criminal and reviewable matters, the Act contains specific rules to clarify the responsibility for the making of representations within the chain of distribution. A representation that is

(a)   expressed on an article offered or displayed for sale, its wrapper or container,

(b)   expressed on anything attached to, inserted in or accompanying an article offered or displayed for sale, its wrapper or container, or anything on which the article is mounted for display or sale,

(c)   expressed on an in-store or other point-of-purchase display,

(d)   made in the course of in-store, door-to-door or telephone selling to a person as ultimate user, or

(e)   contained in or on anything that is sold, sent, delivered, transmitted or in any other manner whatever made available to a member of the public,

is deemed to be made to the public by and only by the person who caused the representation to be so expressed, made or contained and, where that person is outside Canada, a representation described in paragraph (a), (b) or (e) is, for the purposes of the relevant sections, deemed to be made to the public by the person who imported the article, thing or display into Canada.[977]

Subject to the provisions summarized above, a person who, for the purpose of promoting, directly or indirectly, the supply or use of a product

---

[974] *Competition Act,* section 74.04.

[975] *Competition Act,* section 74.05.

[976] *Competition Act,* section 74.06.

[977] See *Competition Act,* subsection 52(2) and (2.1) for criminal proceedings and section 74.03 reviewable matters which is the same save that responsibility for point-of-purchase displays under paragraph (c) is also attributed.

or any business interest, supplies to a wholesaler, retailer or other distributor of a product any material or thing that contains a representation, which is false or misleading contrary to the provisions of the Act, is deemed to have made that representation to the public.[978]

f) Remedies for Reviewable Matters

Only the Commissioner may apply to the Tribunal, the Federal Court or a superior court of a province seeking a remedy relating to a reviewable matter. If the Tribunal or the Court finds that a person has engaged in "reviewable conduct" as defined by the Act, they may make any combination of the following orders:

(a)   A cease and desist order may be granted requiring the person to stop the activity complained of and not to engage in substantially similar conduct for a period of 10 years unless the order specifies a shorter period.[979]

(b)   If the Commissioner has made out a strong *prima facie* case that a person is engaging in reviewable conduct, a cease and desist order may be made on an interim basis for a maximum duration of not longer than 14 days if a) serious harm is likely to ensue unless the order is made; and b) the balance of convenience favours making the order.[980]

(c)   Payment of an "administrative monetary penalty", up to a maximum amount of $50,000.00 for an individual and $100,000.00 for a corporation for an initial order, with doubled amounts possible for subsequent orders. A doubled payment would be appropriate if an order had been previously made against the same person under the same provision.[981]

(d)   An order may require a person to publish, in such manner and at such times as is specified, an "information" or "corrective" notice directed to the class of persons likely to have been affected by the impugned conduct. The notice will include the name under which the person carries on business and the determination made as well as:

(i)   a description of the reviewable conduct;

---

[978] *Competition Act*, subsection 52(3) and subsection 74.03(3).
[979] *Competition Act*, subsection 74.10(1)(a).
[980] *Competition Act*, section 74.11.
[981] *Competition Act*, subsection 74.10(1)(c).

(ii) the time period and geographical area to which the conduct relates; and

(iii) a description of the manner in which any representation or advertisement was disseminated, including, where applicable, the name of the publication or other medium employed.[982]

(e) The Commissioner and the person against whom the Commissioner seeks an order may come to an agreement on the terms of the order and a consent order may be filed with the Tribunal or the court for immediate registration. Once registered, the order has the same force and effect as if it had been issued.[983]

(f) The orders for administrative penalties or publication of corrective advertisements may not be made if the person whose conduct is being reviewed establishes they exercised due diligence to prevent the reviewable conduct from occurring.[984] The Act provides that these orders are to be made with a view to promote acceptable conduct rather than to punish.[985]

In the case of *Canada (Commissioner of Competition) v. P.V.I. International Inc.*,[986] the only reported case to date which has considered these provisions, the Tribunal refused to order corrective advertising. The Tribunal stated that in the United States the Federal Trade Commission uses corrective advertising in only a minority of cases, and that in the specific factual situation before it the complexity of the claims and the evidence showing they were false or misleading would make it exceedingly difficult for a consumer to understand in a short notice why the claims were false or misleading. The result was questioned on appeal.

g) Access to the Competition Tribunal

A person concerned about another person's conduct may only bring the matter to the attention of the Commissioner and hope that the Commissioner

---

[982] *Competition Act*, subsection 74.10(1)(b).

[983] *Competition Act*, section 74.12.

[984] *Competition Act*, subsection 74.10(3).

[985] *Competition Act*, subsection 74.10(4).

[986] (2002), 19 C.P.R. (4th) 129 (Competition Trib.), reversed 2004 CarswellNat 1471, 2004 FCA 197 (F.C.A.).

will take the matter forward for review.[987] It is still possible, however, under section 36 of the Act, to bring a civil action to recover damages actually suffered as a result of another person's conduct which is in violation of Part VI of the Act.

h) Misleading Representations

Section 52 provides that "no person shall, for the purpose of promoting, directly or indirectly, the supply or use of a product or for the purpose of promoting, directly or indirectly, any business interest, by any means whatever, knowingly or recklessly make a representation to the public that is false or misleading in a material respect." The offence also includes permitting a representation to be made which violates the section.[988] For greater certainty in establishing an offence, it is not necessary to prove that any person was deceived.[989]

Under section 52, there is a *mens rea* requirement, as the Crown must prove that the accused knowingly or recklessly made a representation to the public that was false or misleading in a material respect. However, the Crown need not prove that any person was actually deceived or misled. As set out above, a person who permits the making of a representation may be charged. For example, a distributor who prepares an advertisement, which was misleading contrary to the section, and provides it to a sub-distributor who makes the representation to the public will come within the section.

Section 74.01 provides that "a person engages in reviewable conduct who, for the purpose of promoting, directly or indirectly, the supply or use of a product or for the purpose of promoting, directly or indirectly, any business interest, by any means whatever makes a representation to the public that is false or misleading in a material respect." This section also extends to a person who permits the making of a representation.[990] As there is no requirement to show an intentional element and the scope of potential

---

[987] A complaint may also be made to Advertising Standards Canada, which is a national industry association committed to self-regulation of advertising. Consumers may submit complaints relating to violations of the Canadian *Code of Advertising Standards*. In addition, competitors may take advantage of a trade dispute procedure. Advertising Standards Canada cannot award damages or issue injunctive relief but in some cases can be effective in stopping misleading advertisements since the advertiser is required to withdraw or amend advertising which violates the *Code*. For more information see *www.adstandards.com*.

[988] *Competition Act*, subsection 52(1.2).

[989] *Competition Act*, subsection 52(1.1).

[990] *Competition Act*, subsection 52(1.2).

remedies available is wider, the vast majority of misleading advertising cases will be dealt with under this section.

Under either the criminal or the reviewable conduct provisions, the Act specifically requires that the general impression conveyed by any advertisement as well as its literal meaning be taken into account in determining if an advertisement is false or misleading in a material respect.[991]

In determining whether a representation is false or misleading in a material respect, the Court must determine what impression the representation would create, not by applying its own reason, intelligence and common sense, but rather by determining the impression that a fictional ordinary citizen would gain from hearing or reading the representation.[992] The public does not generally carefully study or weigh each word in an advertisement; the ultimate impression on the reader arises from the sum total of, not only what is said, but also that is reasonably implied.[993] However, a number of decisions suggest that the level of known prudence and sophistication which may be expected of an "average" purchaser may be higher if the representation in issue is directed to a more sophisticated audience.[994]

As a result of the application of the general impression test it is the Bureau's position that an advertisement may be misleading if:

(a) The representations made are partially true and partially false, or capable of two meanings, one of which is false;

(b) The representations are literally or technically true but fail to reveal essential information. For example, where a product is offered at a sale or special price but an integral part of the product is not included in the price;

(c) The representation is literally or technically true but creates a false impression. For example, the advertised results of a test of a product are not material to its use but the representation makes it appear otherwise; or

(d) The representation is literally true with respect to the written text but is associated with a visual representation which creates a false impression. For example, the illustration relates to a different product.[995]

---

[991] *Competition Act*, subsection 52(4) and 74.01(6).

[992] *R. v. Kenitex Canada Ltd.* (1980), 51 C.P.R. (2d) 103 (Ont. Co. Ct.), varied (1981), (sub nom. *R v. Fell*) 59 C.P.R. (2d) 34 (Ont. C.A.); *UL Canada Inc. v. Procter & Gamble Inc.* (1996), 65 C.P.R. (3d) 534 (Ont. Gen. Div.).

[993] *R. v. Imperial Tobacco Products Ltd.* (1971), 3 C.P.R. (2d) 178 (Alta. C.A.).

[994] *R. v. International Vacations Ltd.* (1980), 56 C.P.R. (2d) 251 (Ont. C.A.).

[995] *Misleading Advertising Guidelines* available at the Bureau's website at *www.strategis.ic.gc.ca*.

The registration of a trade mark will not ensure that the use of that trade mark in an advertisement will not result in a misleading representation. Where the trade mark is "suggestive" of the products or services in association with which it is used, an incorrect impression can result where the trade mark implies a fact which is untrue or misleading in the context of the advertisement. For example, the use of the registered trade mark FACTORY CARPET OUTLET by a retailer, who did not have a factory, was found to be misleading.[996]

Once charges have been laid or an application for a determination of reviewable conduct is made, the route of adjudication may not be changed with respect to those facts or substantially the same facts.[997]

i) Correction Notices

Paragraphs (c) and (d) of former subsection 37.3(2)[998] of the Act required that corrective advertising take place as part of a statutory due diligence defence. This requirement was found to constitute a reverse onus contrary to the *Charter* and of no force and effect.[999] The requirement was formally repealed in 1999, but somewhat similar considerations are applicable in the context of the exercise of the Commissioner's discretion to prosecute and the advertiser's marketplace response. For example, if a mistaken price is set out in an advertisement the advertiser may be compelled by potential civil liability and potential consumer ill will to take immediate steps to attempt to rectify the problem. It is the policy of the Commissioner that immediate publicized correction notices and action to rectify errors are factors which will be considered with respect to initiating proceedings relating to misleading advertising.

The publishing of a correction notice is, by definition, an admission that the original advertisement was incorrect. Correction notices should not be published until the relevant facts are carefully considered.

When a serious error is detected, immediate steps should be taken to make a correction, preferably in the medium in which the error occurred. When an error occurs in targeted print advertisements, every effort should be made to bring the error to the attention of the customers who were initially targeted. The correction notice should be communicated through the medium originally used in the campaign.

---

[996] *R. v. Discount Broadloom Centre Ltd.* (1976), 31 C.P.R. (2d) 110 (Ont. Co. Ct.).

[997] *Competition Act*, subsection 52(7) and 74.16.

[998] *Competition Act*, R.S.C. 1970, c. C-23.

[999] *R. v. Wholesale Travel Group Inc.* (1991), 38 C.P.R. (3d) 451 (S.C.C.).

Newspaper advertisements are typically corrected by placing an advertisement (correction notice or erratum) in the same newspaper. The notice should be prominently published so that those who were originally exposed to the advertisement may read it. Displaying the correction notice prominently in stores is also helpful, particularly at point of sale.

Errors in catalogues require additional effort to reach consumers likely to have received the catalogue. It is prudent to bring the error to the attention of the purchaser at the time when they order the product, rather than on delivery.

All retail outlets should be notified of errors as soon as they are detected, so that they may pass the information on to their staff and customers.

j) Product Performance Claims

References in advertisements to product performance are very common, including comparative references to competitors' products. Under subsection 74.01(1)(b), it is reviewable conduct for any person, for the purpose of promoting directly or indirectly, the supply or use of a product or for the purpose of promoting directly or indirectly any business interest, by any means whatever, to make a representation to the public in the form of a statement, warranty or guarantee of the performance, efficacy or length of life of a product that is not based on an adequate and proper test, the proof of which lies on the person making the representation. A representation relating to product performance may be subject to both paragraphs 74.01(1)(a) and (b).

The burden of proof for reviewable matters is on the balance of probabilities. The onus under paragraph 74.01(1)(b) of the Act requires the Commissioner to demonstrate that the representation alleged to be reviewable was made. Once the Commissioner does this, the onus shifts to the respondent to demonstrate that the relevant statement, warranty or guarantee is substantiated by an "adequate and proper" test.[1000] The representation will still be reviewable conduct under this paragraph even if it is true.

The use of the words "adequate and proper" has generally been interpreted to mean that the test methodology is objective and complies either with appropriate industry testing standards or is conducted according to generally accepted scientific principles. In addition, the test results should

---

[1000] *Canada (Commissioner of Competition) v. P.V.I. International Inc.* (2002), 19 C.P.R. (4th) 129 (Competition Trib.), reversed 2004 CarswellNat 1471, 2004 FCA 197 (F.C.A.).

be statistically significant. The actual tests do not necessarily need to satisfy the rigid requirements of scientific research.[1001]

Performance claims should not be made unless they are based on adequate and proper test results. The tests must be carried out before the claim is made. In cases involving products supplied to another company which advertises the product, responsibility generally lies with the advertiser, not the supplier of the product, to have proper documentation. If the Court determines that a performance claim cannot be substantiated, the advertiser is liable.

In the case of *R. v. Bristol-Meyers Canada Ltd.*,[1002] the accused represented that clothes softened with Fleecy were three times softer than clothes softened with the recommended dosage of competitive softeners. Although it could be shown that the clothes treated with Fleecy were softer, the claim they were three times softer could not be substantiated since there was no acceptable method of qualifying "softness."

If a performance claim is broad, the existence of proper tests supporting only one portion of the claim or under only one condition of use is not sufficient. Results must not only be significant, but must also be meaningful to the consumer. The test methodology used must be such as to show that the result claimed is not a mere chance or one time effect.[1003] All tests must be completed before the advertisement runs.

The following matters should be considered and complied with, if applicable:

(a) comparative data should not be used to imply general superiority of a product or service, unless such a claim would be accurate over a comprehensive range of normal conditions of use for the product or service;

(b) if superiority is limited to a certain range of conditions, the advertisement should be qualified to reflect this;

(c) comparisons demonstrating the relative effectiveness of competing products or services should be shown under equivalent conditions;

(d) dissimilar products or services should not be the subject of an unqualified comparison; and

---

[1001] For a discussion of the requirements relating to adequate and proper test relating to the previous section of the Act, see *The Misleading Advertising Bulletin*, April 1-June 30, 1993 at 1.

[1002] (1979), 45 C.P.R (2d) 228 (Ont. Co. Ct.).

[1003] *Misleading Advertising Guidelines* available at the Bureau's website at *www.strategis.ic .gc.ca*.

(e)   services should not be compared for a use or under a method of application for which they were not intended.

6. COMPARATIVE ADVERTISING

A comparative advertisement is an advertisement in which the advertiser or features of the advertiser's product or service are compared to others or the product or service of others. Typically, the point of the comparison is a competitor or its product or service. The comparison may be direct in that a specific reference is made or indirect when a general reference is made such as the "leading brand" or "brand x".

Accurate comparative advertising can be beneficial to consumers since they are provided with information which may allow them to make more informed and advantageous purchases. The Competition Bureau encourages appropriate product comparisons.[1004] On the other hand, inappropriate comparative advertising by an overzealous competitor demands an immediate response by the affected brand owner. There are a number of potential causes of action available to the brand owner.

a) The *Competition Act*

We have previously discussed the relevant provisions of the *Competition Act* in Part 5 of this chapter. A brand owner concerned with a competitor's conduct may bring the claims to the attention of the Commissioner and hope that the Commissioner will bring the matter forward for a review. As discussed, only the Commissioner may apply to the Tribunal, the Federal Court or a superior court of a province seeking a remedy relating to a reviewable matter. Interim relief is possible in this context.

If a brand owner seeks to bring an action under section 36 of the *Competition Act*, the brand owner must show that it has suffered a loss or damage as a result of a competitor's violation of the provisions of section 52 of the Act.[1005] Unfortunately from the brand owner's point of view, this requires it to show that the competitor knowingly or recklessly made a representation to the public that is false or misleading in a material respect. A two year limitation period applies. Time commences to run from the time the impugned conduct was engaged in or the day on which any criminal

---

[1004] See *Gillette Australia Pty. Ltd. v. Energizer Australia Pty. Ltd.* (2002), 193 A.L.R. 629 (Aust. F.C.A.).

[1005] *947101 Ontario Ltd. v. Barrhaven Town Centre Inc.* (1995), 121 D.L.R. (4th) 748 (Ont. Gen. Div.).

proceedings relating to such conduct were finally disposed of, whichever is the later.[1006]

If such an action is brought in the Federal Court, there are concerns with respect to the ability of the Court to grant an injunction since the *Competition Act* makes no provision for such relief.[1007] However, such considerations may be less relevant in an action brought in the courts of a province, since typically there is broader equitable jurisdiction in such courts and the cause of the action for breach of the *Competition Act* may be combined with additional tort claims.[1008]

Since an action under section 36 is limited to the criminal breach of the Act, it seems reasonable to assume that the number of actions brought will be limited. Prior to the 1999 amendments of the Act, there were a number of cases which sought interlocutory injunctions on the basis of violation of the then strict liability provisions of the Act.[1009]

[1006] *Competition* Act, subsection 36(4).

[1007] *ACA Joe International v. 147255 Canada Inc.* (1986), 10 C.P.R. (3d) 301 (Fed. T.D.); *Church & Dwight Ltd./Ltée v. Sifto Canada Inc.* (1994), (sub nom. *Church & Dwight Ltd. v. Sifto Canada Inc.*) 58 C.P.R. (3d) 316 (Ont. Gen. Div.), additional reasons at (1994), 1994 CarswellOnt 4525, 17 B.L.R. (2d) 92n (Ont. Gen. Div.); *UL Canada Inc. v. Procter & Gamble Inc.* (1996), 65 C.P.R. (3d) 534 (Ont. Gen. Div.); *947101 Ontario Ltd. v. Barrhaven Town Centre Inc.* (1995), 121 D.L.R. (4th) 748 (Ont. Gen. Div.) and see Neil Finkelstein and Robert Kwinter, *Section 36 and Claims to Injunctive Relief* (1990), 69 Can. Bar Rev. 298, which suggests these cases are wrongly decided.

[1008] *Mead Johnson Canada v. Ross Pediatrics* (1996), 70 C.P.R. (3d) 189 (Ont. Gen. Div.); *B.M.W.E. v. Canadian Pacific Ltd.* (1996), 136 D.L.R. (4th) 289 (sub nom. *Brotherhood of Maintenance of Way Employees v. Canadian Pacific Ltd.*) 136 D.L.R. (4th) 289 (S.C.C.), but see *947101 Ontario Ltd. v. Barrhaven Town Centre Inc.* (1995), 121 D.L.R. (4th) 748 (Ont. Gen. Div.); *UL Canada Inc. v. Procter & Gamble Inc.* (1996), 65 C.P.R. (3d) 534 (Ont. Gen. Div.).

[1009] *Unitel Communications Inc. v. Bell Canada* (1994), 56 C.P.R. (3d) 232 (Ont. Gen. Div.); *Church & Dwight Ltd./Ltée v. Sifto Canada Inc.* (1994), , (sub nom. *Church & Dwight Ltd. v. Sifto Canada Inc.*) (Ont. Gen. Div.), additional reasons at (1994), 1994 CarswellOnt 4525, 17 B.L.R. (2d) 92n (Ont. Gen. Div.); *Maple Leaf Foods Inc. v. Robin Hood Multifoods Inc.* (1994), 58 C.P.R. (3d) 54 (Ont. Gen. Div.), additional reasons at (1994), 58 C.P.R. (3d) 58 (Ont. Gen. Div.); *Beatrice Foods Inc. v. Ault Foods Ltd.* (1995), 59 C.P.R. (3d) 374 (Ont. Ct. Gen. Div.), additional reasons at (1995), 60 C.P.R. (3d) 462 (Ont. Gen. Div.); *Purolator Courier Ltd. - Courrier Purolator Ltée v. United Parcel Service Canada Ltd.* (1995), (sub nom. *Purolator Courier Ltd. v. United Parcel Service Canada Ltd.*) 60 C.P.R. (3d) 473 (Ont. Gen. Div.); *BC Tel Mobility Cellular Inc. v. Rogers Cantel Inc.* (1995), 63 C.P.R. (3d) 464 (B.C. S.C.[In Chambers]), leave to appeal refused (1995), 1995 CarswellBC 1284 (B.C. C.A. [In Chambers]); *UL Canada Inc. v. Procter & Gamble Inc.* (1996), 65 C.P.R. (3d) 534

b) The *Trade-marks Act*

Two sections of the Act are potentially available to an aggrieved brand owner; subsection 7(a) and section 22. Subsection 7(a) provides that no person shall make a false or misleading statement tending to discredit the business, wares or services of the competitor. The statements need only be misleading without being false.[1010]

Neither malice nor knowledge of the falsity of the statement need to be shown in an action under the subsection.[1011] All that need be proved is that the statement complained of has been made by a competitor, that it is false or misleading, and that it tends to discredit the business, wares or services of the plaintiff.[1012]

The subsection has been found to be constitutionally valid federal legislation in the context of false or misleading statements relating to matters constitutionally assigned to the federal government, such as patent litigation.[1013] There is substantial doubt as to its constitutionality outside of the context of patents, trade marks, copyright and industrial design. In addition, it is unclear how closely the statement needs to be linked to the trade mark in issue. If the reference is not direct but by way of inference, such as a reference to the leading brand, this may not be sufficient.

Section 22 provides that no person shall use a trade mark registered by any person in a manner likely to have the effect of depreciating the value of the goodwill attaching thereto.[1014]

It has been held that the verb "use" in section 22 is to be interpreted by reference to the definition of the noun "use" in section 2 and 4. The effect of this is to confine the application, and therefore the prohibition of section 22, to a use which any person may make, in association with goods or services within the meaning of section 4 of another's registered trade mark in such a manner as to depreciate the value of the goodwill attaching thereto. In the leading case of *Clairol International Corp. v. Thomas Supply & Equipment Co.,* where the mark in issue was registered for use in association with wares only, it was found that the presence of the plaintiff's trade marks

---

(Ont. Gen. Div.); *Mead Johnson Canada v. Ross Pediatrics* (1996), 70 C.P.R. (3d) 189 (Ont. Gen. Div.).

[1010] *Rowell v. S. & S. Industries Inc.,* [1966] S.C.R. 419 (S.C.C.).

[1011] *Rowell v. S. & S. Industries Inc.,* [1966] S.C.R. 419 (S.C.C.).

[1012] *Rowell v. S. & S. Industries Inc.,* [1966] S.C.R. 419 (S.C.C.).

[1013] *Reillo Canada Inc. v. Lambert* (1986), 9 C.P.R. (3d) 324 (Fed. T.D,), additional reasons at (1987), 15 C.P.R. (3d) 257 (Fed. T.D.); *ACA Joe International v. 147255 Canada Inc.* (1986), 10 C.P.R. (3d) 301 (Fed. T.D.).

[1014] *Syntex Inc. v. Apotex Inc.* (1984), 1 C.P.R. (3d) 145 (Fed. C.A.), reversing (1982), 69 C.P.R. (2d) 264 (Fed. T.D.) and see **Chapter 5, part 4(b)**.

on the defendant's packages was "use" within the meaning of section 22, but that their presence on the defendant's brochures was not within it.[1015]

This interpretation leads to an unexpected situation. If the mark in issue is registered for use in association with wares only, the result of the *Clairol* case applies and the plaintiff can restrain the defendant's use of its mark which comes within the definition set out in the Act for wares. Under this definition a trade mark is deemed to be used in association with wares if, at the time of the transfer of the property in or possession of such wares, in the normal course of trade, it is marked on the wares themselves or on the packages in which they are distributed or it is in any other manner so associated with the wares that notice of the association is then given to the person to whom the property or possession is transferred.[1016] However, if the mark in issue is registered for use in association with services the broader definition of "use" for services applies and the plaintiff can restrain the defendant's use of its mark in advertising.[1017]

Much has been written about the section by commentators,[1018] but the approach of the *Clairol* case continues to be applied although the section has not been definitively interpreted by an appellate court.

c) The Torts of Injurious Falsehood and Unlawful Interference with Economic Relations

In a number of recent cases relating to comparative advertising, the plaintiffs have asserted claims for injurious falsehood and unlawful interference with economic relations.[1019] In order to succeed with a common law action asserting injurious falsehood the plaintiff must show:

[1015] [1968] 2 Ex. C.R. 552 (Can. Ex. Ct.) and see *Cie générale des établissements Michelin - Michelin & Cie v. CAW-Canada* (1996), (sub nom. *Cie Générale des Établissements Michelin-Michelin & Cie v. C.A.W. -Canada*) 71 C.P.R. (3d) 348 (Fed. T.D.).

[1016] Section 4.

[1017] See *Eye Masters Ltd v. Ross King Holdings Ltd.* (1992), 44 C.P.R. (3d) 459 (Fed. T.D.), where this result was described as bizarre.

[1018] See for example Norman Siebrasse, *Comparative Advertising, Dilution, and Section 22 of the Trade-Marks Act*, (2001) 18 C.I.P.R. 277; James J. Holloway, *The Protection of Trade-mark Goodwill in Canada; Where We Are and Where We Should be Going* (2003), 17 I.P.J. 1.

[1019] *Unitel Communications Inc. v. Bell Canada* (1994), 56 C.P.R. (3d) 232 (Ont. Gen. Div.); *Church & Dwight Ltd./Ltée v. Sifto Canada Inc.* (1994), (sub nom. *Church & Dwight Ltd. v. Sifto Canada Inc.*) (Ont. Gen. Div.), additional reasons at (1994), 1994 CarswellOnt 4525, 17 B.L.R. (2d) 92n (Ont. Gen. Div.); *UL Canada Inc. v. Procter & Gamble Inc.* (1996), 65 C.P.R. (3d) 534 (Ont. Gen. Div.).

(a) the statement made is false,
(b) the statement was made with intent to cause injury without lawful justification,[1020] and
(c) actual economic loss has been suffered as a result of making the statement.[1021]

The key to a claim for injurious falsehood is identity. If the plaintiff is not identified in the comparative advertisement, there is no tort.[1022] However, if the defendant identifies the plaintiff by implication in the offending advertisement, this may be sufficient for purposes of such an action.[1023] The truth of any statement is a complete defence to a claim for injurious falsehood.[1024]

In order to succeed with a common law action for the tort of unlawful interference with economic relations the plaintiff must show:

(a) The defendant intended to injure the plaintiff. It must be shown that the defendant targeted the plaintiff. Negligent interference does not amount to intentional interference;[1025]
(b) The defendant has employed unlawful means. Breach of the *Competition Act* may supply the element of unlawful means;[1026]

[1020] *Church & Dwight Ltd./Ltée v. Sifto Canada Inc.* (1994), (sub nom. *Church & Dwight Ltd. v. Sifto Canada Inc.*) (Ont. Gen. Div.), additional reasons at (1994), 1994 CarswellOnt 4525, 17 B.L.R. (2d) 92n (Ont. Gen. Div.).

[1021] *Church & Dwight Ltd./Ltée v. Sifto Canada Inc.* (1994), (sub nom. *Church & Dwight Ltd. v. Sifto Canada Inc.*) (Ont. Gen. Div.), additional reasons at (1994), 1994 CarswellOnt 4525, 17 B.L.R. (2d) 92n (Ont. Gen. Div.).

[1022] *Unitel Communications Inc. v. Bell Canada* (1994), 56 C.P.R. (3d) 232 (Ont. Gen. Div.); *Church & Dwight Ltd./Ltée v. Sifto Canada Inc.* (1994), (sub nom. *Church & Dwight Ltd. v. Sifto Canada Inc.*) (Ont. Gen. Div.), additional reasons at (1994), 1994 CarswellOnt 4525, 17 B.L.R. (2d) 92n (Ont. Gen. Div.); *Beatrice Foods Inc. v. Ault Foods Ltd.* (1995), 59 C.P.R. (3d) 374 (Ont. Gen. Div.), additional reasons at (1995), 60 C.P.R. (3d) 462 (Ont. Gen. Div.).

[1023] *Church & Dwight Ltd./Ltée v. Sifto Canada Inc.* (1994), (sub nom. *Church & Dwight Ltd. v. Sifto Canada Inc.*) (Ont. Gen. Div.), additional reasons at (1994), 1994 CarswellOnt 4525, 17 B.L.R. (2d) 92n (Ont. Gen. Div.); *UL Canada Inc. v. Procter & Gamble Inc.* (1996), 65 C.P.R. (3d) 534 (Ont. Gen. Div.).

[1024] *UL Canada Inc. v. Procter & Gamble Inc.* (1996), 65 C.P.R. (3d) 534 (Ont. Gen. Div.).

[1025] *Lineal Group Inc. v. Atlantis Canadian Distributors Inc.* (1998), 42 O.R. (3d) 157 (Ont. C.A.), leave to appeal refused (1999), 138 O.A.C. 197 (note) (S.C.C.).

[1026] *Apotex Inc. v. Hoffmann-La-Roche Ltd* (1996), 9 C.P.R. (4th) 417 (Ont. C.A.).

(c)   Actual economic loss has been suffered as a result of the interference.[1027]

Courts of competent jurisdiction in the provinces have jurisdiction to
hear and determine actions for injurious falsehood and unlawful interference
with economic relations, but the Federal Court of Canada does not.[1028]

7. SUMMARY AND CHECKLIST

To ensure that brand advertising complies with relevant laws and is
protected the following matters should be considered.

1. Advertising must be consistent with the brand image it seeks to foster.
    Considerable time and effort should be devoted to ensuring that there
    is consistency between the brand image and the statements made in
    advertisements.
2. If a slogan functions as a trade mark, consideration should be given to
    obtaining a trade mark registration.
3. In order to ensure that brand advertising can be protected, the brand
    owner should own the copyright in the advertising material that is
    prepared at its request.
4. If advertising appropriately communicates information relating to the
    brand components, misleading advertising should not be a concern.
    However, for those cases where mistakes occur or in assessing the
    activities of competitors it is helpful to understand the rules concerning
    misleading advertising.
5. The Commissioner of Competition has the option under the Act to
    enforce the misleading advertising provisions of the *Competition Act*
    as civil matters reviewable by the Competition Tribunal or the civil
    courts, or as offences prosecuted in the criminal justice system. The
    choice to proceed under either regime is entirely within the discretion
    of the Commissioner. The choice of one route precludes proceeding
    with the other.
6. No person shall, for the purpose of promoting, directly or indirectly,
    the supply or use of a product or for the purpose of promoting, directly
    or indirectly, any business interest, by any means whatever, knowingly
    or recklessly make a representation to the public that is false or mis-

---

[1027] *Lineal Group Inc. v. Atlantis Canadian Distributors Inc.* (1998), 42 O.R. (3d)
157 (Ont. C.A.), leave to appeal refused (1999), 138 O.A.C. 197 (note) (S.C.C.).
[1028] See *Janssen-Ortho Inc. v. Amgen Canada Inc.* (2003), 26 C.P.R. (4th) 93 (Ont.
S.C.J); *Mattel Canada Inc. v. GTS Acquisitions Ltd.* (1989), 28 C.P.R. (3d) 534
(Fed. T.D.).

leading in a material respect. This criminal offence also includes permitting a representation to be made which violates the section. In establishing an offence, it is not necessary to prove that any person was deceived.

7. A person engages in reviewable conduct who, for the purpose of promoting, directly or indirectly, the supply or use of a product or for the purpose of promoting, directly or indirectly, any business interest, by any means whatever makes a representation to the public that is false or misleading in a material respect. The prohibition relating to reviewable conduct also extends to a person who permits the making of a representation. As there is no requirement to show an intentional element and the scope of potential remedies available is wide, the vast majority of misleading advertising cases are dealt with under this section.

8. Under either of these provisions, the general impression conveyed by any advertisement, as well as its literal meaning, will be taken into account in determining if an advertisement is false or misleading in a material respect.

9. A representation expressed on a product or physically associated with it or contained in point of sale material is deemed to be made to the public by, and only by, the person who caused the representation to be so expressed, made or contained. Where that person is outside Canada, the representation is deemed to be made to the public by the person who imported the product or material into Canada.

10. It is the policy of the Commissioner of Competition that immediate publicized correction notices and action to rectify errors are factors which will be considered with respect to initiating proceedings relating to misleading advertising.

11. It is also reviewable conduct for any person, for the purpose of promoting directly or indirectly the supply or use of a product or for the purpose of promoting directly or indirectly any business interest, by any means whatever, to make a representation to the public in the form of a statement, warranty or guarantee of the performance, efficacy or length of life of a product that is not based on an adequate and proper test, the proof of which lies on the person making the representation. A representation relating to product performance may be subject to scrutiny as misleading and not based on adequate and proper tests.

12. Performance claims should not be made unless they are based on adequate and proper test results. The tests must be carried out before the claim is made. In cases involving products supplied to another company which advertises the product, responsibility generally lies with the advertiser, not the supplier of the product, to have proper documenta-

tion. If the Court determines that a performance claim cannot be substantiated, the advertiser is liable.

13. Accurate, comparative advertising can be beneficial to consumers in
that they are provided with information which may allow them to make
more informed and advantageous purchases. On the other hand, inappropriate comparative advertising by an overzealous competitor demands an immediate response by the affected brand owner. There are
a number of potential causes of action available to a brand owner.

Chapter 9: Developing Effective Brand Management Policies

1. INTRODUCTION

As discussed in Chapter 1, a brand should be managed like any other economic asset. Someone must be responsible for the management of the brand. This designated responsible individual will have to coordinate management of the brand across the organization of the brand owner including different divisions or business units. In addition, brand execution will have to be coordinated across different forms of media and in different markets.[1029]

Earlier chapters have discussed specific legal considerations relating to choosing a brand name, branding on the Internet and protecting the components which make up a brand. This chapter is directed towards developing policies to deal with these matters and to assist in brand management.

2. SELECTING A BRAND NAME

In Chapter 2, desirable brand name considerations and cautions relevant to choosing a brand name were discussed. In order to consider and apply these considerations effectively, a process must be in place. In smaller companies the process may be carried out by a single individual, but in a larger organization a number of people will be involved. In all cases, the

---

[1029] See David A. Aaker, *Building Strong Brands* (1996), Chapter 11.

process needs to be systematic and the relevant considerations must be objectively considered.

In addition, consideration must be given to the basic concepts relating to the *Trade-marks Act* summarized in Chapter 2. For example, will the proposed brand name actually distinguish the wares or services in association with which it is proposed to be used from the wares and services of others? Will the trade mark be registrable under the *Trade-marks Act*?

If the proposed brand name is a name or surname, if it is potentially descriptive of the character or quality of the wares or services or if it is weak and lacking inherent distinctiveness, these issues must be raised and objectively considered before proceeding any further. Typically, the advice of qualified counsel should be obtained.

3. ONLINE BRANDING

At the same time as the brand name selection process is taking place, consideration should be given to potential online branding and domain name availability. Domain names must be chosen and secured in the appropriate generic and country Top Level Domains. Once chosen, the domain names must be coordinated and managed appropriately. Typically, generic contact information should be developed and maintained. Where appropriate, consideration should be given to protecting domain names as trade marks.

A designated individual must take responsibility for these matters, as well as for dealing with the various Internet concerns, which have been identified in Chapter 3.

4. OBTAINING AND MAINTAINING TRADE MARK REGISTRATIONS

Chapter 4 summarizes how the trade mark registration system works. The key to taking advantage of the system is to understand it, so it can be used to the maximum extent possible to protect the brand name, domain names which function as a trade mark, slogans, the product and, in some cases, product packaging. This can only occur if a specific individual is designated as responsible for compliance with the *Trade-marks Act* and to coordinate with qualified counsel. While brand managers may be busy with the strategic and tactical responsibility for the brand, someone must be in charge and responsible for ensuring that this function is fulfilled.

Once use of the brand name commences, a review should be carried out in association with qualified counsel to ensure that the applied for mark is actually being "used" within the meaning of the *Trade-marks Act.* [1030]

In Canada there is no necessity to file specimens to obtain a renewal of an existing registration. Since the system does not provide any built-in requirements for monitoring whether the registered trade mark is being used in the form in which it was registered or in association with the wares or services the registration was obtained for, brand owners should develop systems to ensure that these matters are reviewed in a timely fashion. It is also prudent to ensure that appropriate trade mark notices or legends are in use.

If significant variations are made in the presentation of the brand name without taking the necessary steps to obtain trade mark registrations, the registration may be at risk of expungement, since the subject matter of the initial registration may be either abandoned or unsupported by any use. In addition, the variant in use may not be protected by a trade mark registration and can only be protected by the assertion of common law rights. In order to avoid this type of situation, actual usage should be audited and monitored on a pre-determined basis to ensure that the brand owner's rights are protected.

Systems should also be established to ensure that trade mark registrations are renewed in a timely fashion. A registration is subject to renewal within a period of 15 years from the date of its registration or last renewal. Unlike other intellectual property rights, a trade mark registration may be renewed any number of times without limitation. [1031]

5. CONTROLLING BRAND EXPRESSION

It can be difficult to control the graphic presentation of a brand since many different parts of an organization may be involved. The promotions, packaging, advertising, marketing and event marketing departments, as well as other areas of the organization, may be involved and will likely be managed by different individuals. In addition, advertising agencies and other outside groups typically have a part to play in the graphic presentation of the brand.

Someone must be responsible for auditing and monitoring brand expression and ensuring it is consistent with the brand strategy and legal requirements. For this reason it is important to ensure that standardized presentations or templates are available and used by all relevant individuals.

[1030] See **Chapter 4, part 3**.
[1031] See **Chapter 4, part 6(e)**.

A brand manual[1032] can help establish uniformity in the display of the visual components which make up the brand. The manual should provide a set of written standards together with specific examples which show exactly how the brand name, design presentation of the brand name and slogans should appear in print advertising and on product packaging. The same standards should also apply to television advertising. Such a manual should deal with the following matters, among others:

(a)   brand name and presentation including specific colours to be used, size and shape of type, style and size of presentation and the relationship of the various parts of the brand name to each other;

(b)   the placement of the brand name on product packaging and in print advertising;

(c)   the placement of slogans or other corporate or sub-brands when used with the brand name;

(d)   emphasizing to employees the importance of monitoring the marketplace concerning the activities of competitors, including the name of a designated contact individual to whom the information should be provided; and

(e)   providing guidelines relating to trade mark use including spelling, capitalization and the use of trade mark notices or legends.

Instructions relating to "use" can help avoid the prospect of a brand name becoming generic through inappropriate use. For example, XEROX Corporation requests that people refer to XEROX brand photocopies and photocopy machines instead of using such expressions as "make me a XEROX of this document".

Similar considerations apply to product packaging which must appropriately express the brand image. The form and content of product packaging can be controlled through the development and implementation of master art work templates. The templates should be used to create all reproductions of product packaging. When such templates are provided to service providers outside the organization of the brand owner, appropriate contractual protection should be in place to ensure that the templates are only used for authorized purposes and are returned together with all copies at the end of the assignment.

The existence of such manuals and master art templates should be brought to the attention of all relevant employees through appropriate seminars and training programs. Companies with intranet capabilities should consider using these facilities to make such information available. Employ-

---

[1032] These manuals are also referred to as a "Graphics Manual", "Brand Book" or "Trade Marks Manual".

ees should know the rules. The use of such material can provide evidence of systematic use of the brand name and assist in establishing the extent to which the brand is known.[1033]

6. LICENSING PROGRAMS

As discussed in Chapter 4, the *Trade-marks Act* allows for the licensing of trade marks so long as the owner has, under the licence, direct or indirect control of the character or quality of the wares or services.[1034] If these requirements are not complied with, the distinctiveness and validity of the brand name may be diminished.

Any brand owner who engages in licensing must control the character or quality of the licensed wares or services. The owner must also be in a position to show that such control was exercised. Control is typically exercised by requiring, at a minimum, that:

(a)   the licensed wares or services conform to standards and/or specifications relating to the character or quality of the wares or services prescribed by the brand owner;

(b)   the licensee be subject to a right on the part of the brand owner to inspect the production or method of delivery of the licensed wares or services;

(c)   all advertisements or other public presentations containing the licensed marks be subject to a requirement to obtain a written pre-approval from the brand owner.

Retained records consisting of approved product samples as well as approved product packaging and advertising and reports relating to inspection and control will allow the brand owner to show that it has in fact exercised control. If a brand owner grants many trade mark licences it should have a licensing/quality control department to monitor and audit the character or quality of the licensed wares or services and retain the appropriate information.

A trade mark notice, in form prescribed by the trade mark owner, should be included in all public presentations of the licensed mark. The brand owner should prescribe such notices and be in a position to show they were used.

[1033] See for example *Enterprise Rent-A-Car Co. v. Singer* (1996), 66 C.P.R. (3d) 453 (Fed. T.D.), affirmed (1998), (sub nom. *Enterprise Car & Truck Rentals Ltd. v. Enterprise Rent-A-Car Co.*) 79 C.P.R. (3d) 45 (Fed. C.A.).

[1034] See **Chapter 4, part 7(b)**.

7. RECORDS RETENTION

It is important for the brand owner and trade mark counsel to have available retained records concerning the brand name's history, including the identity of the owner and the date of first use together with dated examples of product packaging and advertisements showing actual use. These records should be retained in a systematic fashion for the life of the brand in issue.

These records can be extremely valuable in the context of oppositions or trade mark litigation. The initial designs of labels and packaging can help establish claims for copyright relating to such works. In addition, such evidence can show the extent to which the brand name has become known which will in turn affect the brand owner's ability to protect it.

Retained records should include the following representative, dated material relating to the branded wares or services:

(a)   labels;
(b)   bills of lading and other shipping documents;
(c)   invoices;
(d)   advertisements;
(e)   point of sale signage;
(f)   computer control labels;
(g)   catalogues;
(h)   invoices and other bills relating to the preparation and reproduction of labels; and
(i)   other materials displaying the brand name.

Such material together with sales figures can provide the basic evidence required in trade mark oppositions or actions for infringement.

Demand letters and actions taken to preclude third parties from using confusingly similar trade marks or trade names or otherwise misusing the brand owner's intellectual property should also be retained.

This type of record keeping will be particularly important where a trade mark has been assigned, since the trade mark must become distinctive of the new owner. In such cases, the new owner[1035] must engage in a program to bring to the attention of the relevant portion of the public that it is the owner of the mark and the source of the wares or services. If the new owner maintains appropriate records, they will help show that this has in fact occurred. Records retention is also important if the trade marks have been licensed.

[1035] See **Chapter 4, part 7(a)**.

8. EDUCATIONAL PROGRAMS

A brand owner should develop educational programs relating to brand expression and the various matters which make it up. The content of such programs will vary depending on the nature of the business in issue. Such programs need to create an understanding of how the trade mark system works so that it can be used to protect the brand name and the components that make it up. The importance of monitoring the market place concerning the activities of competitors should be emphasized as well.

In-house seminars and training programs can be developed and carried out in order to familiarize employees with the steps necessary to ensure that the integrity of the brand name is fostered and maintained. Companies with intranet capability should consider using these facilities to communicate relevant information.

9. POLICING THE MARKETPLACE

As discussed in Chapter 5, a mark may acquire distinctiveness through extensive use in the market place, which shows that the mark is known to purchasers of the wares or services in issue. The proper management of brand expression can result in increased distinctiveness. However, distinctiveness may be reduced if other competitors are using trade marks or trade names similar to the brand owner's brand name.

The key to managing distinctiveness is obtaining the relevant market-place information. The following steps should be considered.

a) Monitoring the *Trade-marks Journal*

In Canada, trade mark applications which have been approved by the Registrar of Trade-marks are advertised in the *Trade-marks Journal*. The *Journal* includes a summary of the application and a reproduction of the trade mark in issue. Within two months of the advertisement of the application, anyone may, on payment of a prescribed fee, file a statement of opposition.

It is important to review the *Trade-marks Journal*, since a brand owner's assessment as to whether a trade mark is confusing with its registered trade mark may vary substantially from the determination of the Examiner at the Trade-marks Office.

Also, where the Trade-marks Examiner is in doubt whether the claimed trade mark is registrable by reason of a pre-existing registered trade mark, the Examiner may approve the application and, by registered letter, notify

the owner of the registered trade mark of the advertisement of the application.[1036] Such letters should be carefully considered by a brand owner.

In Chapter 5, an overview of the nature of opposition proceedings is
provided. In many cases it may be useful to seek an extension of the time
in which to file a statement of opposition, so that discussions may take place
with the applicant to ascertain whether the application will be withdrawn
or some other settlement can be arrived at.

b) Watch Services

If a brand owner owns registrations of the brand name in a number of
countries, then reviewing the *Trade-marks Journal* or its equivalent in those
countries may not be practical. Watch services can be used to provide this
monitoring function. The watch service will notify the brand owner of
potentially conflicting trade mark applications by sending a watch notice to
the brand owner, who must then determine what steps should be taken.

Clipping services provide for a broader search but may not include trade
mark journals. A newspaper clipping service operator will maintain a constant watch for references to a pre-determined brand name.

The Internet raises a number of concerns, which were discussed in
Chapter 3. As a result, a specific policy should be devised concerning
monitoring and policing the Internet. Such monitoring should include the
use of confusing domain names by cybersquatters, criticism or gripe sites,
the use of confusing metatags and key words, linking and framing and other
related activities. It is also possible to conduct Internet monitoring and
policing through the use of domain name watch services, cyber-clipping
services and other service providers who use customized search tools and
the like.

c) Specific Investigations Carried Out by Brand Owner

A significant portion of market place investigation can be carried out
by the brand owner through its own employees or agents. The brand manual
should emphasize to employees the importance of monitoring the market
place for activities which are potentially infringing and to ensure that such
information is brought to the attention of a specific designated individual
within the organization for action. A brand owner may periodically emphasize to employees the importance of carrying out such activities and, if
appropriate, provide incentives for locating instances of potential infringement.

[1036] Subsection 37(3) of the *Trade-marks Act.*

These activities should be combined with other internal initiatives directed to the market place. For example, searches may be carried out, on a periodic basis, of all existing registrations and applications for a specific trade mark. Once the search results are obtained, the brand owner can then determine what steps should be taken to maintain the position of its trade marks on the register. For example, an application might be noted up to be opposed or if references are disclosed for which no market place evidence is found, proceedings under section 45 of the *Trade-marks Act* may be initiated. [1037]

10. ENFORCING RIGHTS

In some cases, it may be appropriate to enforce a brand owner's rights against third parties. The nature of the potential rights available to a brand owner has been discussed in previous chapters. While it is beyond the scope of this text to discuss all of the procedural aspects of asserting those rights, there are some general matters which should be considered.

First, the importance of carrying out a thorough investigation of the relevant facts cannot be over-emphasized. An appropriate response cannot be developed without full knowledge of the facts. Frequently, this may require the assistance of independent investigators to assist in gathering the evidence. In addition, an assessment of the relevant marketplace should be carried out.

Second, a review should be carried out to determine the nature of the third party's business activities, the intellectual property owned by it, basic corporate information including business name registrations, and its general financial strength including its ability to engage in protracted litigation.

Third, once such investigations have been carried out, it can be determined what type of claims should be asserted, the strength of the claims and the scope of potential remedies available. The most appropriate negotiating position, the claims asserted in a demand letter or statement of claim and the foundation of a litigation strategy, will also be determined by these investigations. Concurrently, an assessment should be made of the appropriate forum for asserting those rights.

Fourth, an assessment should be made of the potential costs of enforcing the rights in issue. This should include the direct costs of retaining counsel and other litigation costs, the indirect costs relating to the loss of employee time devoted to the proceedings, the potential exposure for costs the brand owner will be subject to and the potential recovery.

[1037] See **Chapter 4, part 8**.

Finally, it is important to develop a general strategy to arrive at the desired goal. The strategy, including the specific tactics or steps to be followed, should be committed to writing and not varied without careful consideration. The formulation of a realistic plan and obtainable goal is dependent on the thoroughness of the investigation and analysis described above.

11. PROTECTING PRODUCT SHAPE AND APPEARANCE

In Chapter 6, the potential methods of protecting product shape and appearance have been discussed. The key is to designate a person to be responsible. By virtue of the nature of this task, the individual may be aligned more closely with the manufacturing and development part of a business as opposed to the marketing function. In any event, this person in association with qualified counsel must consider an appropriate method of seeking protection for new products.[1038] This will frequently involve applications under the *Industrial Design Act,* but for established products, consideration can be given to obtaining a registration under the *Trade-marks Act* as a distinguishing guise.

It is important to keep in mind that an application for the registration of an industrial design must be filed in Canada within one year of the publication of the design in Canada or elsewhere in the world.

Finally, steps will need to be taken to ensure that articles are marked appropriately to indicate that they are protected by an industrial design registration or a trade mark registration as the case may be.

12. PROTECTING PRODUCT PACKAGING

In order to protect product packaging, the focus will typically be on the *Copyright Act* as opposed to the *Industrial Design Act.* Once again, a designated individual should be responsible for taking the appropriate steps to ensure protection.

As copyright protection does not depend on registration or other formal steps the timeliness of seeking protection is not relevant. However, care must be taken to ensure that the brand owner is the owner of the copyright in the relevant product packaging. If outside service providers are used the appropriate analysis must be done and steps taken to ensure that the brand

---

[1038] There may be some overlap with protecting inventive new products under the *Patent Act,* but the determination of whether a product should be protected by way of patent typically should be considered at a much earlier point and is not considered in this text.

owner is the copyright owner. In addition, steps must be taken to ensure that moral rights associated with any works have been waived in favour of the brand owner.

It is prudent to use a copyright notice on product packaging.

13. PROTECTING BRAND ADVERTISING

Like product packaging, brand advertising can be protected under the *Trade-marks Act* in some cases but more generally by copyright. The concerns with respect to protection are similar to those for product packaging. In addition, it is wise to designate an individual as a compliance officer for the purposes of ensuring that all advertising complies with the *Competition Act* and other legislation dealing with advertising.

INDEX

Feb 13/07